"Every young woman needs role models. In 1973, my life was forever changed as I witnessed Billie Jean King conquer Bobby Riggs in the Battle of the Sexes. The impact on me was absolute. Never again would being female hinder me from pursuing any activity that interested me. I am grateful to Pat Williams for documenting these unstoppable women who have made a lasting impact on our society and culture. No doubt their inspiration will create another generation of influential women athletes. Pat, start working on the sequel!"

—Jeanie Buss
Executive Vice President of Business Operations, Los Angeles Lakers

"Much inspiration can be found in the lives of our greatest women sports legends, and Pat Williams deserves plenty of credit for bringing these exceptional stories—and all they can teach us—to the forefront."

—Val Ackerman
Former President, WNBA

"Pat Williams's inspiring book takes some of the mystery out of why some people soar while others slog along. The collected life stories of these remarkable athletes and women are a reminder of how passion and will can trump adversity, and how victories are measured not just by trophies, but by living the life you want."

—Johnette Howard
Columnist, *Newsday*, and Author of
The Rivals: Chris Evert vs. Martina Navratilova

"Several years ago, Pat Williams shared his idea with me about this book. I am overwhelmed with the outcome. This book is awesome! I really enjoyed reading about these highly inspirational women. It motivated me and made me want to go out there and coach again. The life lessons at the end of each chapter will powerfully impact everyone."

—Rita Brown
Coach, USA Gymnastics, and CEO, Brown's
Gymnastics and Training Centers

"I enjoyed reading about all these women athletes of influence, especially my protégés Nadia Comaneci, Mary Lou Retton, and Shannon Miller. This book is well written and packs a powerful message."

—Bela Karolyi
Coach, USA Gymnastics

Michelle Akers:
Fearlessness

*"To be successful in any field, two things are required:
have your goal clearly in mind, and be flexible
along the way to make changes when necessary."*
—MICHELLE AKERS

The defender saw Michelle Akers charging hard and smartly did what anyone would do when facing the five-foot, ten-inch superstar, with eyes blazing and hair flying, zeroing in on a soccer ball. She prepared to backpass the ball to her goalkeeper.

Most players would have ceded the play, regrouped, and reloaded for another offensive attack.

Michelle Akers has never been described as most people. The Michael Jordan of her sport, yes, but ordinary? Never.

As the Norwegian defender tried for the backpass, Akers steamrolled into her, knocking down another defender in the process. Before the goalie could get to the ball, it was on Akers' foot, and the charging goalie found herself woefully out of position against one of the greatest athletes ever to play soccer.

She was no match. Akers deftly kicked the ball into the net, giving the United States the 2–1 victory and the 1991 World Cup.

"To me, success is how much of an effort are you going to exert to enjoy the process and become the person you are meant to become," explained

Akers. "I always wanted to work as hard as I could, so I wouldn't have to look back later and have a bunch of regrets."

No worries there. In a career that reads like a women's soccer anthology, Akers has done it all. A four-time collegiate all-American, she won two World Cups and an Olympic gold medal. She reigns as the second-leading scorer (behind only Mia Hamm) in U.S. Women's National Team history, and was named Player of the Century in 1999 by FIFA, soccer's world-governing body.

That she accomplished so much while enduring physical ailments that included thirteen knee surgeries, a fractured cheekbone, dislocated shoulders, and a lengthy battle with chronic fatigue syndrome proves that she was as gritty as she was talented.

Often wrongly diagnosed, chronic fatigue is a debilitating condition that left Akers dizzy, nauseous, and frequently battling fierce migraines. Sleep didn't necessarily help alleviate the crippling and bone-wearying fatigue that came with the condition, and the endless training required to be best in her sport only exacerbated the symptoms.

However, it never slowed her down. In the 1999 World Cup finals, Akers grew weaker and weaker with each step but not until she collided head-to-fist with Brianna Scurry did she leave the game. Two full bags of intravenous fluids and oxygen did little to clear her head.

"Michelle was a legend because on the field she was a courageous player and was absolutely fearless as she attacked her game," said Akers's former teammate, Julie Foudy. "That approach probably shortened her career by four years. Michelle never held back and left everything on the field of combat, including teeth and bone chips."

A striker for most of her career, Akers finished her national team run with 105 goals in 153 games, a ratio that is nothing short of mind-boggling in the goal-stingy sport of soccer.

But it is what she did for her sport—and for women everywhere—that is the real statistic of Akers's career. She opened doors previously barred, ushering in a new wave of lucrative opportunities for female athletes. The first American woman to play professional soccer in Europe (she went to Sweden), Akers was also the first woman soccer player to sign a shoe deal.

Her deals, of course, were far less lucrative than those of her successors—

Praise for *How to Be Like Women Athletes of Influence*

"A celebration of all the memorable women in history—a remarkable resource filled with history and humanity."

—Lesley Visser
Sportscaster, CBS

"Women with the right stuff: Pat Williams has assembled thirty-two of them as an all-star cast in *How to Be Like Women Athletes of Influence.*"

—Bud Collins
NBC/*The Boston Globe*/BudCollinsTennis.com

"Pat Williams, who has made his own impact in the sports world with his storied career—as a baseball *and* NBA executive, an author, and an excellent motivational speaker—has put together a very important collection of the thirty-two most influential female athletes in history. Pat is a visionary in his own right!"

—Ann Liguori
Radio and Television Sports Personality, Author, www.annliguori.com

"Reading *How to Be Like Women Athletes of Influence* brought back a flood of wonderful memories, particularly the chapter about Mia Hamm. As you read about these remarkable women, your life will be forever changed."

—Anson Dorrance
Head Women's Soccer Coach, University of North Carolina

"Once I started reading Pat Williams's new book, I couldn't stop. I hope every young athlete in every sport will dive into the lives of these remarkable women athletes. This book is a life changer."

—Carolyn Bivens
Commissioner, LPGA

"There is so much to be learned from these amazing women, and there is no better person than Pat Williams to impart the lessons. Truly inspiring!"

—Melissa Isaacson
Chicago Tribune

"In this wonderful book, Pat Williams offers us insights and truths that can only be gleaned from the lives of great people who serve as examples of life's most important virtues. The volume is replete with these life-changing and life-enriching discoveries."

—Deborah A. Yow
Director of Athletics, University of Maryland

Other Books in the How to Be Like Series

32 Women at the Top of Their Game and How You Can Get There Too

How to Be Like Women Athletes of Influence

Pat Williams with Dana Pennett O'Neil

Health Communications, Inc.
Deerfield Beach, Florida

www.hcibooks.com

Library of Congress Cataloging-in-Publication Data

O'Neil, Dana Pennett.
   How to be like women athletes of influence : thirty-one women at the top of their
game and how you can get there too / Dana Pennett O'Neil and Pat Williams.
      p. cm.
   ISBN-13: 978-0-7573-0677-8 (trade paper)
   ISBN-10: 0-7573-0677-2 (trade paper)
1. Women athletes—Biography.   I. Williams, Pat, 1940-   II. Title.
   GV697.A1O64 2007
   796.082—dc22

                                                                    2007021567

Publisher: Health Communications, Inc.
            3201 S.W. 15th Street
            Deerfield Beach, FL 33442-8190

Book cover design by Larissa Hise Henoch
Photo of Michele Kwan: Charles Troutman/SportsChrome
Photo of Venus Williams: Rob Tringali/SportsChrome
Photo of Annika Sorenstam: Greg Crisp/SportsChrome
Photo of Mia Hamm: Tom DiPace/SportsChrome
Inside book formatting by Dawn Von Strolley Grove

To Rita Brown and Betsy Nagelsen McCormack, two women of impact in the athletic world and beyond who enthusiastically encouraged me on this writing project from the beginning. I am grateful to both of them for their many contributions.

PW

To my mother, Graceann. She isn't famous, she isn't an athlete, but she has taught me all a woman ever needs to know about grace, dignity, strength, and kindness.

DPO

Contents

Foreword

When I first read the manuscript for this book, the phrases that kept jumping out at me were the same ones that I remember thinking as a young girl, about taking advantage of an opportunity, about overcoming obstacles, about fulfilling your dreams, about chasing your passion.

Growing up, I was a girl on a boys' ice hockey team and the backup goalie no less. Although I did manage to shake the establishment by becoming the only female goalie in a nearby rec league and later on my high school team, I was hardly a world-class athlete. But I still can relate to what the women in these chapters felt and lived.

I think a lot of women and young girls can.

It takes a lot more than talent to achieve what these ladies achieved. Unafraid of challenges or blissfully ignorant to them, they forged ahead because their sport fed them something nothing else could. Outsiders considered them unorthodox, but they realized they had something very special, an opportunity to pursue their dream, and they went for it undaunted.

Most important, they believed in themselves. I'm not sure that can be underscored enough. Believing in yourself, I think, is far more powerful than any physical gifts you may be blessed with.

We don't do enough today to celebrate the amazing female role models we have. We remain a society obsessed with physical beauty, particularly where women are concerned. What these women prove and what I want my daughter, my son, and in fact everyone young and old to know is that you can't be beautiful on the outside until you feel beautiful on the inside. And if you are beautiful on the inside, then your beauty will shine on the outside.

The stories contained in these pages aren't important because someone won a gold medal or set a world record. They're important because they show just how much a person can accomplish by simply believing in oneself, and working like crazy to achieve one's goals.

You, like me, may never compete in an Olympic Games or capture a championship, but that doesn't mean we can't learn from these women. We each measure success by our own personal yardsticks. Their paths to fame may simply become our paths to fulfillment, but that is no less important than crossing a finish line first.

Nowadays, I am an anchor on ESPN's *SportsCenter*, and it isn't a stretch to say that the success and affirmation I got out of ice hockey allowed me to realize I could ace my new professional role as well. Like being a goalie, it never occurred to me that I would be anything less than a success in television. I believed in myself and didn't allow the doubters or the critics to shake that belief.

Inside this book are thirty-two women athletes who never let criticism or doubt or obstacles stop them. Their dreams and their passion always gave them the courage and the strength to push ahead and persevere.

My hope for you is that they will inspire you as much as they have me.

Linda Cohn
ESPN Sports Center Anchor
Bristol, Connecticut

Introduction

❧

Simple Idea,
Amazing Journey

*L*ike a lot of basketball fans, I watched in amazement in June 1998 as Michael Jordan hit the key shot to beat the Utah Jazz and lift the Chicago Bulls to their sixth National Basketball Association (NBA) title. A basketball lifer, I was completely fascinated and blown away by the greatness we had seen embodied in one person and wondered if we would ever see it again.

That summer I took the ideals I thought Michael Jordan embodied and began giving a speech called "How to be Like Mike." The more I gave the speech, the more positive feedback I received about it, and I began to wonder if that premise might not make for a good book.

Fortunately for me, I count Mark Victor Hansen, the cocreator of the Chicken Soup for the Soul series, as a friend, and he introduced me to his publisher, Peter Vegso of Health Communications. Peter loved the idea, and in September 2001, just as Michael Jordan was beginning a comeback with the Washington Wizards, *How to Be Like Mike: Life Lessons About Basketball's Best* was released.

The book was received well, and Peter suggested we think about a series of similar books. We brainstormed a number of ideas, and over the last six years, six more books have followed: *How to Be Like Jesus, How to Be Like Women of Influence, How to Be Like Rich DeVos, How to Be Like Walt Disney, How to Be Like Jackie Robinson,* and *How to Be Like Coach Wooden.*

As that series came to a close, I lunched with Peter one day in Deerfield Beach, Florida, to discuss future projects, and he told me the bestsellers in the series were about sports and women.

The simple idea occurred to me—what if we put those two groups together? Over the next few weeks I hashed out the notion of identifying the world's greatest women athletes and writing a chapter on each for what I thought would be a sensational book. I shared my idea with Peter, and he said, "Good idea. Let's do it," which is always the sweetest of music to any author.

Then came the nitty-gritty. I needed to find a writing partner, and I needed to get the women athletes down to a workable number. The first part was easy. I made a few phone calls to some respected sportswriting friends from my days in Philadelphia: Phil Jasner and Dick Jerardi of the *Philadelphia Daily News,* Mike Sielski of Calkins Media, and Dick Weiss of the *New York Daily News.* I told them about my project and said I thought it would be good to have a woman to work with on this particular book. Did they have any recommendations?

All four, independent of one another, said the same name—Dana Pennett O'Neil, a reporter with the *Philadelphia Daily News* who covers Villanova basketball and the Eagles. That high praise made it a slam dunk for me, so I quickly called Dana and was thrilled when she said she would love to participate.

Next came the hard part. Selecting the best of anything is never easy. It's a subjective process, one sure to inspire debate around the water cooler on Monday mornings. I think that's great. If people are discussing women's athletics because of my book, I'm delighted.

I'm sure as you page through this book, a name might pop into your head that you think belongs in here, or you may even be disappointed that a certain person has not been included.

We started this book with one hundred names—but Peter Vegso quickly reminded me that this wasn't to be an encyclopedia and that thirty chapters needed to be our target number. That didn't make things easy for us. I contacted friends and colleagues, people who have been involved in women's athletics or covered women's athletics for years, to help me whittle the list down. The first cut got us to fifty and then finally to the thirty-two women athletes you see in these pages, as well as the bonus chapter on Pat Summitt, who I regard as the best women's coach of all time.

Certainly others could have made the cut. We debated the merits of more than a few names, but in the end, we believed this was the best thirty-two.

The thrilling part for me came next. I reached out to the women in the book, asking for one-on-one interviews, and of the twenty-nine still living, twenty-one graciously agreed. I chatted with Mia Hamm about her electrifying World Cup title, relived the magic Olympic run with Shannon Miller, learned what makes Serena Williams tick, went back to that moment of perfection with Nadia Comaneci, and had so many other inspiring conversations. If I couldn't interview an athlete personally, I talked with the people who made these women special—the parents, coaches, and friends who helped push them to their greatness.

Every time I hung up the telephone, my heart was racing, and I was just swooning. It was such a treat to talk to these women and feel their enthusiasm, their energy, their passion and sweet spirit.

Sports fan or not, this is a book for you. These women can teach all of us, no matter how we make our living, how old we are, or our personal circumstances, how to realize our full potential and live successful lives. Like us, their lives have not always been perfect. They have faced hurdles and criticisms, but rather than give up, they pushed forward because they believed in their dreams, and more important, they believed in themselves.

That's a life lesson we all can take to heart.

So here it is, my friends, after two years of hard work and research, thirty-two women to learn from. I hope their stories invigorate and inspire you as much as they did me.

Pat Williams
Orlando, Florida

Akers remembers the national team days of $10 in meal money—but Akers's place in soccer history is assured. She is the epicenter from which Mia Hamm and Kristine Lilly and Brandi Chastain emerged.

"Michelle was Mia before there was Mia," former U.S. Women's National Team coach Tony DiCicco used to tell people about Akers.

Today's generation is all about Hamm. It is her poster gracing their bedroom walls and her name that they call when they come to games.

Hamm's generation was all about Akers.

"She was one of the best ever," Hamm said. "Michelle is the ultimate professional, so focused and prepared. She taught me how to be a professional. She worked so hard every day. You're not always going to get a perfect pass, so you've just got to find a way."

Born in 1966, Akers was part of the first generation to truly enjoy the benefits of Title IX, the federal amendment that is credited with opening sports up to women in this country. Aside from tennis and golf players, there were few women to idolize, and so the tomboy from Seattle just played anything and everything as her parents looked to quench her sports hunger.

They couldn't quite answer every request. As a kid, Akers idolized Mean Joe Greene, the defensive lineman from the Pittsburgh Steelers made famous in a Coke commercial, and she decided that she, too, would star in the NFL one day. When a teacher explained that girls couldn't play professional football, the distraught Akers cried and cried.

"A lot of parents will push their kids to find their niches," Michelle's father, Bob, once said. "But we had to back off on Michelle a little."

Ultimately Akers gravitated to soccer, a sport she first began to play when she was eight.

Though her parents divorced

"Michelle tries her best every day. She works hard at life. She gets it because she attacks life with gusto. She doesn't just let it sit."

—Bob Akers, Michelle's dad

when she was young, Akers remained close with both of them and said that today she remains most proud of her relationship with her father, Bob.

"My dad is my number one hero," she revealed. "He demonstrated the importance of getting to know yourself and overcoming your personal demons and shortcomings. He helped me to appreciate the process of 'becoming' and seeing others go through the same thing. My dad always encouraged me as a young athlete and wouldn't let me goof around. He was there for me when I was failing and when I was successful. Dad has always been honest with me and loved me through all the stages of my life."

Akers really started to shine as a soccer player in high school, where she frequently trained with the boys at Shorecrest High School.

Even her father noticed it.

"Michelle was always talented, but it really started to emerge in high school," Bob Akers explained. "She played all the sports, but soccer was her love. It gave her more freedom, and Michelle loved to run."

Awarded a scholarship to the University of Central Florida, Akers was named to the inaugural women's national team in her sophomore season.

That year, 1985, the U.S. Women's National Team was hardly the enterprise it is today. Hastily assembled and given virtually no practice time, the team's total international exposure consisted of four games in Italy. They lost three and tied one. Akers, however, left her mark, scoring the first goal in U.S. Women's National Team history.

A year later, University of North Carolina head coach Anson Dorrance took over the coaching and handpicked his players. The impact was immediate. When the U.S. team returned from Italy that year, the women had won three of their four games.

By 1991, the United States was a dominant force in women's soccer. Buoyed by the growth of the sport at the collegiate level, the roster included a who's who of players, with Akers at the top of the list.

Her teammates called her Mufasa. It wasn't just because of her wild head of curls.

"It's Swahili for lion," Dorrance explained. "The lion was the king of the jungle, and Michelle ruled the game."

Indeed, the U.S. women dominated the qualifying rounds for the first-ever Women's World Cup, beating their opposition by a combined score of 49–0.

When Akers, who would lead the U.S. team with ten goals in the '91

World Cup, swiped that backpass to score in the eighty-eighth minute, she gave the United States its first soccer championship since 1962. Instead of a blaze of glory, though, the women returned from China with little fanfare.

Akers told reporters back then that on her flight home, an old lady sitting next to her asked why she was in China. Told the United States had just won the World Cup, the woman turned, smiled at Akers and said, "That's nice."

Five years later, the reaction was a little stronger. When the women won the gold medal at the Atlanta Olympics in 1996, you would have been hard-pressed to find an American—man or woman, young or old—who didn't know. The U.S. Women's National Team went from unheralded niche players to household names virtually overnight.

* * *

Before all of that, Akers found herself overcome with fatigue. Figuring she might be overdoing it, Akers tried to back off—but nothing seemed to help. During an Olympic Sports Festival in 1993, a dazed Akers collapsed on the field in San Antonio. Originally diagnosed with mononucleosis, doctors later said she had the more severe Epstein-Barr version of the disease.

Not until almost a year later did doctors diagnose her with chronic fatigue syndrome. By then, the United States was in the throes of its training for its home-game 1996 Olympics, and there was simply no way Akers would miss that.

She studied everything she could about the disease and did everything she could to alleviate the symptoms, opting, for example, for a room by herself on the road in case she was exhausted and needed rest or was besieged by migraines and needed quiet.

Nothing helped dramatically. Depressed and at her wit's end, Akers turned to her faith.

"My strength and my inspiration come from my faith," she said. "God put me together as I am, and he likes me that way. He wants to accomplish a lot of things through me, and that keeps me going. My faith allows me to have great days no matter what."

Her inner resolve coupled with a pre-Olympic diet she once labeled disgusting—no glutens, no caffeine, no beef, no sugar, no dairy products, and two pounds of carrot juice per day—allowed Akers to defy the odds and the naysayers who didn't think she'd be able to play in Atlanta.

The thirty-year-old Akers graciously ceded the striker position to Hamm and dropped back into the midfield, but her impact was no less. She played every game and scored on a crucial penalty kick to help the United States get by Norway in the semifinals and pave the way to the gold medal.

"Michelle Akers has an inner drive that is quite uncommon," DiCicco, the national team coach, said. "In fact, I think that was part of her illness. She didn't know how to back off. She'd always leave it on the field. You had to drag her off the field."

Exhausted by the chronic fatigue and in need of yet another knee surgery, Akers took five months off to recover, but refueled her engines for one more run.

It would be the most historic for her sport.

The 1996 Olympic Games ushered women's sports into the mainstream, helping to bring about professional women's leagues in both soccer and basketball. But it was the 1999 World Cup, held in the United States, that really set off the pandemonium.

Akers, who used to be able to find her father in the nearly empty stands at virtually every game, now found herself scanning crowds of almost ninety thousand.

"Michelle teaches us to attack life with zest! Play hard and work hard. She wasn't afraid to roll up her sleeves and get dirt under her fingernails. That's what Michelle did every day with no one watching her, and that's what made her great."

—Julie Foudy, Akers's Olympic teammate

For a woman who shepherded the game from its infancy, no knee pain, no fatigue would keep her away.

"Michelle's life teaches us that nothing comes easy," her father, Bob, said. "There are no free lunches. You've got to focus, dedicate yourself, and then work hard."

Shrugging off the effects of the chronic fatigue, Akers rallied to score the game-clinching goal against Brazil in the semifinals—but when the United States beat China in the historic shootout, punctuated by Brandi Chastain's jersey-tearing celebration, she was in the cata-combs of the Rose Bowl, hooked up to an IV. The collision with Scurry looked like the final blow, but really Akers had been deterio-rating for some time during the game. Akers was still dazed when the U.S. team went to the podium for the national anthem.

"Michelle was a role model for women in soccer. She never fully embraced the spotlight and never sought the limelight."

—TONY DICICCO,
U.S. WOMEN'S NATIONAL TEAM COACH

A year later, done in by a shoulder injury as well, she retired.

"It's not been hard for me to transition to the next phase so far because I was so beat up physically at the end of my career," she told me. "For the last three years of soccer, I just kept going to complete what I was there for."

Akers lives today on a farm in Florida with her husband, lawyer Steve Eichenblatt, and his three children. Akers has horses and time and quiet, luxuries she rarely allowed herself while competing.

She has written a book and started a foundation, Soccer Outreach International, which she uses to teach people to integrate their sport and their faith.

"Chronic fatigue syndrome had always been the most difficult hurdle in my life," Akers told me. "Now, however, it's learning how to work through and understand the next step of who I'm meant to be in this life."

Whatever she decides, expect Michelle Akers to chase down that next phase like an errant backpass.

Michelle Akers's Life Lessons

Hang On to Your Dreams; They're Real

It is so easy to become discouraged, to give up on a dream or simply lose sight of it altogether. Michelle Akers had every reason to let go of her dream. Women weren't superstar athletes, and soccer was never anything more than a second-class sport in the United States. But she believed she could achieve something special and didn't let outsiders, injuries, or obstacles stop her. "God put that dream in your heart, and it's real," Michelle said. "He'll get you where you want to go."

Everyone Needs a Team

A team need not be people in the same uniform, playing for the same organization. A team can be family, friends, coaches, and trainers, whoever helps a person achieve a goal. Michelle Akers was fortunate enough to have every kind of team—friends and family as well as women like her who weren't afraid to blaze a new trail in their sport. "You can't do anything by yourself," Akers said.

Take Baby Steps Every Day

No one picks up a paintbrush and becomes Picasso. No one first kicks a soccer ball and becomes Pelé. Even for people who are naturally gifted, progress is a process. Michelle Akers realized that quickly, and by learning to appreciate the baby steps, she achieved greatness. "I've always had the fire in my belly about sports," Akers explained. "It's just in there, and the drive was apparent to everyone. Not every person is necessarily born with the 'fire' but it can be developed. With me, I came out of the womb with it."

Play Your Guts Out Every Day

Michelle Akers's dedication is almost legendary. Former teammates, coaches, anyone who knows her, talks about how hard Akers worked, how much of herself she gave. "Michelle was completely self-motivated to get to another level," her former teammate Julie Foudy said. "She had her own bag of soccer balls and would go out early to work on free kicks. She had her own trainer. The girl was the hardest worker ever."

∽ 2 ∽

Bonnie Blair:
Humility

"Every day is not perfect, and you will get frustrated. You must be patient and stick around until things get better."

—BONNIE BLAIR

When the closing ceremonies ended and the Olympic flame was extinguished at the 1994 Olympic Games in Lillehammer, Norway, Bonnie Blair stood alone. There was no one like her in her sport, no woman like her in American Olympic history.

Blair made history in the tiny Norwegian hamlet, winning the 500- and 1,000-meter speed skating competitions, her fifth and sixth Olympic medals, to become the most decorated winter athlete in United States history and the country's record holder for the most gold medals (five) by a woman in any sport.

Yet when Bonnie Blair reflects on her final Olympic Games, she doesn't talk about the records or her place in history. Her shining moment, in fact, was in an event she finished out of medal contention.

"My best race in the 1994 Olympics was the 1,500-meter event," Blair said. "I finished fourth and did not medal, but I skated faster than I ever had before. That personal best made me feel successful and proud of what I did. I was very excited about finishing fourth because I felt as if I'd finished first."

That says everything about Blair, a woman so good at what she did that her only real competition was herself. Fueled by a passion and a drive that consumed her, Blair turned a childhood love into legend by never giving up and always reaching higher.

Asked to describe herself in one word, Blair said simply, "Intense."

She stands alone in the annals of speed skating, without question the greatest woman to compete in her sport. Other women have come along to achieve better times than Blair, but no one can replace her. She is the name and the face of speed skating, the tiny spitfire who captured a country's heart with her combination of good-hearted sincerity and take-no-prisoners tenacity. By the time she competed in Lillehammer, the Blair Bunch, the group of supporters that at Bonnie's first Olympic Games in 1988 included just her immediate family, had swelled to some three hundred people in the stands and an entire country back home.

Sports fans always love a winner, so Blair was easy to love. No woman had ever won consecutive 500-meter races at the Olympics before Blair won three in a row. She left her sport with nineteen World Sprint Medals to go along with her Olympic jewelry and world champion titles in 1989, 1994, and 1995.

But to become a true Olympic darling, the "It" girl in a Games distinguished by amazing competitors, it takes that extra something. Blair had "It," and in her case, "It" wasn't an effervescent smile or a pogo-stick personality. Blair's "It" was her genuineness while the world spun around her.

"Bonnie Blair is the gal next door," her former coach, Nick Thometz, said. "She is a pure person who never let fame go to her head. She has time for people because she is so down to earth. The woman has no ego. It's never about Bonnie."

Of course, growing up as the youngest of six children, it's easy to see why it could never be just about Bonnie. There were five other kids to root for, each with his or her own special talents, each lauded and praised by their parents, Eleanor and Charlie.

Eleanor, who grew up in Flushing, New York, skated as a little girl on a nearby pond, and Charlie had done some skating as well, so when they had their children they put them on skates and sent them into competition from their New York home.

In fact, when Bonnie was born, her older brothers and sisters were in a speed skating competition and Charlie was the timer. He dropped off his wife at the hospital and went on to the meet.

"In those days, husbands weren't allowed in the delivery room, so Dad figured instead of waiting for me to be born, since Mom had been through this five times before, that he'd take the rest of the kids to a skating meet," Blair told ESPN.com.

When Blair was born, the public address announcer told the crowd, "The Blair family has just added another skater."

If he only knew. . . .

When Charlie Blair got a new job as a civil engineer, the family relocated to Champaign, Illinois; the kids kept up with their speed skating, but none seemed to be as taken with it as little Bonnie. Her big brothers and sisters, anxious to bring their kid sister into the family sport, stuck her in her first pair of skates at the age of two. Her feet were much too small, so they just put the skates on her, shoes and all.

"We still have pictures of her in those little white skates," Eleanor Blair told the *Washington Post* in 1992. "She loved it."

By four, she was racing.

"I don't even remember learning how to skate," Blair once told the *New York Times*. "It comes almost as naturally to me as walking."

After trying to compete in pack-racing, where the tiny Blair had a hard time jockeying for position in the front of the pack, she finally tried distance racing, where skaters are paired off and basically race against the clock.

Blair, though, is just like most people. Skating was a passion, but there were often other things tugging at her. As a teenager, she said she was lazy, more interested in going to the movies than practicing, and she once told *Chicago Tribune* reporter Philip Hersh that a growth spurt that rendered her "clumsy and cloddy" nearly pushed her out of the sport.

"I finally listened to people who said, 'You're just growing; give yourself a chance to get used to your body,'" she told Hersh.

Fortunately for her and for everybody else, she did just that. On her first trip to an Olympic track in 1979, Blair finished 500 meters in 47 seconds and made the national team.

"I thought, 'Maybe I can go to the Olympics. That would be really cool,'" Blair said. "My career had a slow pace with a nice, gradual up climb. I never had too much too soon. I always had a passion that kept my inner fire burning."

Blair needed help to make her Olympic dream a reality. She needed to move to Europe to train, a move that would have emotional costs as well as financial ones. The Champaign Policemen's Benevolent Association took care of the latter, raising the $7,000 necessary and beginning a lengthy sponsorship of Blair.

In 1984, Blair made her Olympic debut, finishing a respectable eighth in the 500 meters. She was only nineteen.

"When I was younger, the skaters above me were a real inspiration in my life, especially the East Germans," Blair said.

Indeed, before Blair's rise, East Germany owned women's speed skating, accounting for the gold medal in the 500 meters in 1980 and the gold and silvers in the 1984 500-meter and 1,000-meter competitions.

Four years later, East Germany had merged with its western democratic neighbor. The Germans were still good, but Blair was even better. Blair took her first of seven consecutive U.S. sprint championship titles in 1985 and, two years later, scored her first world record in the 500 meters, setting the stage for the 1988 Games in Calgary.

Buoyed by her family, some thirty strong, who wore blue jackets and called themselves the Blair Bunch, and her traditional peanut butter and jelly pre-race sandwich, Blair beat her German rival, Christa Rothenburger, 39.10 to 39.12 in the 500 meters to not only win the gold, but set a new world record.

"That was an unbelievable feeling of power and impact," Blair said, adding that winning that first Olympic gold was her greatest thrill.

Before she left Canada, Blair added a bronze in the 1,000 meters and carried the American flag in the closing ceremonies. The only American woman to leave Calgary with more than one medal, she came home to a huge hometown party. With endorsements from Xerox, Visa, and Jeep, she freed the police department from their sponsorship.

Gifted with almost flawless technique, Blair combined talent with hard work. A sweet, good-natured person away from the ice, she was a fierce competitor on it. As an athlete, Blair owned an uncanny ability to seize control of her goals. As much as she admired the East Germans, she told me she also knew that to be a success she had to look beyond them to realize her own potential.

"I will always remember Bonnie's fierceness as a competitor," Thometz, her coach, said. "She'd have that intensity and fire in her eyes, a look that said, 'I'm going to conquer today!'"

Hardly satisfied with her medal haul in 1988, Blair steamrolled into Albertville, France, for the 1992 Games. By then she was more than a favorite. She was expected to win. She came to Albertville with a string of eighteen consecutive victories in the 500 meters and had won every 500- and 1,000-meter race on the World Cup circuit that year.

It brought a new kind of pressure to Blair, but one she easily kept in perspective. Three years earlier her father, Charlie, had died, and in 1992 her brother Rob had been diagnosed with an inoperable brain tumor.

In him, Blair saw what really mattered, what fighting really was about.

"He has been a real inspiration to me because the glass is always half full with him," Blair said of Rob, who's now fifty. "He never asks, 'Why me?' He's at peace with his situation."

In Albertville, the Blair Bunch came back in full force. This time the jackets were purple—Rob had them made—and the Blair Bunch numbered closer to fifty. They coaxed the Albertville, France, crowd into singing "My Bonnie Lies over the Ocean" and greeted each race with ringing cowbells.

Outsiders thought all of that family could only add to the load on Blair's shoulders. Those who knew Blair knew differently.

> *"Bonnie had the uncanny ability to prepare for every race like it was an Olympic event. She'd put herself in the frame of mind that this was the biggest race of the year."*
>
> —NICK THOMETZ, BLAIR'S FORMER COACH

"Bonnie has the ability to drop everything around her and focus on the task at hand," her husband and fellow speed skater Dave Cruikshank said. "Once she was on the line, nothing would rattle her. When you saw that burning intensity in her eyes, you knew she was ready to conquer. She was so intense that nothing else mattered."

To the joy of her family and American fans back home, Blair won both the 500- and 1,000-meter events in Albertville, becoming the first woman to win back-to-back 500 golds.

Later that year she was named the winner of the James E. Sullivan Award, presented to the country's best amateur athlete.

"Bonnie is very big on people having goals in life. She'll tell you, 'Don't be afraid to take a risk. Don't be afraid to lose. Be committed to your decision.'"

—DAVE CRUIKSHANK, BLAIR'S HUSBAND

After the Olympics, Blair's mother told Hersh that her daughter's glory would matter little back home. "She will still have to do the dishes and make her bed and all the things she did," Eleanor Blair said, summing up exactly why people have always loved Bonnie. She is extraordinary yet ordinary all at once.

Two years later, Blair, along with the Blair Bunch—numbers swelling into the hundreds by now—made their Olympic swan song. The 1994 Lillehammer Games were tinged with a trace of sadness for Blair because she knew this was the end for her, but Blair had spent a lifetime learning how to block everything else out. She wasn't about to let her emotions cloud her competitive spirit in her last Olympic Games.

She came to Norway to win.

Naturally, she did.

Blair breezed to her third consecutive 500-meter gold medal and then raced around the 1,000-meter track in 1:18.74. She told Thometz, her coach, afterward that she wasn't sure it would be enough for gold but "it was all I had."

It was plenty good enough. In a sport usually decided by the length of a skate blade, Blair won by 1.38 seconds, the largest margin of victory in Olympic history for the 1,000 meters.

With her fifth gold medal and sixth of her career, Blair unseated her hero, Eric Heiden, as the most decorated American athlete at a Winter Games.

"She brings out the best in her competition," Canadian Susan Auch once said of Blair, "because we're always chasing her."

✳   ✳   ✳

The awards poured in for Blair after the 1994 games: *Sports Illustrated's* Sportsperson of the Year, *Glamour* magazine's Woman of the Year, and the Associated Press Female Athlete of the Year. But Blair wasn't finished. Not quite. Though 1994 brought an end to Blair's Olympic experience, it did not end her racing career. She had one more mountain to conquer. She wanted to become the first woman to skate the 500 meters in less than 39 seconds.

Why, was the logical question? Why bother? With a houseful of medals and her place in history firmly intact, why race more? What was left to prove?

"I loved what I did," Blair explained. "It wasn't about the dollars because there was no money involved in speed skating. I stuck with my sport for years because I wasn't ready to give it up. I enjoyed what I was doing. It wasn't about medals with me. I stayed with it because I loved it."

And so in March 1994 in Calgary, Blair lined up against the clock again. She skated the 500 meters in 38.99.

Was that good enough? Could she go off and relax now?

Not quite for Blair. A year later she stepped onto the Calgary track again, this time blazing to a 38.69 finish, another world record.

"I try to be better than ever before. I want to be the best I can in whatever I'm doing"

—BONNIE BLAIR

Finally on March 18, 1995, her thirty-first birthday, Blair skated a personal best, an American record 1:18.05 in the 1,000 meters. It would be her final race. She hung up her skates and went off and began the rest of her life.

"I went out when I wanted to go out," Blair told *Investor's Business Daily* in 2004. "That helped in the transition process. A lot of athletes do something for so much of their lives. They stop and then wonder if they were ready. They wonder, 'What if I would have kept going?' I never had to 'what if' myself."

Of course, there will never be another Bonnie Blair, but Blair's legacy lives on in American speed skating.

As she was making her farewell at Lillehammer, Chris Witty was beginning her Olympic career. Since Blair's retirement, Witty has won a silver and a gold in the 1,000 meters plus a bronze in the 1,500 meters.

"Bonnie has inspired me," Witty said once. "She inspires me to this day."

And Blair continues to inspire others as well. Married since 1996 to Cruikshank, she has two children: son, Grant, is seven and daughter, Blair, is five. She works today as a motivational speaker where she challenges people to be dedicated, to take risks, and to have a sense of balance.

A sense of balance really is what is most amazing about Blair. Despite her successes, her trophies, and the gushing reports of her talent, she always remained grounded.

"My legacy?" Bonnie said to me. "Bonnie loved what she did and was successful at it at the same time."

To hear the humble Blair tell it, her success sounds like happenstance, a funny by-product of doing what she loved.

Then again, maybe Blair is right. Maybe the true lesson of her life is that only by pursuing a passion can a person realize his or her true abilities.

Bonnie Blair's Life Lessons

Love What You Do

The demands—physical and emotional—of being an athlete on the scale of a Bonnie Blair are far too great to just go through the motions, but the same can be said of any profession or hobby. The burdens somehow seem less and the rewards always appear greater when there is passion for what you're doing. As Bonnie explained, "I lived my life for skating."

Plan Ahead

Settling was never on Bonnie Blair's agenda. There was always another goal on the horizon, another task to accomplish. To say she planned her success would be a stretch—no one could truly anticipate that sort of greatness—but Bonnie did lay out groundwork for herself, a chart that pushed her further and further every day. "When you are involved with a training program, you have to make out a list and then check things off when they're completed," Bonnie said. "I still do that today as a wife, mother, and speaker. I try to be better than ever before."

Discipline Yourself

Distractions are everywhere in life. The temptation to take a day off, to rest, or to ignore your passion is always there. But as Bonnie Blair realized, excellence means more than talent and hard work. It means being consumed by your passion, sometimes to the exclusion of everything else. As Bonnie explained, "I had to give up some fun things because I'd dedicated my life to my task; as a competitive athlete, that's how I lived my life."

Make Good Judgments and Good Decisions

As a kid growing up, Bonnie Blair loved a lot of sports. She enjoyed gymnastics and swimming, softball, and bicycling. At an early age, though, she made an important decision, one that would affect the pattern of her life. "I didn't have the same killer instinct for those sports that I had on the ice," she later said. "The eye of the tiger wasn't there."

～ 3 ～

Nadia Comaneci:
Perfection

*"To me, success is believing in yourself and
being comfortable and confident with who you are."*

—NADIA COMANECI

e remember her as an elfin fourteen-year-old girl, shy and quiet, hiding behind soulful brown eyes that told a story her language and her country refused to allow her to tell.

We can hear the piano opening from the theme song to the *Young and the Restless* playing in our minds while we see her gracefully leaping across the floor to thunderous applause and worldwide adulation.

She was a ten, a symbol of perfection in a sport that routinely denies perfection because of slightly bent toes; she inspired thousands of little girls to head to their nearby gymnastics school and ignited a revolution in the sport. She was the first pixie, so to speak, the one who spawned Mary Lou Retton and Shannon Miller and Kerri Strug and all of the rest of the young women who hold a nation rapt at every Summer Olympic Games.

The real inspiration of Nadia Comaneci, however, began long after her triumphant run of three gold medals and seven perfect scores in 1976.

It began on a dark and lonely night in 1989 when Comaneci slipped out of Romania and into Hungary, walking away from the medals that had made her famous, from the home she had always known and into a life where she was guaranteed nothing except the one thing she wanted most—freedom.

Finally free in the United States and free to visit her liberated Romania, the mystery of Nadia is gone now, her unease and distrust replaced by a quick humor and genuine happiness. When asked what she knows for sure, Comaneci pauses before laughing, "My age."

She is a treasure, but not one tucked away in a box. Rather, she is a living, breathing treasure, one who shares her past and helps pave the way for the future.

"I will always be remembered for my performance in Montreal," Comaneci said. "But I want to be remembered as a woman who opened the door for other women to achieve their dreams in sports. Make the impossible possible. That's a good way to say it."

Making the impossible possible is a lesson Comaneci learned from her parents. A working-class family in Romania, the Comanecis didn't have a lot of money. Gheorghe Comaneci, Nadia's father, was an auto mechanic who walked twelve miles a day to and from work because the family didn't have a car of their own.

Despite their own financial hardships, the Comanecis allowed their daughter to dream big.

"I was extremely fortunate that my family supported me and allowed me to follow my dreams of becoming a gymnastics champion," Comaneci wrote in *Love You, Daddy Boy: Daughters Honor the Fathers They Love,* a compilation of famous daughters honoring their fathers. "Sure, it was a lot of hard work, but it was easy compared to the sacrifices that my father made to provide for our family every day."

The legend goes that a little girl was playing on the schoolyard one day with her friends, jumping and flipping for fun during recess when a gymnastics coach by the name of Bela Karolyi spied her.

Before Karolyi could talk to the young girl, though, the bell rang, and he lost her in the sea of children. Determined, Karolyi marched into the school and went from classroom to classroom asking, "Who here likes gymnastics?" until he found the girl he had seen on the play yard.

Her name was Nadia Comaneci.

Whether the tale is true or one of Karolyi's famously embellished tall tales really isn't important. What matters is that Karolyi and Comaneci met, a pairing that would change the course of a sport.

"She and Bela were a magical pair whose lives intersected in the right time in history," Comaneci's husband, Bart Connor, said.

Karolyi then was not the gymnastics' guru he is today. Russia ruled the gymnastics roost, and though Karolyi would coach the Romanian Olympic team in 1976, he had yet to step onto the international stage.

But what separated Karolyi—and turned him into the coach of champions—is that he believed young girls should be treated no differently than young boys when it came to athletics, a notion that was nothing short of outlandish in an age before Title IX and the concept of women as athletes.

"Bela Karolyi and I together created something special," Comaneci remembered. "It was a 50/50 kind of thing. He's a great motivator. Lots of talented people don't have the right people around them. Bela and I both needed each other."

Indeed, in Comaneci Karolyi found the perfect sponge to his feverish approach. The daughter of a mechanic from a factory town in the mountains of Romania, she was raised to believe in the merits of hard work and, at a young age, learned that the rewards were worth the work.

"When I was five years old, I won a bike competition," Comaneci said. "I liked that, and I enjoyed how people reacted to me. Every kid likes that."

If Karolyi told her to do a trick ten times, Comaneci proudly boasted that she would do twenty.

"She had excellent physical abilities but also a very powerful mental approach," Karolyi said. "That combination made her very successful. Her determination and desire to win built Nadia's self-confidence and helped put her over the top."

A year after enrolling at the Gymnastics High School, where she split her day equally—four hours for class work, four hours at gymnastics training—the nine-year-old Comaneci won the Romanian junior national title.

In 1970, she competed for the first time in senior competition.

The young woman who sought perfection long before it was awarded to her in Montreal was devastated at that meet when she fell off the balance beam three times.

"I sat alone in my room and brooded," Comaneci wrote in her autobiography.

The pity party ended quickly, though, and Comaneci instead used her mistakes as motivation.

"I told myself I was never going to be humiliated in such a way again," she wrote.

By 1975, Comaneci had put the world on notice, winning the all-around title at the European Championships. Only thirteen, she was the youngest competitor in the field.

Before the 1970s, gymnastics belonged to women, not young girls. Hard as it is to believe today, competitors usually were in their midtwenties, some even returning to competition after they had children.

In 1972, Olga Korbut began the youth movement, winning three gold medals and a silver at the Munich Games. Only seventeen, she delighted crowds with her showman's personality and megawatt smile.

Comaneci was the antithesis of Korbut. Reserved and quiet, she competed with a businessperson's demeanor.

It didn't matter. Fans fell in love with her anyway, and thanks to her, gymnastics would never be the same again.

"Nadia changed our sport," Mike Jacki, the former executive director of the U.S.A. Gymnastics Federation told the *Los Angeles Times* in 1989. "She did everything—or at least tried to do everything—perfectly, and that was not something you could say for everyone in the sport before she came on the scene. Nadia put the emphasis on technical mastery."

On the first day of Olympic gymnastics competition at the Forum in Montreal, Comaneci swung onto her favorite apparatus, the uneven bars. Twenty-three seconds later when she dismounted the world had witnessed something it had never seen in the sport before—perfection.

"I finished my routine, and I thought I was one of the best and that maybe I would get a 9.9," Comaneci remembered of her first perfect ten to the *New York Times*. "Then I went back and started to prepare myself for the beam. I wasn't looking for the score, and I heard the crowd explode."

The scoreboard actually read 1.00. It wasn't set up to accommodate tens.

Overnight Comaneci went from an unpronounceable name to a household name. The darling of the Olympics, she would appear on virtually every magazine and newspaper cover in the world. That *Young and the Restless* theme that ABC used for her performance footage ultimately was renamed *Nadia's Theme.*

"She helped bring the sport alive to the masses with that little pixie look and that cute ponytail," former Olympic coach Rita Brown said.

For the next two weeks, Montreal—and really the world—revolved around Comaneci. Officials scrambled to adjust their scoreboards as Comaneci went on to capture six more perfect tens (three on uneven bars, three on balance beam).

Her medal haul grew daily: three individual golds, a silver for her team, and another bronze for herself.

By the time the all-around finals came around—a showdown between Comaneci and the still-popular Korbut—$16 tickets were being sold for $100.

"In 1976 Nadia was this mysterious young girl from Eastern Europe," her husband Bart Connor, an Olympic medalist himself, said. "That was a magical time when Nadia came out of nowhere and did what she did."

Comaneci spoke no English, so her interviews were short and fairly uninformative. That only lent to the mystery of the little girl from the communist country who had captured everyone's hearts.

Back home in Romania, she was the perfect symbol for a political party desperate to prove its merits. She became the youngest person to be designated a Hero of Socialist Labor. *Sportul,* the national sports newspaper, cried "Nadia, the Golden Girl of Romanian Sports, a Symbol of the Free Life of Our Youth" in its headline.

Four years later, when Comaneci returned for the Olympic Games in Moscow, the pixie was gone, replaced by an eighteen-year-old woman who had grown four inches and gained twenty pounds. She won four more medals there, losing the all-around title to Russian Yelena Davydova in a decision many considered to be Moscow hometown judging.

A year later, in 1981, Karolyi defected to the United States and Comaneci retired and returned to Romania. In 1984, International Olympic Committee president Juan Antonio Samaranch presented Comaneci with the Silver Medal of the Olympic Order, the Games' highest honor. She would receive the prestigious award again in 2004, making her the first person to be honored twice.

Gymnastics continued to blossom and grow, but the woman who helped start it, faded away into obscurity.

Hers was a communist country, run by a cruel dictator named Nicolae Ceausescu. Because of her fame, Comaneci lived a good life, but for other Romanians life was oppressive. The secret police patrolled with rigid control, extinguishing free speech and any opposition with cruel force. Food was scarce, and the economy, except for those in Ceausescu's good graces, was disastrous.

And though Comaneci had more material rewards, she had no more freedom. The Romanian government allowed her to travel to Los Angeles for the 1984 Olympic Games, but was fearful that she would defect; the government kept her under constant secret-police surveillance and would not allow her to even speak with Karolyi, who was then coaching the U.S. team.

For the next five years, Comaneci gave private gymnastics lessons while her government forbade her to travel. In 1988 organizers for the Seoul Olympic Games asked Comaneci to attend, but the request was denied.

A year later, Comaneci walked six hours to the only European border that was still manned by guards and lined with barbed wire. She slipped through into Hungary.

Comaneci left everything behind—her mother, her brother, even her medals.

"Romania was a communist country then, and I had to get away," Comaneci explained simply. "I knew I might never see my family again."

Her new life was not, at first, a ten. The man who helped her flee, Konstantin Panait, turned out to be every bit the dictator that Ceausescu was. Married to someone else, he painted a lurid tale about his relationship with Comaneci that proved to be untrue. He made her a virtual hostage by threatening her with extradition back to Romania and took her money, arranging interviews for her but pocketing the appearance fees himself.

The media, at first unaware of Panait's hold on Comaneci, painted an unfavorable picture of Comaneci, and the distrustful Comaneci retreated even further.

Only after her friends—Karolyi and Connor foremost among them—interceded did Comaneci finally escape the last shackles of her life.

"My life teaches people that it's possible to strive for your dreams and achieve them," she said. "So many people give up when times get hard. You must overcome your difficulties and keep on trucking."

The reconnection with Conner was the last step on Comaneci's road to a fairy-tale life. The two had met originally years earlier—a photographer during the 1976 American Cup prodded Conner to peck Comaneci on the cheek while posing for a picture—and when Comaneci moved to Oklahoma to work with coach Paul Ziert in 1991, Connor wasted no time contacting her.

She got the first perfect ten in the Olympics, proving that we can all go for a ten in life.

—RITA BROWN, FORMER OLYMPIC GYMNASTICS COACH

The couple married in 1996. To the delight of Comaneci, the wedding was held in the now-liberated Romania.

"I was wrong," Comaneci said of the climate in her homeland. "Romania changed."

She even has her medals. The day after he learned she had fled the country, Ceausescu ordered soldiers to her home to seize them. What they didn't realize was that Comaneci had far more than her Olympic medals. She had a room full of medals, close to two hundred. The confused soldiers didn't know which to take and instead cordoned off the room, planning to return to confiscate the medals.

A day later, the revolution broke out. Ceausescu never got the medals. Comaneci's brother, Adrian, did, and when he came to America, he returned them to their rightful owner.

"Nadia is passionate about life," her husband said. "She has a unique ability to focus on the objective and ignore all the distractions. She goes after what she wants, and nothing can break her concentration."

Today Comaneci and Connor, the First Couple of Gymnastics, run the Bart Connor Gymnastics Academy in Oklahoma and travel the world as sort of ambassadors for their sport. In 2006, they welcomed their first child, a son, Dylan, or Gogosel, as Comaneci calls him. That's Romanian for "little donut."

Comaneci is as revered and adored now as she was thirty years ago.

It is the appreciation that she gets today at forty-four, though, that really resonates with Comaneci. It is an appreciation for a life, complete with warts, that has taken Comaneci from the precipice of perfection to the cruelty of communism.

That she has emerged from it all with her dignity intact, with her inner strength even stronger, and her joy for life even deeper, really is her legacy.

"One word to describe my life?" she said. "Ten. Perfection."

And now it is.

Nadia Comaneci's Life Lessons

Dream Big, but Go Step by Step

Nadia Comaneci dreamed of being a great gymnast and aimed for the top. That is what fueled her and motivated her, but to achieve the dream, Comaneci kept her focus on one meet, apparatus by apparatus. "You need to have goals," she said. "But I like the little ones, not the big ones. I always expected less, and then when good things happened, everything was much more than I expected."

Don't Be Afraid

More difficult than any tumbling pass or routine on the balance beam, Nadia Comaneci made the most daring move of her career when she defected from Romania in 1989. Of course she was frightened, but she wasn't afraid to push onward. Sports taught her that. "My life teaches people that everything is possible if you just go for it," she said. "Don't hold back. Go after your dreams."

Be Yourself

Before Nadia Comaneci, there was Olga Korbut, a Russian teenager who ignited the world with her bright smile and huge personality. That wasn't who Nadia was, nor did she try to become that. Instead she stayed true to herself and became a star in her own right.

Remember Your Roots

For so long, Romania was a lost country. Its people were down-trodden, its economy in shambles. Nadia Comaneci was the one bright spot. When she left she easily could have turned her back on the country that had caused her so much pain. Instead she has embraced her homeland, maintaining a home there and maintaining her pride in her culture. "I'm proud to go back to Romania," she said. "They still remember me. My people are proud of me and what I did. I want to help them."

Pay Attention to Detail

Gymnastics is easily one of the most disciplined of all sports. It requires attention to every detail, from extended fingers to pointed toes. A momentary lapse of concentration can equate to a disastrous fall. Those are lessons that Nadia Comaneci believes are equally important off of the gymnastics' mat. "Gymnastics taught me to be dedicated to all you do," she said. "It motivated me to make good choices and organize my life."

Keep Your Sense of Humor

Nadia Comaneci is a delight, a joyous woman who is truly amazed that people still remember, let alone revere, her. She is witty and genuinely funny, traits she easily could have lost during the more difficult periods of her life. When asked her what she is afraid of, she laughs: "I have a fear of heights now. Can you believe that? I didn't as a kid."

～ 4 ～

Gail Devers:
Conquering

*"My philosophy of life is to conquer your circumstances or be
conquered. I have always elected to conquer them."*

—GAIL DEVERS

When she was told she had Graves' disease, an autoimmune disease that causes overactivity of the thyroid gland, Gail Devers asked, "How do we control it?"

When she was told that the medication usually used to treat Graves' disease, a beta-blocker, was on the banned substance list issued by the International Olympic Committee (IOC), Devers asked for another solution.

When the alternate treatment, radiation, caused her feet to swell, blister, crack, and ooze to the point that one podiatrist said her feet were so damaged she risked amputation, Devers simply found another option.

And then she went on to win three gold medals, three world championships, and secure a place in Olympic track history.

In her charity work, Devers often refers to the "Gail Force." Never has a nickname been so appropriate. The track superstar is indeed a force to be reckoned with.

"My philosophy of life is to conquer your circumstances or be conquered," Devers explained. "I have always elected to conquer them."

More like blowing through her circumstances like bursting a tape at the finish line.

Sports history is littered with historic comebacks and epic triumphs over difficult circumstances. Few, however, can compare to the hurdles that Devers faced.

In the span of one year, Devers went from a woman who might never walk again to a sprinter dubbed the Fastest Woman in the World. Hers is a story of incomparable spirit and determination, a will that not only never quit, but also saw endless opportunities instead of impossible obstacles.

"It may take a while for the bulb to go off in Gail's head," her longtime coach Bob Kersee told *Sports Illustrated* in 1993. "But once it does and she sees what she can do, she's unstoppable."

Only two women have won the 100-meter dash in back-to-back Olympics.

Devers is one of them.

Only two women have won both the 100-meter dash and the 100-meter hurdles in a single world championship.

Devers is one of them.

Throw in nine Pacific-10 conference titles and two NCAA championships during her collegiate career at University of California, Los Angeles (UCLA), plus two more world 100-meter championships and a high school track championship where Devers alone finished fourth in the team competition, and you can begin to see the outline of a resume that puts Devers among her sport's elite.

What separates Devers from her peers, though, is her ability to hurdle more than just the sawhorses in her lane. Not everyone will become a track star like Devers, but everyone can learn from the faith in both herself and God that allowed Devers to overcome odds stacked firmly against her.

"You can never give up or get down on yourself," Devers once said. "A true champion keeps his or her chin up and always takes life one race at a time."

Raised in San Diego by Larry, a Baptist minister, and Alabe, a teacher's aide in elementary school, Devers once described her childhood as an episode of *Leave It to Beaver*. The Devers' family did everything together, and the children—Gail and her older brother, Parenthesis (P.D. for short)—enjoyed an idyllic upbringing.

"My mom and dad have been my mentors, role models, and heroes," Devers said. "My parents have always supported me. They are my everything."

Unlike so many preachers' kids, Devers never chafed at her father's rules and religious bearing in the community. An old soul, she was content as a youngster to read or crochet and watch one of the few television shows her father permitted, *I Love Lucy*. When the streetlights began to flicker in their neighborhood, a sign that the Devers's kids needed to head home, it was Gail tugging P.D. into the house.

Devers loved to teach, and in the summers welcomed other children into the house for lessons. Though hers was a pretend school, she had a gift. One mother bragged that in the span of one summer under the tutelage of young Gail Devers, her son had gone from a first-grade reading level to third.

"I wanted to be a teacher, and if it was my choice, I'd have had twenty-eight students in my classroom without a teacher's aide," Devers said. "As it turns out, I've been a teacher with a much bigger classroom."

Devers said she never liked to run, but what she liked even less was being beaten in a footrace by P.D. Determined to best her older brother, she began to train on her own, eventually outrunning her brother to the finish line.

Devers never really ran competitively until high school, but when she got started it was quickly clear that she was a natural. At the age of seventeen, in her senior year at Sweetwater High School, Devers won the 100-meter dash, and the 100-meter hurdles, and took second in the long jump, earning enough points on her own to finish fourth in the team competition at the California state track championships.

Recruited by a number of colleges, she chose UCLA, intrigued in part by its new coach, a man by the name of Bob Kersee.

A legend in track circles today, Kersee is known for his exuberant coaching style and his unflinching faith in his pupils.

Kersee instantly recognized what could be done for Devers, promising her success at both the collegiate and international levels.

"Regardless whether his predictions were going to be true, I liked them," Devers told *Sports Illustrated* in 1996. "I hadn't run track until high school.

I hadn't had much coaching. So I thought if he had faith in me, he'd coach me well. For quite a while, Bobby believed in me more than I believed in myself."

Challenged by the coach who had a reputation for screaming, ranting, and raving his protégés to the finish line, Devers soon began to believe in herself. When, as a sophomore at UCLA, she set an American record in the 100-meter hurdles to qualify for the Olympic Games in Seoul that year, Devers was a convert.

But in Seoul, Devers competed poorly, finishing eighth in the semifinals. By then she had been suffering from strange symptoms for some time: vision loss and acute migraine pain, uncontrollable shaking, and seemingly endless menstrual cycles. Her weight had been fluctuating wildly, and no matter what she tried, Devers didn't have the gusto she once had.

For two years, she persisted through the pain, with one doctor after another failing to come up with an explanation. Finally in 1990 she received an answer. She had Graves' disease, a rare thyroid condition that counts former President George Bush and his wife, Barbara, among its sufferers.

The good news for Devers was that simple medication and careful attention to her diet would keep the disease under control. The bad news was that the beta-blockers normally prescribed were banned substances in the eyes of the IOC, and even though she would be taking it for a diagnosed medical condition, the presence of the drug in her system would render her ineligible.

Devers went for a more drastic solution, radiation treatment designed to shrink the cyst in her thyroid gland. But by 1991, Devers could hardly walk, let alone compete. For months she had trained with four and sometimes five pairs of socks on to quell the pain in her swollen, bleeding, and oozing feet, but finally not even that worked. Her parents moved in and literally carried their only daughter from room to room.

Eventually she went to a podiatrist who explained that had she walked for even another week on her feet in their current condition, she likely would have lost them.

That doctor finally discovered the obvious cause of her problem—the radiation had all but destroyed her thyroid gland. Doctors changed Devers's treatment, and slowly her feet returned to normal. By April 1991, Devers took a painful walk around the UCLA track in a pair of socks, her first "workout" in two years.

By May 1991, she won a hurdles competition, and in August, at the world championships in Tokyo, she took home a silver medal.

"Use me as an example," Devers told *Jet* in 1992. "When the walls are closing in, when someone doesn't know where to turn, tell them I was there. I kept going. So can others."

Fully back to training, Devers eyed a return to the Olympic Games, setting her sights on Barcelona in 1992. At the urging of Kersee she added the 100-meter dash to her repertoire and qualified to compete in both the dash and the hurdles in Barcelona.

As she prepared to step into the blocks for the 100-meter dash, Jackie Joyner-Kersee, a two-time gold medalist herself by then, whispered quietly to Devers.

"You've worked hard for this," she said. "You better get it."

The 1992 women's 100-meter was among the closest in Olympic history, with five women crossing the finish line within six one-hundredths of a second of one another. The cacophony of an excited fan base in the stadium had come to near silence when the race ended, with everyone breathlessly waiting to see who had won. Within minutes the television cameramen started sprinting toward Devers, signaling what soon would be an official announcement.

The woman who less than a year earlier had nearly lost her feet had just won Olympic gold. Taking the wind into account, Devers's time of 10.82 was second only to Florence Griffith Joyner's world record run of 10.49.

Days later, Devers caught her toe as she leapt across the final hurdle in the 100-meter hurdles. Leading the race until the mishap, she dove across the finish line but had to settle for fifth.

Where others would have been despondent, Devers, who had overcome far more than that, responded philosophically, "It wasn't meant to be."

Between the 1992 Games and the 1996 Atlanta Olympics, Devers became the easy favorite in both the 100-meter dash and 100-meter hurdles. In 1993 she won both events at the world championships in Stuttgart, Germany, becoming only the second woman to achieve such a feat in forty-five years. In the process she broke her own American hurdles record, finishing in 12.45.

In Atlanta, Devers again survived a narrow finish to win gold in the 100-meter dash, joining 1940s American star Wyomia Tyus as the only women to win gold in track's featured race in back-to-back Olympics. Devers's bad luck in the hurdles, however, continued. She finished fourth, just out of medal reach.

"Each individual must define success for themselves," Devers said. "It's not wins and losses. To me, success is giving your all. I say, give 100 percent and a little oomph."

Devers qualified for both the 2000 and 2004 Olympics—rebounding from an Achilles and hamstring injury to lower her American hurdles mark to 12.33 at the 2000 Olympic trials—but each time was snakebit by injury. In 2000, Devers' hamstring problem resurfaced, and in 2004, a calf injury forced her out of competition.

Fans figured Devers had retired following the 2004 Athens Games, but in 2006, Devers returned to competition with the explanation for her absence. At a post-race press conference, Devers introduced Karsen Anise, her daughter with husband Mike Phillips, born on June 20, 2005. The baby, who arrived via caesarian section, kept her mother out of commission for six months.

But she wasn't down long. After a fourth-place finish in February 2006, Devers stunned the racing community by winning the 60-meter hurdles at the 2007 Millrose Games, only nineteen months after Karsen's birth. The forty-year-old Devers blew by a field that included defending Olympic champion Joanna Hayes, one-time world champion Perdita Felicien, and her own student, Danielle Carruthers, to take first in 7.86, the best time in the world for the season and just 0.12 off Devers's 2003 U.S. record.

"I wanted to come back at forty and do something for my great fans, for the people who supported me having a baby, saying please don't retire," Devers said after the race. "I say forty is the new twenty."

Though not retiring, Devers remained noncommittal about her future plans. She came back specifically to compete in the one hundredth running of the Millrose Games but also said she looked forward to more ordinary challenges.

ᏯᎾ ˙⬩˙ ᏔᏯ

"Keep your dreams alive.
Understand to achieve anything
requires faith and belief in
yourself, vision, hard work,
determination, and dedication.
Remember all things are possible
for those who believe."

—Gᴀɪʟ Dᴇᴠᴇʀs

•⬩•

"I was doing ballet with my daughter earlier today in her little tutu," she said after her surprising win, "so I'll go back to that."

In the meantime, she continues to bring her inspirational story to children everywhere. The author of three books, Devers also runs her own philanthropy organization, the Gail Devers Foundation, whose motto is F.O.R.C.E, for Focus On Respect and Commitment to Excellence. Along with a community center, Devers's foundation is responsible for renovating her high school track and annually offers a character-building camp for children.

And in 2000, Devers testified before Congress about the problems that the original misdiagnosis of her disease presented, urging Congress to combat medical mistakes with action.

Even without her charity work, Devers is an inspiration. Whether she places first, second, or dead last, Devers is a champion every time she stands in the blocks, sprints down a track, and crosses a finish line.

"A perfect day for me is to get up, put my feet on the floor, give thanks to God, and move on," Devers said.

Gail Devers's Life Lessons

Focus on Being the Best You Can Be Every Day

Sometimes progress for Gail Devers was painfully slow. Recovering from the radiation treatments that ravaged her body, the world-class sprinter had to settle for simply walking around a track. But rather than wallow in self-pity, she instead celebrated her small successes. Eventually those small victories became much bigger. "The lessons I've learned from sports have taught me about dedication, setting realistic goals, and never giving up," Devers said.

Be Respectful to Yourself and Others

In a society where athletes are celebrated, pampered, and idolized, Gail Devers never has failed to give of her time or of herself. A favorite among her running peers, she also earned USA. Track & Field's Humanitarian Award in 1999 for the good works she's done for others. "The most important trait to be successful is integrity," Devers said. "Be true to yourself."

Be Committed to Something

Not everyone can cross finish lines in record time or stand on a podium to receive an Olympic medal, but everyone can find a passion and commit themselves fully to it. Before Gail Devers ever ran a step, she fell in love with teaching, and though she didn't grow up to become the elementary school teacher she had once dreamed of being, she has used her status as an Olympic athlete to teach children and commit herself to their causes. "The lessons I've learned from sports have taught me about dedication, setting realistic goals, and never giving up," Devers said.

Excellence Is Defined By You and Not Others

In a world where success is measured by tenths of seconds, and medals and ribbons determine who is the best and who is second best, Gail Devers always took her parents' advice to heart. "The best advice I ever got came from my parents," Devers said. "They told me to always be true to myself and not worry about what others think." By truly believing that, Devers was able to shrug off near misses in the 100-meter hurdles, misses that others would have deemed disappointments but Devers simply said weren't meant to be.

Age Is Just a Number

It is never too late to start and certainly always too early to quit. Gail Devers proved that in 2007 when she stunned the racing world by winning the 60-meter hurdles at the Millrose Games. Only nineteen months removed from the birth of her daughter and at the age of forty, Devers blew away the field and turned in the fastest time of the year.

5

Teresa Edwards:
Trailblazing

*"We define success for ourselves. Each individual
has to ask, 'How far and how high do I want to go?'"*

—TERESA EDWARDS

The house where the bicycle rim served as a hoop is still there. So is the backyard, the one where the rough-and-tumble tomboy played tackle football with the boys.

It's easy to find, actually.

In Cairo, Georgia, if you're looking to find Teresa Edwards's roots you need only drive down Teresa Edwards Street.

She is not the most famous person to come from tiny Cairo. That honor belongs to Jackie Robinson, the baseball pioneer who integrated America's pastime. But make no mistake: the city of ten thousand is every bit as proud of its daughter as it is of its son.

And rightly so.

It is commonplace today to call athletes the "Michael Jordan" of their sport. In Edwards's case, the comparison may be lacking. She is the only American basketball player—male or female—to compete in five Olympic Games and reigns as the most decorated Olympic basketball player with four gold medals and one bronze. A rookie on the team in 1984 and a wily veteran in 2000, she is both the youngest and oldest American to earn an Olympic gold medal.

As a member of Team USA, she competed for eighteen medals in international competition. She won fourteen gold, one silver, and three bronze.

More like Cal Ripken than Jordan, Edwards boasts a longevity record that likely never will be matched, with 216 international games that produced 2,008 points, 890 assists, 576 rebounds, and 372 steals.

"Teresa is probably the greatest woman player of all time," former Women's National Basketball Association (WNBA) president Val Ackerman said. "Five Olympics set the standard forever. Teresa goes down in history for all her contributions to the game, on and off the court."

Respected equally by her predecessors, successors, and peers, Edwards is as important to her sport as Cairo's other native child was to his. Edwards's name may not go into the history books as a person to forever change sports and society as Jackie Robinson's did, but she is every bit as much a pioneer.

"Teresa will be the Wilma Rudolph of women's basketball," Andy Landers, Teresa's University of Georgia coach, said. "This is a country where if you have a dream and pursue it with all you've got, those dreams will come true. Teresa Edwards personifies that."

When the WNBA tried to entice Edwards to its league but refused to pay her and her peers wages comparable to what they had been making in the defunct American Basketball League (ABL), Edwards said no. Even after the ABL folded, Edwards resisted until the WNBA upped its financial ante.

"The greatest lesson from my life is positive perseverance," Edwards told me. "We all have to learn how to persevere in a positive manner, and that's not easy to do."

If anyone was built for such a battle, though, it was Edwards. A tomboy who early in life dashed her mother's hopes of a daughter flitting around in pretty dresses, she ran rough and tumble in Cairo with the boys. If she wasn't playing softball or football in the yard, she could be found in the nearby park playing basketball.

Life wasn't easy for Edwards. Her mother, Mildred, got pregnant with her only daughter when she was just sixteen. Forced to drop out of high school, she went to work in the nearby vegetable fields, and though Edwards's mother never married her father, Leroy Copeland, the couple had three more children—all boys. Money was scarce, and mother and daughter shared a bedroom for much of Edwards's life.

"My mom was the strongest influence on my life and still is today," Edwards remembered. "She's been the prime motivating factor for me. She was a one-day-at-a-time person, and I'm sure that's where I learned that. I always wanted to help her have a better life. To this day, my mother teaches me about life, and this is a woman without a high school degree."

For her part, Edwards became the first in her family to go to college and subsequently the first to earn a college degree, graduating in 1989 from the University of Georgia with a degree in leisure studies.

"That's the biggest example I could make for my brothers," Edwards told *Sports Illustrated* in 1992 about her college diploma. "It means much more than any shot I could ever take."

In the seventh grade, Edwards tried out for and made the middle school basketball team, news that her mother could hardly believe.

"She kept coming home late from school and laying it off on some teacher. 'I'm helping Miss So-and-So,'" Mildred Edwards told *Sports Illustrated* in 1992. "Then she said one day, 'I need a new pair of sneakers because I made the team.' I said, 'Girl, you can't play basketball.' She said, 'Mama, I made the team.'"

Clearly gifted, Edwards wasn't afraid to play with the boys. Frankly, she welcomed it, figuring that was the best way to get better.

It worked. Edwards led Cairo High School to a 58-3 record in her final two seasons and lifted the Syrupmaids to the Class AAAA state title as a senior.

"I don't remember not having a passion for athletics," Edwards said. "I wanted more from myself, so I played with and against the guys. I always had a passion to play and compete."

Georgia's Player of the Year in her senior season, Edwards decided to stay close to home and attend the University of Georgia. On her application to the school, a newspaper once reported, Edwards's scribbled "All-American" next to career goals.

"Teresa is the greatest competitor to ever lace them up," Landers said of his collegiate star. "There have been better players, but she has no peers in competitiveness, and she competes with a purpose. If we won, and she had six points, she was tickled to death. She always came to the arena to compete and didn't care about self-promotion."

She was smart and an adept point guard with lots of basketball savvy but had the added bonus of a five-foot, ten-inch frame that allowed her to be even more effective than the traditional guard. A perfect fit for an already talented Georgia team, she helped the Lady Bulldogs to four NCAA Tournaments and two Final Fours, becoming the all-American she set out to become, but doing more than even she had imagined.

She was named an all-American twice.

"I've always had wonderful coaches, from junior high to high school to college to international play," Edwards said. "It seems I had the right coach at the right time throughout my career."

 formula ..+. formula

"I'm most proud that I made it out of Cairo, Georgia, to make a life for my family and me. Changing your history is a hard thing to do."

—TERESA EDWARDS

Asked to join the national team at the age of seventeen, Edwards was invited to try out for the Olympic team following her sophomore season at Georgia.

She made that 1984 squad and at twenty was the youngest player on the roster. In the Los Angeles Games, she played sparingly but nonetheless returned to Georgia with an Olympic gold medal around her neck.

"When I was in the eleventh grade, I saw her at the Team USA tryouts," basketball superstar Lisa Leslie said. "Two girls trapped her at half-court, and she threw a perfect behind-the-back pass down the floor to a teammate. It was amazing. Teresa was an awesome leader, an extraordinary competitor, and a winner."

Determined to become more of a factor at the next Olympics, Edwards returned to college and concentrated on becoming as good a scorer as she was a playmaker.

"She's a student of the game and is always studying the sport," former WNBA senior vice president for player development Renee Brown said. "She knows the game of basketball inside and out."

After graduating from Georgia—and becoming the second woman to have her jersey retired there—Edwards played professionally in Europe and Japan, earning sizeable paychecks in the only places where professional basketball was available for women.

Honing her game overseas, in 1988 she again donned the red, white, and blue but this time as a more complete player. When the United States took home the gold medal, Edwards soared as the team's second-leading scorer, averaging 16.6 points per game.

Disappointed after a bronze medal finish in Barcelona in 1992, Edwards contemplated retirement. She waffled as late as 1994, but when the twenty-nine-year-old was named to the all-tournament team following the world championship she decided to press on for another Olympic run.

"Teresa hates to lose more than she loves to win," former Olympic coach Nell Fortner said.

This one, of course, would be on American soil and, more important, in Georgia. The 1996 Atlanta Games would be played less than a four-hour drive from Cairo, a fact that brought Edwards to tears when she was officially named to the Games' roster.

Now the oldest player in a United States. uniform at the age of thirty-two, Edwards led the Americans flawlessly. A floor general in every sense of the word, she dished out 8 assists per game, scored 6.9 points, and pulled down 3.8 rebounds, helping the United States not just win Olympic gold but usher in a new era in women's team sports.

"We define success for ourselves," Edwards said. "Each individual has to ask, 'How far and how high do I want to go?'"

Following the Atlanta Olympics, the clamor for professional women's leagues finally reached fever pitch in this country.

The clamor, however, was disorganized, and in the span of one year the United States went from having no professional women's basketball leagues to two. The WNBA had the backing and marketing arm of the National

"I see so many young people who are so easily discouraged when they don't see success right away. They're afraid to go after their dreams. That never happened with Teresa."

—ANDY LANDERS, EDWARDS'S COACH AT THE UNIVERSITY OF GEORGIA

Basketball Association (NBA), but the American Basketball League offered a lengthier season, bigger paychecks, and a more traditional basketball schedule.

Edwards opted for the ABL, serving as coach, star player, and drawing card for the Atlanta Glory. In two full and one abbreviated seasons in the ABL, Edwards shone, averaging 20.7 points per game, 6.5 rebounds, and 6.5 assists. But overshadowed by her sisters in the WNBA who had the television package and the assistance of the NBA, Edwards remained anonymous.

She didn't care. After nine years in basketball exile that took her from Italy to Spain to Japan, Edwards was playing at home.

"With Teresa, what you see is what you get," Houston Comets coach Van Chancellor said. "She never got the big head."

Edwards's joy, however, was short-lived. In December 1998, the inevitable happened. One of the leagues had to go, and it was the ABL. The WNBA offered to take in the ABL refugees but insisted they would pay them only the equivalent of rookie contracts, a substantial pay cut for Edwards and others at the top of the ABL food chain.

She declined, opting instead to train on her own in the hopes of making another Olympic Games.

"The lessons I've learned through sports are the same as in the rest of my life," Edwards said. "The challenges I've faced in basketball, I've just considered part of life."

Instead of the bright lights of television, Edwards trained in anonymity at a gym in Atlanta, pushing herself through grueling workouts and games with men who had no idea who she was and why she was beating them so badly.

"She was way ahead of her time, a true trailblazer. In women's basketball, she was knocking down barriers and cutting a swath not cut before."

—Former Olympic Coach
Marianne Stanley

It all was rewarded when Edwards was named to her fifth Olympic Games at the age of thirty-six. A co-captain in Sydney, Edwards not only averaged 6.1 points in the Olympic Games, she guided the young players by example.

"Someone of her stature, who is as good as she is, you'd expect her to be more involved with herself. Teresa is down to earth," Theresa Grentz, who coached Edwards in the 1992 Olympics, once said. "She can't be bought. Her values are important to her. Her humility and her simplicity of life make her very special to be around."

When the gold-medal game finally ended, Edwards sat alone for what seemed like forever, savoring the moment until teammate and close friend Dawn Staley came to her side.

"She's more competitive than I am," Staley said about Edwards. "And that's saying a lot."

Finally, in 2003, with former Olympic teammate and Minnesota Lynx coach Suzie McConnell-Serio urging both Edwards and Lynx management, Edwards joined the WNBA. The rookie was thirty-eight when she was drafted in 2003.

By the end of the season, the Lynx rewrote its record books as Edwards, a starter in all thirty-four games, shattered the season's assist mark with 148. A year later, the forty-year-old Edwards suited up for the Lynx again.

"You can rely on her," legendary *New York Daily News* basketball writer Dick Weiss said. "For sixteen years, Teresa played at the Olympic level and in her forties was still terrific. We'll never see another one like her."

"I don't care about my basketball accomplishments because they'll be forgotten. I hope I've left something that has helped others."

—TERESA EDWARDS

In 2005, however, she became a free agent, but when no one picked up her contract, she unofficially retired.

Of course with Edwards that unofficially could change any day now.

"Life itself is my biggest hurdle," Edwards said. "Now I've got to walk away from the game and make that adjustment. Crossing over is a tough battle. In the gym, I've always had an automatic passion, and now I've got to find that with the rest of my life."

Few doubt Edwards will find a direction. Friends and colleagues remark not only at Edwards's humility but her ability to overcome humble beginnings and the spiritual strength that serves as her constant foundation.

A genius with a basketball, Edwards serves today as an inspiration that anyone can go from humble beginnings to international stardom.

"Teresa came from a little high school in Cairo, Georgia, but made it to the big time," Van Chancellor said. "If you want to accomplish things like her, you've got to get out and work hard."

Teresa Edwards's Life Lessons

Have Faith

When the American Basketball League (ABL) closed its doors and the Women's National Basketball Association (WNBA) refused to pay Teresa Edwards the salary she had earned previously, she simply said no. It could have marked the end of her career, could have put her in jeopardy of missing the cut for her final Olympic Games. Edwards, however, believed in herself and believed that someone else had her back, and those beliefs allowed her to take the unpopular stand. "My mom gave me the best foundation a child could receive—a life built on faith in God and prayer," Edwards said. "To this day, that's all I have that matters. Without it, I'm nothing."

Dream Beyond the Box Society Keeps You In

Age and logic argue that no one can play on five Olympic teams, that to be competitive for that long is simply impossible. Teresa Edwards defied the Olympics by not merely competing in five Olympics but by being a decisive and important factor in each one. "With Teresa, I think about longevity," WNBA senior vice president Renée Brown said. "She's played on five different Olympic teams and was the leader on each one. She took the responsibility and held herself accountable."

Be Disciplined and Passionate About Something Every Day

Teresa Edwards calls herself a "one-day-at-a-time" person, but with Edwards that doesn't mean being complacent and letting life come at you one day at a time. In her case it means finding a reason to wake up every morning, a purpose to each day, and a goal to fulfill. "Your character is being built in everything you do on a daily basis," Edwards said.

Go for It

The saying has become a cliché, but really the desire and drive to persevere is what guides greatness. Within every athlete, within every great man or woman, there is a fearlessness and a determination to pursue a dream. It is what pushed Teresa Edwards out of the confines of tiny Cairo and into the world of international basketball. It is what allowed her to ascend the Olympic medal podium five times. "I possessed a passion and a heart to be the best at what I did," Edwards said. "I don't think you can coach that. The discipline it took to be the best was a part of who I was. You've got to want it so bad nothing will stop you or deter you."

∾ 6 ∾

Janet Evans:
Everyday Champion

"I was steadfast, worked hard, and kept plugging."

—JANET EVANS

The young woman jumped out of the pool, invigorated after a forty-five-minute swim.

As she was walking along the pool deck, the lifeguard approached her with some advice.

"If you want to swim faster," he suggested, "you've got to bend your elbows."

The woman smiled politely, thanked the lifeguard and then, almost as an afterthought, said, "Wasn't there an Olympic swimmer a while back who had a stiff-armed stroke?"

The lifeguard thought about it and the two chatted back and forth amiably for a while.

Eventually the woman went on her way, grinning to herself.

Unbeknownst to him, the lifeguard had just offered up swimming advice to Janet Evans, a woman who owns five Olympic medals, forty-five U.S. national titles, and three world records, two of which still stand eighteen years later.

"Janet loved [that encounter]," said her agent, Evan Morgenstein, who remembered the conversation with the lifeguard. "It was about her fun spirit and her total lack of ego."

It is Evans's records and medals that define her, but it is her personality that endures. Her gigantic grin lit up the Olympic stage in 1988 for the first time and continued to wow the crowds in Atlanta in 1996, when she passed the torch to Muhammad Ali. Blessed with talent, Evans also was graced with humility. Before she was able to vote she already owned world records, but not once did Evans allow fame and glory to change her. Nicknamed "Just Janet" by her father, Evans lived up to the moniker. She was a normal teenager and a normal adult who just so happened to swim better than anyone in history.

She told me of meeting legendary swimmer Tracy Caulkins in 1985 and how kind Caulkins was to the fourteen-year-old Evans.

"She was so nice to me," Evans said to me. "She showed me her gold medal and acted in such a classy and gracious manner. I've always tried to treat people like Tracy treated me."

She succeeded. Despite more glory than even Caulkins achieved—three gold medals in Seoul in 1988, another gold and a silver in 1992 in Barcelona, forty-five U.S. titles, three world titles, the first woman to break the sixteen-minute barrier in the 1,500-meter freestyle, and the first woman to hold three world records concurrently—Evans remained and still remains true to herself.

"Think about Janet's life," Morgenstein said to me. "Every day she's gotten up, and all she has to do is be Janet Evans. She hasn't had to answer to anyone, but still she is the most gracious person you'll ever meet."

That she did any of it, really, is a testimony to the steely determination that lurks behind the megawatt grin. Told she was too tiny to swim, told her style (that stiff-armed stroke the lifeguard noticed) was too unorthodox, Evans put her head in the water and reached for the wall. She wanted to win, of course, but more than that she wanted to do what she loved.

"Describe myself in one word?" Evans asked me. "Tenacious. I had so much to overcome, including my lack of size, but I was steadfast, worked hard, and kept plugging."

Janet was a precocious toddler who took her first steps at eight months and hula-hooped her way through her parents California home at the age of two. At the age of one, Evans toddled along with her older brothers, David and John, to swim lessons at the North Orange County YMCA but made such a commotion watching from the bleachers that her mother, Barbara, begged the instructor to let little Janet swim as well.

"Janet was always very active right from birth," Barbara Evans told me. "She didn't like to be contained by a car seat or a crib. She wanted to go and keep moving and do it her way."

Though her parents were clearly out of their element—her veterinarian father, Paul, "can only float" and her mother, "can't swim," according to Evans—they recognized early that their daughter had a passion for the pool and fueled that passion however they could. By age three, little Janet had mastered the breaststroke and butterfly and, not long after, competed with the swim team of Placentia.

By age ten, the diminutive sprite set a national record for her age group in the 200-meter freestyle and, a year later, qualified for the U.S. Junior Olympics in the 1,650-yard freestyle.

The national meet, however, was in Wisconsin, and Barbara Evans wasn't keen on her daughter going.

"After qualifying, Janet snuck up in the bleachers and said, 'Daddy, can I go to the nationals?'" Barbara Evans told *Sports Illustrated* in 1988. "And Paul said, 'Of course you can, sweetheart.'"

Younger than every competitor by a year, Evans nonetheless finished forty-seventh out of eighty-one swimmers.

In 1984, Barbara and Paul made the quick thirty-mile drive from their Placentia home to Los Angeles, so their daughter could watch the Olympics.

"I came home and announced that I wanted to be an Olympic champion, and their first comment was, 'What do we need to do?'" Evans told me of her parents' reaction.

Swimming is not an easy sport, not for the swimmer, not for the parents. It requires solitary hours of training and a rigorous schedule that would make most adults blanche, let alone teenagers who hate nothing more than early alarm clocks and demanding schedules.

But as much as she hated the 4:30 AM wake-up calls and the 8:00 PM bedtimes, Evans loved to swim more, and so she and her parents endured the marathon days that produce champions.

Each morning at 5:00 AM, Paul drove his daughter to the pool, and two hours later, Barbara picked her up and brought her home for breakfast. Evans would head to El Dorado High School for the day and, when school was over, went either directly to the pool or to a health club for weightlifting and then on to the pool. Eventually she'd come home to finish her homework and go to bed.

"For the rest of my career, they encouraged me and nudged me when I needed it," Evans told me of her mother and father. "I wanted to do it, but my mom and dad were vital to my success. They attended every one of my meets in the world unless they couldn't get a visa behind the Iron Curtain. My brothers made a lot of sacrifices, too. We didn't take normal family vacations, but I always knew that I was loved."

"I know it sounds pretty silly, but to me, I'm Janet. I just see it as me swimming, not as doing something overwhelming."

—JANET EVANS

The sacrifices were endless. While her friends pushed midnight curfews, Evans was tucked in by 8:00 PM. She missed her sophomore homecoming dance because of a swim meet in London, sent regrets to another formal because she was competing in Berlin, and begged out of her prom in lieu of a regional high school championship.

"Janet understood the importance of self-discipline," her father, Paul, said. "She knew she would have to say no to a lot of good things if she was going to be a world-class swimmer. It's called tenacity, the ability and desire to stick with something through thick and thin."

The payoffs for the hard work came swiftly.

Because of her size, Evans compensated by taking more strokes than her competitors. Hers was not a stroke for the swimming purist—newspapers called her a "windmill in a hurricane,"—but it worked.

"People forget how little Janet really is and was when she swam competitively," her husband, Bill Wilson, said. "She was five foot, six inches, maybe, and weighed less than one hundred pounds and was going up against those

East German machines. Those ladies weighed 180 pounds and had mustaches! Janet's sheer will and passion to win was the difference."

By fifteen, Evans owned her first world records in the 800-meter and 1,500-meter freestyle.

By seventeen, she had obliterated the record books. The teenager packed up world records in the 400-meter, 800-meter, and 1,500-meter freestyle and the year's best finish in the 400-IM for Seoul.

She came home from the Olympic Games a star. Evans won the 400-IM gold medal and, three days later, topped her own world record in the 400-meter by 1.6 seconds to easily win that event. The mark stood until 2006 when Frenchwoman Laure Manaundo finally topped it.

Evans added one more piece of gold to her jewelry box when she defeated East Germany's Astrid Strauss by more than three meters to win the 800-meter freestyle.

"Janet Evans is in a different dimension," East Germany's Heike Friedrich said in 1988. "A swimmer like Janet comes around once every twenty-five years."

Evans came home to parades and banquets and the requisite rounds of interviews. Named the USOC Athlete of the Year, Evans also was honored with the prestigious James E. Sullivan Award, presented to the nation's best amateur athlete.

She could have cashed in on her stardom and accepted the endorsements laid at her feet. No one would have blamed her.

But Evans didn't want that life. She wanted that normalcy again and instead opted to go to college, choosing to enroll at Stanford. Evans was thrilled that the school didn't shepherd its athletes off to private dorms and even more excited to learn she was the only swimmer in her entire building.

"My inspiration comes from within, knowing all the people who are standing with me."

—Janet Evans

Normalcy, however, never extended to the pool where Evans was concerned. In 1989 she set another world record, this one a still unattainable mark in the 800-meter freestyle, and won seven more U.S. titles.

A year later she won three more U.S. titles plus two NCAA crowns for Stanford and, in 1991, matched those efforts stroke for stroke.

In 1992, Evans emerged from the cocoon of college, moving to Austin to train with Olympic coach Mark Schubert.

A bona-fide star this time, she arrived in Barcelona with an amazing seven-year win streak in the 400 meters.

It came to an end in Spain. Dagmar Hase of Germany caught Evans in the final lap, beating Evans in her favorite race by mere inches. The young woman who set personal standards far more reaching than the expectations anyone else could ever set for her was devastated.

"That was really tough for me," Evans told me. "It took me three or four years to get over that loss, even though I won the silver medal."

With one event left—the 800 meters—Evans had two choices. She could wallow in her disappointment or swim for the podium. Not surprisingly, she chose the latter. Three days after her disappointing loss to Hase, Evans led from start to finish, winning the 800-meter freestyle gold by a ridiculous eight-meter distance.

"The biggest obstacle I've had to overcome in my career is learning how to lose. It's okay, " Evans said.

Still licking her wounds from her defeat in the 400, though, Evans left Barcelona and left the pool for four months, her longest break since that day her mother first tossed her in with her brothers.

No one really expected her to come back, not for another Olympics anyway. By 1996, Evans would be twenty-four, and in swimming, as in gymnastics, age is a handicap not an advantage.

But buoyed by the emergence of another upstart—a fourteen-year-old kid by the name of Brooke Bennett, who was winning the events that had defined Evans' career—Evans dove back in the water.

"I didn't want my career to end after Barcelona because other people thought that I was finished,"

"No one doesn't like Janet Evans, and in such a competitive world, that is amazing. She is just so comfortable with who she is."

—EVAN MORGENSTEIN, EVANS'S
LONGTIME AGENT

Evans told *Sports Illustrated* in 1996. "I wanted it to end on my terms, which I'm going to do. No matter what happens in Atlanta, I'll be satisfied because I'm the one who's deciding this in the end."

By then, Evans was more than just a swimmer. She was a popular motivational speaker, a woman who crisscrossed the country to tell people her story, and she wasn't interested in giving that up. So she and Schubert agreed that Evans could train on her own at whatever pool she could find. The deal led to some strange pit stops for Evans, including a session in a senior citizens' complex in Washington state.

"My brother was getting married," Evans told *Sports Illustrated* in 1996. "I told him I would go if he found me a pool for training. He found this twenty-five-meter pool at a senior citizens' complex. I paid the five bucks and went through my workout in the middle of all these senior citizens, and nobody knew a thing. Then I went to the wedding.'"

The year before the '96 Games, Evans and Bennett went head-to-head, but the upstart got the better of the veteran. Bennett won gold in the 400, 800, and 1,500, while Evans finished second, fourth and fifth.

"Here's a woman who spent eight hours a day in the pool her whole life, yet feels a need to give back to the sport she loves so much."

—BILL WILSON, EVANS'S HUSBAND

Earlier in her career Evans would have been devastated by the losses. Age, however, does have one benefit: it brings wisdom. Evans saw the defeats not as disappointments but as personal challenges.

"The key to being successful in life is having a great attitude and a positive outlook," Evans said. "We're always going to have obstacles and bumps, but you have to work hard to get through them. I tell people to be persistent and stay positive."

Reality, however, has a way of crashing dreams. In Atlanta, Evans was outdone by her young competitors. She failed to qualify for the finals of the 400-meter freestyle and finished sixth in the 800 meter.

Bennett won the gold medal in the 800. Tabbed the "next Janet," the sixteen-year-old Bennett demurred.

"Janet Evans is always going to be the queen of swimming, even twenty years down the road," Bennett told *Chicago Tribune* reporter Philip Hersh. "Maybe I've moved up now, but I've only started, and Janet has been there since 1988. Even now that she's gone, she's still the queen."

Evans retired shortly after the Olympic Games, and though a huge chapter of her life was closing, she opened others.

"People say to me, 'Aren't you going to be sad without swimming? Aren't you going to miss it?'" Evans told *Sports Illustrated*. "It's like a part of me is dying. I say, 'Hey, I'm twenty-four years old. Life is just starting.'"

Indeed.

The name Janet Evans still resonates in America, a name that automatically brings to mind swimming excellence as well as that broad hundred-watt smile. It is the latter even more than her swimming achievements that have allowed Evans to flourish in her latest career. People naturally flock to Evans because she makes them comfortable and because she seems so kind, so, well, so ordinary.

"I tell young athletes today that winning is not the most important thing. It's a journey to try your hardest and do your best in everything you do. That gets your mind off just winning and you'll enjoy it a lot more."

—JANET EVANS

She is a sought-after speaker for people of all ages, but especially with children.

"I book Janet to do a lot of swimming clinics, sometimes with up to two hundred kids," Morgenstein, her agent, said. "Unlike a lot of stars we deal with, Janet never complains about anything. She likes to interact with the young swimmers and pushes us to get her more work."

Married since 2004 to Wilson (the couple wed at an aquarium, naturally), Evans also serves on the Special Olympics Southern California board and is a television commentator. Recently she joined forces with USA Swimming to promote its Make a Splash Campaign, a program designed to teach children and families about the importance of proper water safety and swimming instruction.

It is a different life, but a busy life and a gratifying life. Evans fell in love with swimming because it was fun, not because she won titles and medals, and now she has the pleasure of sharing her joy with others.

"I'm most proud that I've been able to share my success with others," Evans told me. "As an Olympic champion, I feel I have an obligation to inspire other people I meet."

Janet Evans's Life Lessons

Find Something You Enjoy Doing

Janet Evans told me about watching the 1976 Olympic Games, about being an enthralled kid just like millions of others at the sight of Nadia Comaneci. Evans decided she would be a gymnast. "I went out and tried to be a gymnast," Evans said. "And I couldn't even do a somersault." Swimming was different. She was good at it, yes, but she also felt more comfortable in the pool, freer and more at ease, and that feeling as much as her God-given skills turned Evans into a champion.

Give Your All

Janet Evans told me a wonderful story about a swim meet she competed in when she was ten, called the Pumpkin Patch Meet. Every kid who won a race got a pumpkin, and since her father's veterinary practice was next to a pumpkin patch, Evans really wanted a pumpkin. Race after race, Evans lost. "My mom kept saying, 'Janet, it's all right. We can get plenty of pumpkins,'" Evans said. But Evans wanted a pumpkin from that meet, and in her last race of the day, she got it. "The last race was the backstroke, my worst stroke," she said. "Well, I won the race and got my pumpkin. I guess that says something about my tenacity."

If You Don't Achieve Success Initially, Use Those Lessons to Improve

With her distinguished resume it is hard to believe Janet Evans ever knew anything but success. Nothing could be further from the truth. No one goes through life without failure, but as Evans learned, it's what you make of those failures that matter, most. When she lost her featured event, the 400-meter freestyle at the 1992 Olympics, Evans was shattered, but then she was inspired. "That loss was the inspiration for me to keep training and swim in the '96 Olympic Games in Atlanta," Evans said.

You Can Be a Champion Even Without the Medals

Sports naturally reward winners. There are trophies and ribbons, first-place finishers, and runners-up. Janet Evans collected her share of trophies and ribbons and first-place finishes, but along the line she learned an invaluable lesson. Those medals aren't who she is, and they don't make her a champion. She is a champion, but not because she swam faster than anyone else. She's a champion because of who she is. "The one thing I know for sure," Evans shared, "is when the sun goes down, I'm still loved . . . even without any gold medals."

Have Fun

With the demands that sports present, with the disappointments that come hand-in-hand with defeat, sometimes it's hard to remember why you started something in the first place. Dig deep, Janet Evans said, and you'll remember. It's something you enjoyed. "I tell young athletes today that winning is not the most important thing," Evans said. "It's a journey, so try your hardest and do your best in everything you do. That'll get your mind off just winning, and you'll enjoy it a lot more."

7

Chris Evert:
Sensational

"I was always determined to be the best."

—CHRIS EVERT

$\mathcal{T}$he nickname never really fit.

"Little Chrissie," implied a girl you could pat on her head and send on her way, a sweet-natured pushover who played tennis like most young girls played Barbies.

Chris Evert was never that girl.

Yes, she was young and sweet and feminine, with ribbons matching the lace entwined on her tennis outfit and a ponytail that bobbed like a teenager's.

That, however, is all about appearances. It is not about heart and determination.

It does not define the person.

Chris Evert was a fierce competitor, a perfectionist whose steely drive belied her wholesome looks.

She dressed pretty, but she played mean—and that's a huge compliment.

"I wanted to be tough, and I wanted to be a woman," Evert said in *The*

Rivals, a book chronicling the epic Evert/Martina Navratilova battles. "I wanted both."

Throughout the landscape of women's tennis, athletes have come along who have changed the game. Althea Gibson and Billie Jean King, Martina Navratilova and Steffi Graf—all left indelible marks on the game, and at their intersections with history provided pivotal changes to the sport.

What Evert did was introduce the game to everyone, or more precisely, to every girl. Coming into herself just as the United States was grappling with Title IX, she was the ideal vision for what the new law intended. She was not big and strong or blessed, as she would be the first to admit, with extraordinary talent. She was a hard worker and a mental tactician, a young girl who looked like every other young girl prowling the mall.

"She brought the same commitment to tennis every day," sportswriter Johnette Howard, author of *The Rivals,* said. "She was not the quickest or the fastest player, but she had the strongest will. She was also the best female ambassador tennis ever had."

Like a teen idol fresh off the pages of *Tiger Beat,* Evert was a girl who liked McDonald's and once had a pet rabbit named Rufus and even had a famous boyfriend in Jimmy Connors. Tennis fans flocked to see Evert, and young girls mimicked her two-handed backhand, desperate to become her.

"She was like the girl next door, so trim and attractive," longtime tennis analyst and *Boston Globe* columnist Bud Collins said. "She set style points, but was a killer on the court. What a tremendous little competitor!"

Today we would call Evert a crossover star, an athlete who appealed to people of all ages, races, and genders.

"Chris brought grace and elegance to the sport of tennis," tennis analyst Betsy Naglesen McCormack said.

Back then she was simply a sensation.

"She's the future of tennis," tennis umpire Frank Hammond told *Sport* magazine's Tony Kornheiser in 1972.

And for years, Evert was also tennis's present. Winner of eighteen Grand Slam tournaments, Evert became the first player to win one thousand singles matches. In her first thirty-four Grand Slam events, she never failed to reach the semifinals, and for one thirteen-year run, won at least one Grand Slam title.

Her career began with Billie Jean King and finished with Monica Seles and Steffi Graf, but really it is her rivalry with Martina Navratilova that defined her. The two squared off eighty times, sixty of them in finals, and from 1975 to 1986, one of the two women stood as the number one tennis player in the world.

That the pair forged a friendship despite such heated battle says everything about the people involved.

"Chris was like a perfect blonde goddess who was challenging Billie Jean King and Virginia Wade," Navratilova said in her biography, *Martina*. "Before I even met her, she stood for everything I admired about this country: poise, ability, sportsmanship, money, style."

Evert certainly didn't come by all that naturally. A painfully shy child born on December 21, 1954, Evert didn't have a real affinity for any one sport, but as the daughter of a tennis pro, she quite naturally found herself on the court, racket in hand. Her father didn't have aspirations to turn his daughter into a superstar. He just wanted her to have a hobby.

"Kids need goals," Jimmy Evert told *Tennis* magazine in 1971. "Kids without goals come home from school and just wander."

So he brought Chris to the Holiday Park Courts in Fort Lauderdale, where for weeks the six-year-old couldn't even return a shot.

"Then I remember liking it a lot," Evert told ESPN. "My dad made fun out of it. He'd say, 'Okay, ten over the net and I'll buy you a Coke."

Not until she turned eight did Evert even play a game.

By eleven, Evert was nationally ranked, appearing in *Sports Illustrated*'s "Faces in the Crowd." At the age of fifteen, Evert was invited to play in a tournament in Charlotte, North Carolina, alongside such great players as Margaret Court, Nancy Richey, and Francoise Durr. Awed by the competition, her mother, Colette, packed just one change of clothes for Evert.

"I figured she'd be home the next day," Colette said.

Instead Evert beat Durr, 6–1, 6–0, and then beat Court, the number-one player in the world at the time, 7–6, 7–6, before losing in the final to Richey. A year later the United States Tennis Association (USTA) invited the sixteen-year-old Evert to the U.S. Open.

Just like that, a star was born. The bubbly teenager was invited to Forest Hills for the 1971 U.S. Open and took over the tournament, running all the way to the semifinals, much to the joy of a giddy media. The *New York Times* dubbed Evert, "Cinderella in Sneakers," while the *Daily News* drooled over its "Little Miss Sunshine."

King, who watched Evert stun Mary Ann Eisel in the second round, 4–6, 7–6, 6–1, knew what was happening instinctively.

"You could tell by the way the crowd was connecting to her," King said in *The Rivals*. "Even then, she was good under pressure. You can look at kids and see how they play pressure situations, how they respond. Do they like being on Center Court, or would they rather be on Court 55 at ten in the morning? She was a star. A star was born in my eyes in that match."

What people missed as they lauded Evert's sweetness, but King immediately recognized, was her killer instinct. Players took to calling it "The Look," a squinty-eyed gaze that never left Evert's face as she played a match. With an uncanny ability to concentrate and never show her emotions, Evert not only beat players athletically. She beat them mentally.

She learned how at an early age. Like most teenagers, Evert wasn't very good at disguising her feelings. If she was angry or frustrated, she'd voice her opinions loudly on the practice court. Once she pouted and whined so much that her brother simply stormed off the practice court, refusing to play until she regained her composure.

It was then that a lesson her father long had been preaching finally sank in.

"It's a psychological advantage to always seem unfazed and to remain cool and in control," Evert recalled her father teaching her.

Evert lost to King in the semifinals, but a year later, she stomped King, 6–1, 6–0, in a tournament in Fort Lauderdale, proving she was no flash in the pan.

"The worst thing you can do to yourself is beat Chris, because the next time she plays you she goes out of her way to make it her business to really let you know who's boss," tennis great Virginia Wade once said of Evert.

She wouldn't turn pro until her eighteenth birthday, but Evert nonetheless dominated the tennis pages. Most of the news had little to do with her game. At the 1972 Wimbledon, she shared a Coke with another tennis player, and the two began to date. It was straight from the tabloid textbook —America's tennis sweetheart and America's tennis rebel, the nineteen-year-old Jimmy Connors.

The two continued their relationship for two years, and Evert, now riding the crest of celebrity, matched her off-court excitement with on-court victories. She won two Grand Slam titles in 1974—the French Open and Wimbledon—climbing to number three in the world. By the summer of 1975, the Evert-Connors dream match had run its course, with the two officially ending their engagement.

Evert's tennis, however, was just beginning to soar. She won both the French and U.S. Open in 1975, vaulting to number one in the world for the first time and held onto that perch until 1978. What happened next is what happens so often to idols. We break them down. Without a well-publicized romance to entertain and no tennis rival to challenge her, Evert became boring.

She won too much, won too easily, and never let outsiders in. She was stoic, an Ice Maiden, the press began to call her.

The fact was, Evert's demeanor was nothing more than a strategy. She had no intention of being cold or distant, but on the court she needed to concentrate on the task at hand, not play to the crowd like an entertainer. And off the court she was still a young woman, still a shy girl who hadn't yet figured herself out.

"In a lot of ways, I was given a public personality before I had a chance to develop one myself," Evert said in *The Rivals*. "Even today when I do corporate appearances, people always say to me, 'My God, I had no idea you had a sense of humor!' They're so surprised. But I couldn't play my best tennis if I let everything out. It would have been nice to be free and loose on the court, to have that exchange with the crowd that Billie Jean or Martina had. But I couldn't. So my control became associated with winning. But it was also one of the things that allowed people to put me in little boxes that were hard to escape. And it hurt."

The best savior, though, to a perceived bore is a rival, and just as Evert needed one most, Navratilova filled the void. The

ເໜໆ .ᴥ. ໓ນ

"I'm not the most versatile natural athlete in the world, so I had to make up for it mentally and put all my eggs in one basket as far as concentrating and really being determined."

—Chris Evert

•◆•

two had met as early as 1973, but it's hard to call their early matches a rivalry. Evert owned a 21–4 advantage through 1977.

But Navratilova wasn't the same player in 1978. Thinner and fitter, she came to the Wimbledon championship against Evert ready to win. Their epic battle for the

championship remains one for the ages, a 2–6, 6–4, 7–5 slugfest that signified the start of something special.

The fans flocked back to tennis. Navratilova—bigger, stronger, and Czechoslovakian—served as the villain, while Evert—small, sweet, and American—was the hero. For four years, the winner would be as difficult to predict as a rainstorm.

But in 1982, the tide slowly began to change, and in 1983, when Navratilova bested Evert for her first U.S. Open title, tennis reluctantly hailed its new queen.

"Being number one is an ego thing—I mean you've got to be frank about it," Evert said in *The Rivals.* "It's a power thing. You're the woman of the hour. You get used to it. And then, all of a sudden, when you're on top and somebody starts taking it away, it's difficult. The press wants to talk to somebody else. You're not the first priority."

Despite Navratilova's dominance, Evert rebounded for two astonishing upsets, proof of her mettle and commitment to the game. On her favorite surface—clay—she beat Navratilova in the 1985 French Open, 3–6, 7–6, 7–5, and again in the 1986 French championship.

"We brought out the best in each other," Navratilova said simply. "No matter how catty we get with each other in private or public, I still have a closeness with her that I will never have with another human being because of what we went through together, on and off the court."

Divorced in 1986 from John Lloyd, Evert traveled to Aspen for the holidays that year at the urging of none other than Navratilova. On New Year's Eve, Navratilova introduced Evert to former Olympic skier Andy Mill. Nineteen months later, the two were married.

In 1989, Evert made her last appearance at the U.S. Open, retiring from the game that had brought her to the height of popularity and to its ugly cellar, after losing to Zina Garrison in the quarterfinals.

She left the game with a 1,309–146 record, a .900 winning percentage that is the best in professional tennis history, and in 1996 she took her rightful place in the International Tennis Hall of Fame.

"Chris will always be remembered for her tenacity and her incredibly strong will. She is a very strong person."

—FORMER TENNIS PLAYER AND CURRENT ANALYST ROSIE CASALS

"When I think of Chris, these words come to mind: focus, concentration, dedication, and mental strength," former tennis player Mary Joe Fernandez said. "She was an extremely graceful player who could adapt to the times. That helped provide the longevity of her career."

A slave to the game for so long, Evert has thrown off the shackles of competition in retirement. Never tempted to return to the game, she instead has immersed herself in her family. Though Evert and Mill divorced, the couple remain devoted to their three boys—Alexander, Nicholas, and Colton—and Evert's only real tennis is playing with them, though they, like any children, are loathe to take lessons from their mother.

"I think I was meant to be the mother of three boys," Evert told *Sports Illustrated* recently. "They're not high maintenance. They don't fight over flowery dresses. They have one favorite T-shirt and a favorite pair of pants, and that's it. If I had a little Chrissie, I'd be too critical."

Her time is spent not only as a mother, but as a television analyst, philanthropist, and entrepreneur. In 1996 she opened the Evert Tennis Academy. Built in conjunction with the premiere sports marketing firm, IMG, the Academy is home to twenty-three courts and is geared toward international and national junior tennis players.

Aside from her children, what makes Evert most proud is the Chris Evert Pro-Celebrity Tennis Classic. Begun the year of Evert's retirement, the classic raised $350,000 in its first year for a drug treatment facility in South Florida. Since then Evert has partnered with the Ounce of Prevention Fund in Florida, which raises money for at-risk children and their families, getting the Florida governor to promise a dollar-for-dollar match for any money Evert raises. Last year's Classic earned $1.2 million and since it's inception has donated more than $14 million to needy children in Florida.

"If you can react the same way to winning and losing, that's a big accomplishment. The quality is important because it stays with you the rest of your life, and there's going to be life after tennis that's a lot longer than your tennis life."

—CHRIS EVERT

One of the top fifty athletes of the century as named by ESPN, *Sports Illustrated*'s 1976 Sportsman of the Year, a four-time Associated Press Female Athlete of the Year, and a March of Dimes Lifetime Achievement Winner, Evert boasts a resume that can only begin to tap into her impact.

"Losing hurts me," Evert once said. "I was always determined to be the best."

Little Chrissie?

Hardly.

Chris Evert's Life Lessons

Stay Calm Even If You Feel Otherwise

No one, no matter how supremely talented, gets through life without a case of the jitters. Chris Evert certainly had her fair share of nerves as she rose to the top of the tennis world and became her sport's favorite daughter. But remembering advice her father long ago taught her, she never let them see her sweat. "It's a psychological advantage to always seem unfazed and to remain cool and in control," Evert once said.

Thrive Under Pressure

Great athletes, great businesspeople, and great actors separate themselves from the pack because they can succeed in the most difficult of circumstances. Only a teenager when the world first discovered her, Evert welcomed the chance to play on Center Court at the U.S. Open, even though it meant all eyes were upon her. "You can look at kids and see how they play pressure situations, how they respond," Billie Jean King recalled of a young Evert. "Do they like being on center court, or would they rather be on court 55 at ten in the morning? She was a star."

Be Gracious, but Don't Accept Defeat

In her epic rivalry with Martina Navratilova, Chris Evert lost her fair share of matches. She never pouted or blamed officials but instead warmly embraced Navratilova at midcourt. That model behavior though, didn't mean Evert went home and thought, *Oh well, no big deal.* To be a winner, losing always has to be a big deal. "Losing hurts me," she once said. "I was always determined to be the best."

8

Lisa Fernandez:
Tenacity

"I want to give everything I've got and more."

—Lisa Fernandez

*L*isa Fernandez walked off the field completely shattered and straight to the consoling arms of her mother, Emilia.

Her softball debut hadn't gone exactly according to plan. Fernandez's team lost, 25–0. The eight-year-old pitcher walked twenty-four batters and hit another twenty.

As only a mother can, Emilia Fernandez found the silver lining and encouraging words in such a dismal performance.

"The next game, work on only walking twenty-three instead of twenty-four," Lisa's mother told her.

And so twenty-four became twenty-three, twenty-three became twenty-two, and soon the walks were eliminated, and then went the hits and eventually the runs. Buoyed by her parents' love and support and a fierce determination to always be better, Fernandez went from perhaps the worst softball player in the world to the best.

Other athletes have mastered other sports, but it is hard to imagine anyone can rival what Fernandez did in softball. From high school through college and into an Olympic career, Fernandez owned the game. When she wasn't blowing away opposing batters from her position on the pitcher's mound, she was swatting balls over the fences from the batter's box.

Her statistics are almost comical, Bunyanesque numbers that seem straight out of a tall tale.

She owns three Olympic gold medals, a 7–2 Olympic record and 0.38 ERA. In eleven Olympic Games, she gave up four runs and twenty hits. She earned the save in the gold-medal game against China in 1996, pitched both the semifinal and gold-medal victories in Sidney in 2000, in Athens in 2004 tossed a four-hitter in the gold-medal game, and in her spare time, batted .545 for the tournament.

In four years at UCLA, Fernandez went 93–7, threw one of only three perfect seasons in NCAA history in 1992 (29–0), posted a career ERA of 0.22, the second best in NCAA history, and at one point won forty-two consecutive games and threw ninety-two consecutive scoreless innings. Her Bruins won two College World Series titles and finished as runners-up in the "down" years.

Want to go back further? Okay. Let's check out high school, where the teenaged Fernandez left other kids quaking at the plate. At St. Joseph's High School in Lakewood, California, Fernandez threw twelve perfect games and thirty-seven no-hitters, and posted a career ERA of 0.07.

Oh, and on the days she didn't pitch, Fernandez played third base. Naturally she hardly ever committed an error.

But unlike a lot of incredibly gifted athletes, as her first game implies, Fernandez didn't just saunter into her greatness. She got there the old-fashioned way.

"Lisa's motto is 'Never be satisfied,'" said Kelly Inouye-Perez, Fernandez's catcher from the time the two were middle-schoolers. "Her work ethic is above and beyond the norm."

Indeed, on her second date with her then boyfriend (now husband) Michael Lujan, Fernandez explained unapologetically, "I have to hit. Do you mind?" Consequently their date was spent at the UCLA batting cages.

From high school to college to the Olympics, you'd think somewhere along the line Fernandez would have relaxed a little bit and rested on the laurels she worked so hard to earn.

It never happened. Up until the day Fernandez, who perfectly used the word "tenacious" to describe herself, threw the last pitch to seal a 4–1 victory over Australia in the 2004 Olympic gold-medal game, Fernandez never eased off the throttle.

Despite a resume of gaudy success, it was never the wins that counted to Fernandez. It was the losses. She remembers each one vividly.

Perfection, of course, is impossible. Every pitcher loses. Every batter makes an out.

Really? Tell that to Fernandez. Dot Richardson, Fernandez's Olympic teammate, explained to the *Washington Post* in 1995 what makes Fernandez tick.

"I remember one time when she had pitched a perfect game, and we were driving home, and she looked sort of sad," Richardson said. "Someone asked, 'What's wrong? You just pitched a perfect game.' Lisa said, 'Yeah, but I didn't get a hit.' And then there would be a night when she would go four-for-four and be upset that she didn't get to pitch."

Every child is raised to believe anything is possible. Fernandez, however, saw that firsthand. Her father, Antonio, fled Cuba in 1962, and after a stint in the U.S. Army, forged a new life for himself, his Puerto-Rican born wife, Emilia, and two daughters in California. He worked in a factory, so the hours were long and the money not great. But it was enough to get by, and the young girls flourished.

Fernandez's family—the thing she says she is most proud of—demanded hard work and accountability but also instilled in Lisa that boundaries and limits were meant to be pushed through, that the only expectations that mattered were the ones you set for yourself.

"My mother and my grandmother encouraged me to play and get my education," Fernandez told me. "They said, 'There's more a young woman can do than get married.'"

Softball was to the Fernandez family what baseball is to the Ripkens. Antonio played semipro baseball, Emilia played slow-pitch softball, and big sister, Elsie, played the game, too. As a youngster, Lisa was the batgirl for her mom's team but eventually decided she'd play the game herself.

After that disastrous debut at eight, Emilia spent every day after school working with Lisa, stepping out the required distance and drawing a pitcher's mound with chalk in the backyard.

As Fernandez progressed, so did her mother's level of protection. She started off sitting on a milk bucket, graduated to using a glove, and then added a little padding to the glove. Next came a catcher's mask, then a chest protector, followed shortly by shin guards.

And then mom said enough.

"By eleven she was too fast," Emilia Fernandez told *USA Today* in 1998. "We had to get someone else."

The next year Fernandez went to meet with a local pitching coach, hoping he could mold her into a superstar. The coach never even asked her to pitch. He took one look at the twelve-year-old Fernandez and said it wasn't going to happen.

Once more she came home to her mother in tears.

"My coaches told me I wasn't good enough," Fernandez said. "I wasn't the right size, and my arms weren't the right length."

Just as she did after her daughter's first game, Emilia Fernandez consoled her daughter, but also prodded her. She reminded Fernandez that only she could decide what she could and couldn't do.

That was all Fernandez needed to hear.

"Lisa has tremendous drive and motivation," Emilia said. "She doesn't say 'no.'"

Indeed, instead of letting the coach's words destroy her, Fernandez used them to inspire her. If her body naturally wasn't built for greatness, she would overcome it by working harder than anyone else. If someone didn't think she could, she'd spend extra hours proving that she would.

> ❧ ⋅✦⋅ ☙
>
> *"Lisa leads her own life.*
> *Her goal is to achieve her best.*
> *She doesn't go around*
> *comparing herself to others."*
> —EMILIA FERNANDEZ, FERNANDEZ'S MOTHER
>
> •✦•

And so the girl with short arms didn't just become good, she became ridiculously good.

At St. Joseph's High School, an all-girls Catholic school, Fernandez rarely struggled. As a freshman she pitched a memorable 29-inning, 1–0 victory.

But asked about her high school career, Fernandez not surprisingly remembers a loss.

"When I was in high school, we won a title and thought we'd automatically win the next year," she said. "We cut corners and lost in the first round. That will never happen again. I wake up every morning and work out. There are some days I just want to stay in bed, but then I think, *If I miss this workout it may cost me a title somewhere down the line.* It all parallels."

When Fernandez enrolled at UCLA, the Bruins already were a softball power. They had just won their second consecutive NCAA Championship in 1989, running their total to ten titles since 1982.

Never, however, had they seen a player like Fernandez.

She rewrote both the UCLA and NCAA record books in her tenure at Westwood, winning the Honda Award, presented to the nation's top collegiate softball player, for three years, and the Honda-Broderick Cup, awarded to the top collegiate female athlete, as well as earning all-American status in each of her four years.

Her pitching prowess was matched only by her work at the plate, where she batted .510 in her senior year.

"She just spoils you rotten," Fernandez's UCLA coach Sharron Backus, who coached the Bruins to eight national titles, told *USA Today* in 1993. "She does whatever is necessary, and does it so classy, so effortlessly."

Her greatness and domination, though, came at a time when softball was still somewhat of a fringe sport and filled with critics who equated the game to the slow-pitched game played by beer-bellied men.

Fernandez, of course, liked nothing better than proving people wrong, and in her senior season got to quiet at least one naysayer for good. Kevin Williams, a UCLA running back in 1993, spent the better part of his senior season good-naturedly trash talking at Fernandez, telling her that he could hit her easily.

"To be successful, you must be mentally tough and accountable for your actions. Also you must be willing to self-evaluate, particularly after you win. Even if you are winning, you still must keep improving."

—LISA FERNANDEZ

So, as Shelley Smith retold the story in *Sports Illustrated* that year, Williams dug in at the plate and stared down Fernandez. She offered him thirty pitches. He made contact on two, each infield taps that landed foul.

Fernandez's 69 mph softball may not sound impressive, but pushed back to a baseball regulation mound, that would equate to a 101 mph fastball whizzing by.

Fernandez, however, isn't just about mowing down the competition. She is a softball student.

cᴏ .◆. ᴏ

"You've got have it between the ears. The mind is powerful, and you have to discipline it. Many times I'vt hit the breaking point, buy your mind can tell you what to do."

—LISA FERNANDEZ

•◆•

"She studies and analyzes her opponents, and when she spots their weaknesses, she goes out and takes advantage of all she's learned," Richardson explained. "Then Lisa gets down and dirty and gets the job done."

Blessed with good timing, Fernandez came of age just as softball became an Olympic sport. In the Atlanta Games in 1996, Fernandez threw a three-hitter in a ten-inning semifinal game against China and came in for the save to clinch the gold medal in softball's debut season.

Naturally she barely remembers the medal ceremony. What does linger, however, is a qualifying-round extra-inning game against Australia. The United States took a 1–0 lead into the bottom of the tenth. After an Australian runner was placed on second per the international tie-break rules, Fernandez, flawless through nine and two-thirds innings, gave up a two-run homer to Joanne Brown, and Australia won the game.

That summer Fernandez received a postcard with a picture of a victorious Brown atop her teammates' shoulders. The card wasn't signed. It just said, "See you in Japan," site of the world championships.

In Japan, Fernandez hit a home run and pitched a one-hit shutout to help the United States beat Australia for the title.

"I admire her willingness to face challenges head on," Richardson recalled. "She doesn't run away or shy from the pressure situations. In fact, she wants the responsibility on her shoulders. It's not a selfish thing. It's always for the team. Lisa says, 'You guys believe in me, and I'll help you get there.' She doesn't have a cocky me-first attitude; she wants to help the team."

Four years later, Fernandez continued her revenge, beating Australia in the semifinal game with thirteen strikeouts and coming right back for a three-hit complete game victory over Japan to win the gold medal.

Fernandez capped off her Olympic run in Athens in 2004. An elder statesman of thirty-three at the time, she nonetheless set the standard. Fernandez set an Olympic record with her .545 batting average through nine games and went 4–0 on the mound, allowing one run and five hits.

It was the exclamation point to a career that still continues. A mother now, Fernandez is still part of the U.S. National Team and one of a number of women fighting to have softball, dropped in the summer of 2005, reinstated as an Olympic sport in time for the 2012 Games.

"She is the ultimate competitor," Michele Smith, Fernandez's Olympic teammate, said. "She had some early setbacks and challenges, but she never gave up. Lisa pushed her teammates and helped us challenge each other to maximize our abilities. She had great strength physically, mentally, and emotionally."

Fernandez has developed a new passion as well—golf. She plays with the same tenacity she used in softball, outworking the competition so she can constantly get better. She told me she admires Annika Sorenstam, not for Sorenstam's successes but "the way she constantly challenges herself."

"Ten years from now I could see Lisa on the LPGA Tour," Inouye-Perez said. "She's terrific, and with her work ethic, the sky is the limit."

Despite a life full of success that few can match, Fernandez remains

"Lisa's life and career teaches us never to be satisfied. When you're told 'no,' overcome your setbacks by working harder to achieve your dreams."

—MICHELE SMITH, FERNANDEZ'S
OLYMPIC TEAMMATE

humble and gracious, more amazed at her accomplishments perhaps than anyone else.

It is not that Fernandez doubted herself. But somewhere in the back of her mind, that eight-year-old kid who left the mound in tears, that twelve-year-old girl who was told she didn't have what it took to be great, still lives.

And she still pushes Fernandez to be even better.

"I'd like people to remember me as being determined and always giving my all," Fernandez said. "I've never been satisfied and still push the envelope, on the field and off."

Lisa Fernandez's Life Lessons

Work to Get One Step Better

Emilia Fernandez's words to her daughter after a horrific start to a softball career, "The next game work on only walking twenty-three instead of twenty-four," framed Lisa Fernandez's life. She took challenges incrementally, ticking off accomplishments slowly but steadily en route to a career of near perfection. "My parents taught me how to deal with losses and come back," Lisa said of her mother, Emilia, and her father, Tony. "It was more than just a game. It was a way of life. Study the reasons why after setbacks, so you can do better the next time."

Never Be Afraid of a Challenge

When Australian Joanne Brown launched a two-run homer to not only end Lisa Fernandez's perfect game but earn the Aussies a victory in an Olympic-qualifying round game in 1996, Fernandez could have run away from the powerful Australian team. Never. She lived for the chance to go toe-to-toe with Brown again, and when the chance came, Fernandez pitched a one-hitter and belted a home run to help the United States to victory. "You won't always win," Lisa said to me. "But you must be prepared."

Overcome Adversity

There is no smooth road to glory. There are bumps in every road, even one seemingly paved with perfection. Lisa Fernandez met adversity at every intersection, but she met it head on. "You've got to have it between the ears," Lisa explained. "The mind is powerful, and you have to discipline it. Many times I've hit the breaking point, but your mind can tell you what to do."

Don't Let Anyone Tell You What You Can and Can't Do

If Lisa Fernandez trusted others instead of herself, her career would have ended when she was twelve years old. A respected pitching coach told her she didn't have what it took physically to succeed in softball. Lots of people would have written off the sport. Fernandez instead took the criticism as a personal challenge. "My biggest fear is disappointing myself, my family, and my fans," Lisa said. "That's what gets me up in the morning. I want to give everything I've got and more."

Never Say, "What If?"

What if . . . Lisa Fernandez had quit after her first game? What if . . . Lisa Fernandez had listened to the pitching coach who said she'd never make it? Lisa Fernandez could have spent her life asking "What if?" But she never has. To her, not trying is worse than not succeeding. "Don't be afraid to fail," she said simply.

Know What a Champion Is

The trophies and plaques that cover every path on the road to softball glory can all be found in Lisa Fernandez's trophy case: high school championships and College World Series honors, world championship awards, and Olympic medals. Those, however, don't define what a champion is. "It's not about the wins and losses," Lisa said, "but about the process. All you can do is sacrifice, work hard, and then let God take care of the rest."

Stick to the Plan

Her peers thought Lisa Fernandez was crazy. She worked morning until night to get better, running, lifting, practicing with such single-mindedness that she even spent her second date with her future husband at a batting cage. That, however, is how success is born, with an eye always to the goal and a never-wavering dedication to getting better every day. "Work on your weaknesses, and make them your strengths," Lisa said. "Leave no stone unturned."

9

Peggy Fleming:
Graciousness

"Life is not about one shining moment.
You can't just kick back and put your feet up on the desk."

—Peggy Fleming

With television cameras for the first time offering coverage of the Olympic Games, Peggy Fleming was the first darling of the ice, the first figure skating doll to capture a nation's heart.

When Fleming's music ended and her stardom began on the ice in Grenoble, France, in 1968, many considered that moment to be the pinnacle for Fleming.

She thought it was merely a beginning.

"I've had some wonderful successes in my life, but I must move on and keep challenging myself," Fleming said. "Life is not about one shining moment. You can't just kick back and put your feet up on the desk."

Indeed, the challenge for Fleming has been about taking that shining moment and making it a life. She has more than succeeded. A champion, a respected broadcaster, and a breast cancer survivor, Fleming has used her celebrity to enrich her own life as well as empower others. Rather than fade into the backdrop, she has remained an integral part of her sport while expanding her reach to others who don't know a triple axel from a camel spin.

Her athletic resume—five U.S. Championships, three world championships, and that historic gold medal—speaks to her place in sports history, but her gentleness and kindness are what truly set her apart.

"Peggy is interested in life and involved in life and is young at heart," Christa Fassi, wife of Fleming's longtime coach, Carlo Fassi, said. "She teaches us not to let life pass us by."

Really, figure skating was blessed. The first ice diva wasn't a diva at all, but instead a sweet, shy girl from California. Had someone else skated onto that ice in France, someone with less poise and generosity of spirit, the sport might never have captured the masses as it has since her world debut.

Seven years earlier, in 1961, the entire U.S. delegation was killed in a plane crash on the way to the world championships. The United States really scrambled to push its juniors into senior competition, hoping to simply stem the tide.

Instead it found not just an Olympic champion but a young woman who captured everything that was right and beautiful about the sport.

"She launched figure skating's modern era," *Sports Illustrated* wrote of Fleming in 1994. "Pretty and balletic, elegant and stylish, Fleming took a staid sport that was shackled by its inscrutable compulsory figures and arcane scoring system and, with television as her ally, made it marvelously glamorous. Ever since, certainly to North Americans, figure skating has been the marquee sport of the Winter Games and increasingly the staple of prime-time television."

Today, figure skating is second only to professional football as the most popular spectator sport in the United States.

"For thirty years, she was the personification of world figure skating in the United States, both as a champion and then through her television work," longtime *Chicago Tribune* Olympic reporter Philip Hersh said.

The woman who would later be described as graceful and elegant was anything but as a child. Fleming said she was an awkward girl who lacked confidence, the kind who'd rather melt into the school desk than raise her hand and answer questions.

Fleming only came out of her shell when she got to play outside with her sisters.

"I've always had energy and loved doing things as a young girl," Fleming said. "I'd run the hills for the fun of it and see how high I could climb a tree. I'd jump off the top of the roof just to see if I could do it. I'd do flips off the monkey bars at school."

Fleming's parents, Doris and Al, were active if not outwardly athletic. A former Marine who was injured by a Japanese grenade, Al held a variety of jobs during Fleming's childhood, including running the presses at the *San Jose Mercury News*.

In 1957, when Fleming was nine, her mother spied an ad in the newspaper for an ice skating rink that was opening in the Bay Area. Fleming wrote in her autobiography, *The Long Program*, about her father's love for skating. "When my folks were courting, he had even taken a job setting up bowling pins to earn extra cash to go skating."

Naturally, when Doris showed the ad to her husband, the Fleming girls quickly found themselves packed in the car and on the way to the rink.

And for Peggy Fleming, on the way to a new life.

She was not a natural. She fell down a lot on that first skating adventure, and at nine, Fleming hardly realized she had found her true calling, but skating did awaken something new in Fleming. The tomboy in Fleming, the one who had to be the best and most daring, made her work, but a new Fleming emerged on the ice. Suddenly the girl who didn't give a lick about her looks, and frankly was never impressed by her own reflection in the mirror, felt pretty.

"It felt so good and blended in with all the other athletic things I was doing," Fleming said of her first time skating. "I loved the musical part of skating and loved the beautiful dresses and the feeling of being pretty. When I started skating, I pushed myself as far as I could go and felt alive with a real feeling that I was expressing myself. There was a feeling of electricity inside me."

With a new passion feeding her confidence, Fleming blossomed. Her family signed her up for skating lessons, and when at the age of eleven, she moved to Pasadena, her parents secured her two precious hours of private ice time in the early morning hours.

Fleming's new love presented difficult financial strains for the family. One hour of ice time, Fleming explained in *The Long Program*, cost more than Al Fleming could make in one hour at the *San Jose Mercury News*. Add to that the cost of lessons and costumes and, well, the Flemings were clearly out of their element.

"My family didn't have much money, and all the champion skaters were coming out of the New England area in those days," Fleming said. "Skating was a 'wealthy sport.' But my parents encouraged me to keep going."

Al Fleming, in fact, taught himself how to drive the Zamboni while Fleming trained in Pasadena, to not only defray the costs of the ice time but to give his daughter a perfect surface to practice on.

Parents and daughter saw the reward for their hard work and sacrifice almost instantaneously. With coach Gene Turner, a former men's national champion and one-time partner of legendary Sonja Henie, directing her, Fleming entered her first competition.

Unsure really of how the whole competitive world worked, Fleming simply went out and skated her routine at the Bay Area Juvenile Girls Championship

She won.

"Sports helped me overcome my shyness and go out and compete and try to get better every time out," Fleming said. "It's forced me to overcome my nervousness and fight through my fears. I love the challenge of doing that and am proud I could do it."

During Fleming's era, skaters were required to do more than flawless routines. They had to complete tension-packed school figures, where they were given six figures to master, all under the watchful eyes of judges standing within inches. At Fleming's next competition, the Pacific Coast Championships, a free and loose Fleming did her figures without much care or concentration and finished dead last, failing to even qualify for the free skate.

That wouldn't happen again.

A year later, in 1960, she returned to the Pacific Coast Championships, acing the figures and winning the competition.

"Peggy teaches us what hard work is all about," her good friend, Martha Neumann, said. "Everything she has accomplished is due to her dedication and serious commitment to her sport."

In 1961 the plane crash that jump-started Fleming's career also took the life of her coach at the time, Bill Kipp. Forced to find a new coach, she eventually landed with Bob Paul, who taught Fleming the grace and balletic movements that would become her trademark.

Under Paul's tutelage, Fleming won her first of five consecutive U.S. championships, earning a spot on the 1964 Olympic team in Innsbruck.

Completely overwhelmed by her first international competition, Fleming nonetheless finished sixth in Austria, the highest American finisher.

She was only fifteen.

As talented as she was in her free programs, Fleming still struggled with her school figures, and so in 1965 her mother (her father had since passed away) decided the entire family would relocate to Colorado Springs, take up residence in the Broadmoor Hotel, and work with legendary Italian coach, Carlo Fassi.

"They had a beautiful skating rink on the grounds," Fleming said of the Broadmoor. "My dad had died, and Thayer Tutt, who ran the place, took me under his wing. My coach, Carlo Fassi, was very patient and understanding with me. He made practicing fun and was still demanding. That was a crucial point in my career, and I was living in the perfect setting."

Indeed, Fassi changed Fleming's life in many ways. In 1965 Fassi sent Fleming on a summer exhibition in Davos, Switzerland. He asked one of his other students who was visiting Europe with some college friends to check in on the young Fleming.

His name was Greg Jenkins. On June 13, 1970, Jenkins became Fleming's husband.

"I'm most proud of my marriage and my children," Fleming said of her and Greg's two boys, Andy and Todd. "I was twenty-one when we were married, and now our children are grown, and we have grandchildren. I have had a wonderful life."

The year after Fleming met Jenkins, 1966, she won her first of three consecutive world championships.

The tomboy was now an ice queen.

At the 1968 U.S. championships in Philadelphia, Fleming officially captured a country. Flawless and breathtaking, she easily won the title, and in the postcompetition exhibition, her performance to *Ave Maria* literally left the crowd speechless.

"I remember extending my arm on the last note, a long, languid lift of the arm and a wave of the wrist," Fleming wrote in *The Long Program*. "I made it last as long as possible—long after the last note had died. For a long instant the crowd was as quiet as a congregation in prayer. And then, when I broke the spell, the applause filled me with joy."

ꙮ ..◆. ꙮ

"Peggy was very graceful and pleasing to watch, but she also had athletic ability so she had it all. That's a package very few skaters possess."

—CHRISTA FASSI, WIFE OF FLEMING'S LONGTIME COACH, CARLO FASSI

•◆•

Fleming not only was coming into her own as a skater, but as a young woman. An "item" now with Jenkins, she, like any teenager, craved independence, which was difficult to come by in a world where her mother ruled her career. Though Fleming would never outwardly buck her mother, she did, like any teenager, chafe at her restraints.

Christa Fassi, Carlo's wife, told me of the skater and mother routine that occurred almost every day at practice.

"When Peggy was young, she'd get on the ice late at practice," she said. "Her mother was sitting in the stands getting more and more nervous. Then she'd get up and stalk toward the locker room, and just as she got there, Peggy would gracefully step on the ice to start practice. Then her mother would turn around and walk back to her seat. It happened every day like clockwork."

But if mother and daughter butted heads on occasion, it did nothing to fracture their bond. When it came time for Fleming's moment in Grenoble, she turned of course to her favorite costumer for the perfect outfit. Doris Fleming stitched together a dress that now lives in time, a chartreuse, high-necked outfit with rhinestones at the cuff and collar. Doris Fleming chose the color because she learned that not far from Grenoble was the monastery that made Chartreuse liqueur.

"She thought that dressing me in chartreuse would send a subliminal message to the French people and that they would root for me, which in turn would help my confidence and endear me to the French fans," Fleming explained in her autobiography.

Turns out, Fleming could have skated in day-glo orange, and she would have enthralled everyone. Fleming built an almost insurmountable lead in, ironically, the school figures, and though her long program wasn't as flawless as the one in Philadelphia, it was enough to win her a gold medal.

Feted on the covers of *Life* and *Sports Illustrated,* she returned home a hero and a star.

Really, Fleming was the perfect antidote for the American public. Caught in a year more turbulent than any other in history—Martin Luther King Jr. and Robert Kennedy had been assassinated, the Vietnam War raged on, and the counterculture hippie movement swept the nation—the United States almost craved someone like Fleming, a sweet, good-natured kid from a modest background.

She behaved as gently and as gracefully as she skated, carrying herself with the dignity of the women she told me she admired: Jacqueline Kennedy (with whom she shares a birthday) and Audrey Hepburn.

"Peggy has a grace so deep and totally integrated to who she is," Martha Neumann said. "She's never out of character. What you see is who she is. Peggy is so genuine, a real human being. Peggy is a gentle spirit."

And fans couldn't get enough of her. After winning her final world championship in 1968 after the Olympics, Fleming began a long and prosperous professional career. Her first TV show, the Sun Valley special, won two Emmy Awards and paved the way for four more television specials, including a 1973 production filmed in the U.S.S.R., the first joint effort by Americans and Soviets to be filmed in the U.S.S.R. during the Cold War.

> *"To be successful you have to think positively, look ahead, and believe in yourself. That's hard to do sometimes."*
>
> —Peggy Fleming

Most fans today, of course, know Fleming from her role in the television booth. She joined ABC Sports in 1981 and since has offered her analysis at world, national, and Olympic events.

"I get up with something to do on my agenda," Fleming said. "I can't wait to accomplish things every day."

Nothing, of course, prepared Fleming for what would be her greatest challenge. On February 10, 1998, thirty years to the day after she won her gold medal, Fleming lay on an operating table, undergoing breast cancer surgery. She had discovered the lump while preparing to work for ABC at the U.S. nationals in Philadelphia, the scene of her biggest triumph. Fleming tried to dismiss it, arguing she had just had a mammogram, but when the nationals ended and she returned home, she immediately went to the doctor.

"You've got to have wins in life to gain the confidence to go on, but wins are not the true measure of success."

—PEGGY FLEMING

She had a lumpectomy and went about her business while she waited for the result she assumed would be benign. She went to Boston to film a skating special and returned home, where her husband called from a conference in Florida. He already had received the results. The tumor was malignant.

"I hung up the phone and cried," Fleming wrote in *The Long Program*. "It couldn't have been too long, maybe just a couple of minutes, but even now I remember that moment."

Fleming, though, isn't the type to dwell on negativity. She said she's endured her share of hardships and dark moments, but never languishes in them, refusing to let them drag her down.

And so the initial diagnosis momentarily knocked the wind out of Fleming, but the moment didn't last. Instead Fleming attacked cancer as she attacked the ice. She endured the treatments, the added tests to make sure the cancer hadn't spread (it hadn't), and eventually the radiation with the same grace and determination that had served her well in her career.

"When I think of Peggy, I think of grace under pressure," her longtime friend and personal assistant, Jean Hall, said. "Things can be totally chaotic, and that's when she blossoms. She won't crumble and is actually better when the chips are down."

Dealing with cancer is an intensely private battle, but celebrity doesn't allow much to stay private long. News reports were soon out that Fleming was battling breast cancer, and national magazines were asking for comments for stories.

What she found, though, was that sharing her story brought her together with other survivors, that there was a sorority waiting to welcome her. She was featured not once, but twice, in *People* magazine and later agreed to appear on the *Oprah Winfrey Show*. Inspired by other women more ravaged than she who had beaten breast cancer, Fleming quickly realized that she could make a difference.

The woman always remembered for her gentleness now has become a fighter and crusader for women's health. Along with speaking up about the need for early breast exams, Fleming has become a strong voice in the fight against cardiovascular disease. Fleming lost both her father, only forty-one when he died, and her sister, just fifty at the time of her death, to heart disease and has watched another sister endure a triple bypass.

Fleming has attacked her heart health as a way to ward off whatever genetics may be working against her. She carefully monitors her diet, works out frequently, and takes cholesterol-lowering medication daily. But like her advocacy on behalf of breast cancer awareness, Fleming isn't content to just take care of herself. She has shared her story with national magazines, hoping that others will follow her lead.

"I want to be around a lot longer than my father," Fleming said in a recent issue of *Heart Healthy Living*. "We can prolong our lives so much more than in the past. I go every year for checkups and take care of myself. I want to be a good example for my kids."

"I now do TV work with Peggy, and she is just as great as you'd hope she would be. She's just like your best friend in college."

—*USA Today* COLUMNIST
CHRISTINE BRENNAN

Remembered still as the teenager in chartreuse who forever changed a sport, Fleming is today adored for the full woman she has become.

"My purpose in life is to share all my gifts with audiences," Fleming said. "And that includes athletics and the importance of positive thinking in all your circumstances. The one thing I know for sure is none of us get out of here alive, so do the best you can. Make a difference. Enjoy your life. Love people."

Peggy Fleming's Life Lessons

Find Your Gift as Early as Possibly; It's There, Because We All Have One

A gift needn't be an athletic skill or an artistic one. It can be something as simple as the ability to talk with people or to understand them. Teachers are every bit as gifted as athletes, nurses every bit as blessed as pianists. "I loved sports as a child but never dreamed it would be my career," Peggy Fleming said. "I always thought I'd be a schoolteacher because I loved children."

Think Positively

If ever Peggy Fleming learned the power of positive thinking, it was after she was diagnosed with cancer. Although doctors fortunately caught her cancer early, she still was every bit as overwhelmed by the words "cancer," "malignant," "tumor," and "radiation" as anyone would be. Instead of wallowing in her sadness, though, Fleming decided to fight, and as so many cancer survivors will attest, positive thinking is as much a cure as chemotherapy. "I try to learn from my low points," she said. "Sometimes it's hard to pull yourself back up out of a hole, but I don't like it down there. When you go through bad times, don't ever feel sorry for yourself."

Work Hard

Peggy Fleming was challenged by her coaches and pushed and prodded by her mother, but she succeeded on her own. She wanted to skate and practice for four hours a day. She wanted to scrape herself off the ice after falls and keep going. "My biggest fear is letting myself down and not working my hardest," Fleming said. "I don't want to disappoint the people who believe in me."

Be Grateful for All Your Accomplishments

Perhaps Peggy Fleming's greatest gift isn't her skating after all. Perhaps, instead, it is her quiet dignity and her humility in the face of stunning worldwide successes. Every person who meets her remarks at how kind she is, how gentle, and yes, how grateful. It is telling that it is those attributes, not her gold medal and sport-altering performance that she most wants to be remembered for. "I'd like my legacy to be that I was a nice person and grateful for all my gifts," she said. "I hope to be remembered as a person who gave back to my sport and others. That's what makes me feel good about me and my life."

Always Keep Moving Forward

For a woman who has accomplished so much, Peggy Fleming is not nearly satisfied. She is still striving and challenging herself, still searching for other avenues to explore, ways to be a better person, friend, professional, mother, and grandmother. The goal no longer is a gold medal but self-improvement, and yet Fleming approaches it with the same vigor she applied to her training. "I've tried never to forget where I came from and to look to the future while learning from the past," she explained. "I always want to challenge myself and keep learning constantly."

❧ 10 ❧

Althea Gibson:
Pioneering

"Who could have imagined? Who could have thought?"

—ALTHEA GIBSON

The tennis stadium at Flushing Meadows Park bears the name of a great man, a man who overcame two diseases, one social and the other physical.

Arthur Ashe was a true pioneer in American tennis, a man who conquered racism with grace and attacked AIDS with the same grace later in his life. That the United States' greatest tennis stadium, the site where the U.S. Open is played annually, honors Ashe makes perfect sense.

But tennis history long has overlooked the person who set the stage for Ashe, who made it possible for him to compete.

Her name was Althea Gibson, a woman forgotten as she receded from society in her illness-plagued final years but who, thanks to the rise in prominence of two powerful sisters, is finally getting her due.

"Her accomplishments set the stage for my success and through players like myself, like Serena, and many others to come, her legacy will live on," Venus Williams once said of Gibson.

Althea Gibson's tennis success alone would be enough to earn a place in history. She won five Grand Slam singles titles, two each at Wimbledon and the U.S. Championship, and once at the French Championship (renamed the French Open in 1968).

But each of those Grand Slam titles includes an addendum: *the first black person to win the French Championsihp, to win Wimbledon, to win the U.S. Championship.* That is Gibson's legacy, a legacy that, as Williams said, lives on in her and her sister, Serena, as well as Zina Garrison, MaliVai Washington, and Jeff Blake, and in Chanda Rubin and Alexandra Stevenson.

Three years after Jackie Robinson made his historic debut with the Brooklyn Dodgers, Gibson strode onto the courts at Forest Hills to face Barbara Knapp in the first round.

The year was 1950. Tennis would never be all-white again.

"Her contribution to the civil rights movement was done with her tennis racket," longtime friend Fran Gay told the *Associated Press* upon Gibson's death in 2003. "Althea came up in a hard time. Segregation was no easy thing. It was a feat that she accomplished under really devastating and debilitating odds because she wasn't wanted."

No one sets out to become a pioneer, and the reserved, guarded Gibson certainly didn't intend it. Her approach to her career was rather simplistic.

She was very good at tennis. She happened to be black.

"I see myself as an individual," she told *Sport* magazine in 1963. "I can't help or change my color in any way, so why should I make a big deal out of it? My attitude has always been that I could do more for the Negro by making good, and being accepted because I had made good, then I ever could by popping off."

Her refusal to yell louder, to crusade for the cause, frustrated black leaders, but ultimately Gibson's methods worked. Barriers came down. The game changed.

"Who could have imagined? Who could have thought?" Gibson said in 1988, when she donated her trophies to the Smithsonian Institute's National Museum of American History. "Here stands before you a Negro woman, raised in Harlem, who went on to become a tennis player and finally winds up being a world champion, in fact, the first black woman champion of this world. And believe it or not, I still am."

Born in 1927 to sharecroppers in South Carolina, she moved to Harlem at age three and quickly distinguished herself as, well, a bit of a thorn in her parents' side. She didn't get into trouble, but she didn't exactly work on her academics, either. "Me and my friends used to regard school as a good place to meet and make our plans for what we would do all day," she told *Sport*.

Some nights she would ride the subway all night, in part to escape her father's whip and in part to enjoy the warmth in the winter or the blowing fans in the summer.

Though life was hard, Gibson had the good fortune to live on 143rd Street, a Police Athletic League (PAL) play street, which meant the police set up barricades to close the street to traffic during the day so kids could play.

The big game on the block was paddle tennis and Gibson was among the best. A PAL coach and aspiring musician by the name of Buddy Walker spotted Gibson playing in the streets and introduced her to the game of tennis. He bought her two secondhand rackets for $5 and convinced her to join him at the Harlem River Tennis Club.

Gibson was a natural. She beat older, more experienced boys and tromped the girls. With Walker's help and a collection to cover her membership fees, Gibson joined the Cosmopolitan Tennis Club—"the ritzy tennis club in Harlem," Gibson called it.

"I just found that I had a skill at hitting that ball," Gibson told a biographer in 1965. "And I enjoyed the competition."

To her parents' chagrin, Gibson quit high school and began competing in girls' tennis tournaments. Tennis, though, was segregated in the late 1940s, so Gibson was forced to compete in the all-black American Tennis Association (ATA) instead of the United States Tennis Association (USTA).

Still there was no denying her natural ability. She won seven consecutive New York state championships and for seven years reigned as the ATA's top-ranked player. Her prowess caught the eye of two prominent doctors, Walter Johnson of Virginia and Hubert Eaton of North Carolina. Johnson, active in the black tennis community, became her tennis patron, getting Gibson better instruction and competition. Years later, he would do the same for Ashe.

Eaton put Gibson back on the proper academic track. She lived with the Eaton family during the school year and, in 1949, earned her high school diploma in Wilmington, North Carolina.

Armed with her ATA credentials, Gibson and Johnson lobbied the USTA to allow Gibson to compete in the U.S. nationals at Forest Hills, the precursor to the U.S. Open. Their pressure, coupled with a strong editorial by four-time champion Alice Marble in the *American Lawn Tennis Magazine,* swayed the USTA.

"If tennis is a game for ladies and gentlemen," Marble wrote, "it's time we acted a little more like gentle people and less like sanctimonious hypocrites."

The USTA acquiesced, essentially ending tennis segregation.

Discrimination, however, wasn't so easy to put to rest.

The road Gibson now traveled was a difficult, lonely one, particularly for a woman who was only twenty-three.

Remember, the civil rights movement was a decade away; segregation was commonplace. Some tournaments simply pulled up their stakes rather than admit Gibson, and while traveling to compete in tournaments, Gibson frequently was denied hotel rooms.

"I tried to feel responsibilities to Negroes, but that was a burden on my shoulders," Gibson told *Time* in 1957.

But she loved tennis too much to shirk the added burden.

In her 1950 debut at Forest Hills, Gibson nearly did the improbable. She faced defending Wimbledon champion Louise Brough in the second round and led 1–6, 6–3, 7–6 when a tremendous thunderstorm struck. The powerful storm not only ended the match, a lightning bolt knocked one of the concrete eagles perched atop the stadium to the ground.

When the match resumed, Brough held serve and went on to win the match, but the loss didn't diminish what Gibson had accomplished, and she knew it.

"When that lightning put down that eagle, maybe it was an omen that times was a-changing," she said later. "Brough was a little too experienced for me in that situation, but my day would come."

It didn't come as swiftly as Gibson would have liked. Though a year later Gibson again made history by becoming the first black person to play on the hallowed grounds of the All England Club, site of Wimbledon, she wasn't playing tennis to make history. Fiercely competitive, she played to win, and frustrated by the gap in her game and the more seasoned amateurs

ஃ .⟶. ௸

"Most of us who aspire to be tops
in our fields don't really
consider the amount of
work required to stay on top."

—ALTHEA GIBSON

•⟶•

in the Grand Slams, Gibson contemplated joining the Army in 1955 and walking away from the game.

Fortunately, her coach talked her out of it.

A year later she would be hoisting a French Championship plate.

So began a run that was every bit as dominant and overpowering as the Williams sisters' era. Lithe and athletic, Gibson played with a physicality that the women's game hadn't seen before.

But dominance doesn't usually make for fast friendships on the tennis tour, and the fact that Gibson was black made her all the less popular. Fortunately, along the way she encountered Angela Buxton, an Englishwoman who, as a Jew, experienced the same ostracism as Gibson. The two originally met in India and, at the '56 French Open, decided to become a doubles team.

"She was still fighting the black barrier," Buxton told the *Observer* in 2001. "At that time, Americans weren't going to ask her to play. You can't imagine what it was like. I remember her sitting on the sideline when I was playing the 1956 Wightman Cup against America at Wimbledon. She was staying with me at the time, and I was thinking, 'What is she sitting there for? One of the best players in the world, and she wasn't chosen.' She came up in a different society altogether from those American girls who were playing. They wouldn't have dreamt of asking her to play."

Perhaps fueled by an us-versus-them mentality, the pair were unstoppable on the tennis courts. They won the French Championship in 1956 and went on to capture the Wimbledon crown that same year.

"Minorities Win," one British newspaper headlined after the pair's historic win at Wimbledon.

"It was in very small type," Buxton told the *Observer*, "lest anyone should see it."

Theirs was a partnership that reached far beyond the tennis courts. Gibson and Buxton would remain lifelong friends.

Buoyed by her success on the doubles courts, Gibson flourished on her own as well. She reached the finals at the U.S. Open in 1956, losing to Shirley Fry in the title match.

But 1957 belonged to Gibson. Already in possession of a trophy from Roland Garros, she set her sights that year on Wimbledon. As described in *Born to Win: The Authorized Biography of Althea Gibson*, the ATA threw their star a huge farewell bash, enticing the likes of Sammy Davis Jr. to serenade Gibson from the piano. She flew across the pond to Buxton's flat in Paddington where she would stay while she played a handful of Wimbledon tune-ups.

"Her road to success was a challenging one, but I never saw her back down. Althea did a lot for people in tennis, but she did even more for people in general."

—Tennis legend Billie Jean King

On July 6, 1957, with the heat hovering around 100 degrees, Gibson sent a forehand return past Darlene Hard. Hard couldn't chase it down, and Gibson screamed, "At last! At last!" as she claimed a 6–3, 6–2 victory and tennis' most heralded championship. Queen Elizabeth II, on the throne only five years and making her first official appearance at Wimbledon, presented the tearful Gibson with her trophy.

"Shaking hands with the Queen of England was a long way from being forced to sit in the colored section of the bus," Gibson told her biographers, Frances Clayton Gray and Yanick Rice Lamb.

At the traditional Wimbledon ball that evening, Gibson told the crowd, "In the words of your own distinguished Mr. Churchill, this is my finest hour."

Gibson returned home a hero, particularly to the black community. With the help of the *New York Amsterdam News,* Gibson was fêted with a ticker-tape parade down the Canyon of Champions, an honor only one other black American had been afforded at the time—Jesse Owens.

"At that time we didn't have people who could run for the president of the United States," L. Garnell Stamps, who watched Gibson play as a child, told Gray and Lamb. "We did not have many nationally known people. There were a few in the arenas and on the field of play and in other things. We had to look up to those."

As much as she reveled in the excitement and adulation, Gibson wasn't satisfied. There was still one championship to conquer, the one that had gotten her started. "Winning this [Wimbledon] title is the greatest thrill since I started playing tennis," Gibson said at the time. "I'm not going to be satisfied, however, until I win at Forest Hills."

Two months later, she did just that. On September 8, 1957, the woman who had made international tennis history in England did the same in her own country. Gibson defeated Brough, 6–3, 6–4, to become the first black woman to win the U.S. Championship.

At the end of the year the *Associated Press* named Gibson its Female Athlete of the Year, the first black to earn the honor.

A year later Gibson did the improbable, defending both her Wimbledon and U.S. titles.

Despite her successes, Gibson was by no means wealthy. She competed in the pre-Open Era, which meant that Grand Slam competitors were considered amateurs and not eligible for prize money. So after capturing her second U.S. title, Gibson, already thirty-one, decided to turn professional and say good-bye to Grand Slam tennis.

Left to forge her way, Gibson tried golf, becoming the first black woman in the Ladies Professional Golf Association (LPGA). She took money to play exhibition matches in a tour with the Harlem Globetrotters and even recorded an album.

"She made an impact on what was considered a white, rich sport. She was a true pioneer who made it to the top due to her inner strength and persevering attitude."

—Tennis analyst
Betsy Nagelsen McCormack

But really, what place was there for a retired black tennis player, a woman to boot? There was no ESPN for a ready-made career as a tennis analyst. No one was interested in signing Gibson up for endorsements.

"If she had been a half-step later [in her tennis career], she would have been a multimillionaire," former New York City mayor and longtime friend David Dinkins said of Gibson.

She wandered through the rest of her life, serving as New Jersey's state commissioner of athletics for ten years, her tennis career slowly erased by time.

Struggling and in poor health, Gibson disappeared from the collective conscienceness, confined to her East Orange, New Jersey, home while tennis, and really the world, went on without her.

"It's sad that she missed her best years as a player," longtime tennis analyst and *Boston Globe* columnist Bud Collins said. "Later on she became kind of a curiosity, having to tour with the Harlem Globetrotters to make a living. That had to be rather demeaning to her.

In 1997, the same year that Venus Williams became the first woman since Gibson to reach the U.S. Open championship match,

"People thought I was ruthless. I was. I didn't give a darn who was on the other side of the net. I'd knock you down if you got in the way. I just wanted to play my best."

—ALTHEA GIBSON

Time included a poignant piece on what had happened to Gibson. The same week that the U.S. Open inaugurated the Arthur Ashe Stadium, a reporter set out to find Gibson in New Jersey. East Orange residents weren't sure who she was, wondering aloud if she had been a track star, while a woman in city hall insisted Gibson already had died.

That same year, Gibson contacted her old friend, Buxton.

Buxton shared the conversation with the *Guardian* in 2001.

"Angie baby, I can't last much longer. I'm going to commit suicide. I've got no money. I'm very ill. I've got no medication because I can't pay the bills. I can't pay the rent," Buxton recalled Gibson saying.

Buxton already had contacted a number of tennis people about Gibson's plight. Those letters, coupled by an article that appeared in *Tennis Week* magazine, changed Gibson's life. Within days of the story written by Paul Fein, Gibson's mailbox was crammed with letters, all stuffed with money.

Gibson lived another six years, long enough to see Serena Williams hoist a U.S. Open trophy in 1999 and Venus Williams claim a Wimbledon title in 2000, long enough for their arrival to reintroduce her name and her contribution to a new generation.

Finally On September 28, 2003, Gibson succumbed to respiratory fail-ure. She was seventy-six.

Her legacy lives on.

"If it hadn't been for her," tennis legend Billie Jean King told *Time*, "it wouldn't have been so easy for Arthur or the ones who followed."

Gibson titled her autobiography, written upon her retirement in 1958, *I Always Wanted to Be a Somebody.*

She was and still is.

Althea Gibson's Life Lessons

Believe First in Yourself

Althea Gibson walked a difficult road. She had help, and she had friends, but ultimately in a sport like tennis, where it is you, a court, a net, and your opponent, Gibson had only herself. She had to believe that she could play, and more important, she had to believe that she belonged. "I was nervous and confident at the same time," she once said. "Nervous about going out there in front of all of those people with so much at stake and confident that I was going to go out there and win."

Defy the Odds

Althea Gibson succeeded at a time when no one expected her to, when really no one wanted her around. Surviving in a segregated world was difficult enough. Succeeding in the face of such long odds was unprecedented, but Gibson forged ahead not because she wanted to further her cause, but because she wanted to further her-self. "I'm playing tennis to please me," she said.

Realize That Doing Nothing Sometimes Is the Best Solution

Faced with horrific racism, Althea Gibson likely wanted to scream and rattle the rafters. Black leaders sometimes wish she had. But Gibson believed that yelling and fighting wouldn't accomplish nearly as much as stoic single-mindedness. She wasn't afraid to ruffle feathers, but chose wisely when she should ruffle them and when she should leave things alone. "She had an elegance about her and a humble spirit," former pro tennis player and TV analyst Betsy Nagelsen McCormack said of Gibson.

Stay Humble

Despite the honors and accolades, the excitement she generated, and the regal treatment she received, Althea Gibson never put on airs. She lived in the same modest East Orange, New Jersey, apartment for years and treated every person she met with the same civility, regardless of their station in life. She loved being a tennis champion, but knew it wasn't everything. "Being champion is all well and good," she said. "But you can't eat a crown."

Don't Be Afraid to Win

There is a place for political correctness. Althea Gibson knew it had no place in competition. She did not merely want to compete in tennis. She wanted to win her tournaments, and she never apologized for it, knowing that only those who strive to win will win. Later in her life, when she taught children how to play the game, she always told them, "Focus on what you're supposed to do, not what's around you."

Never Be Satisfied

After winning both Wimbledon and the U.S. Championship, Althea Gibson could easily have walked away from tennis. No one would have blamed her; no one would have chided her. She didn't. She came back a year later and won them each again. "In sports you aren't considered a real champion until you have defended your title successfully," she said. "Winning it once can be a fluke; winning it twice proves you are the best."

~ 11 ~

Steffi Graf:
Strength

*"There is a reason you go through different things in life.
They make you who you are."*

—STEFFI GRAF

he former tennis prodigy (who shall remain nameless to protect her foolishness) couldn't help but sound a little catty. After summarily disposing of the thirteen-year-old wunderkind from Germany, she brushed the upcoming tennis player aside with a snarky, "There are hundreds of players like her in America."

Somewhere the United States Tennis Association (USTA) sighs, "if only."

There were few, if any, anywhere like Steffi Graf. Dubbed "Fraulein Forehand," her fearsome right-handed shot left an entire generation in its wake. In a sport with a rich history of dominating performers, Graf stood out. Ranked number one for a record 377 weeks of her seventeen-year career, Graf stood atop the women's rankings for 186 consecutive weeks, from mid-1987 to 1991. She won 107 titles, including twenty-two major events, and in 1988 became the first woman since Margaret Court in 1970 and only the third woman in history to win the Grand Slam.

That same year, Graf one-upped her peers by adding an Olympic gold medal to her Australian Open, French Open, Wimbledon and U.S. Open crowns, a stunning run of victories that was named the Golden Slam in her honor.

She was only nineteen.

"Steffi Graf is the best all-around player," Chris Evert said once to ESPN. "Martina [Navratilova] won more on fast courts, and I won more on slow courts, but Steffi came along and won more titles on both surfaces."

So much better than her peers, Graf's greatness sometimes was overlooked. Save for a brief challenge from Monica Seles, she went unrivaled for the better part of her career, her dominance so overwhelming it was almost boring. In 1987, she went 75–2 and for the next eight years never failed to win less than fifty matches. Six times the WTA Tour named Graf its Player of the Year, a stunning run from 1987 through 1990 and again from 1993 to 1996.

Chastised much like Pete Sampras for being boring and stoic, Graf actually was nothing more than intensely private. Hardly one to flail and rail at officials, she possessed a steel will, an asset she would call on frequently during a career beset by chronic injuries—legendary tennis commentator Bud Collins once wondered if any great champion "ever played hurt so often"— and family crises.

Graf now has gracefully slipped into retirement, somehow managing to stay out of the spotlight despite being half of sport's most powerful pairing. Her 2001 marriage to Andre Agassi produced nothing less than tennis royalty, but Graf intentionally eschewed the spotlight while her husband finished his career, all but hiding in private boxes at the bigger tournaments.

"Two minutes around her and you forget what she's done in tennis," Agassi said of his wife to the *New York Times*.

Determined to raise their children, Jaden and Jaz, with as much normalcy as they can muster, the couple has no nannies, no live-in help. A visit to their home would yield no mantles lined with Wimbledon platters or U.S. Open trophies. They are ordinary parents who happen to be extraordinary tennis players.

That really is how Graf was raised. Though her father, Peter, groomed her to be a great tennis player, handing his daughter her first wooden racket when she was three, Graf was more like her mother, Heidi, quiet, unassuming, and reflective.

"I want to stay in the background and build the best family for all of us," Heidi told *Sports Illustrated* in 1989.

It wasn't easy, not in Germany where Graf would become a superstar on par with Michael Jordan in the United States. In Bruhl, her hometown, leaders had named a park after her before she was out of her teens, and during Graf's tennis reign, German telephone operators, trying to distinguish between the two towns named Bruhl, often would ask, "Do you want Steffi's Bruhl or the other one?"

That all would come later. In the beginning, there was just a little girl who loved to run and work out and who, despite barely being able to see over the net, was awfully good at tennis. Graf won her first tournament at the age of five and by thirteen had claimed the European Championship. Though working her tirelessly on the practice courts—often as long as four hours a day—her father, Peter, purposefully limited the number of tournaments Graf played in to avoid burnout.

"She was very intense," former tennis player and Graf contemporary Mary Joe Fernandez said. "I first played with her when I was nine and she was eleven or twelve. Even then she was focused, intense, and athletically gifted."

The tactic worked. While no one was paying much mind to the teenager from Germany, Graf slowly climbed the rankings. She was 124th when she first turned pro as a thirteen-year-old, up to number ninety-eight by the end of that 1983 season, twenty-second the following year, and all the way up to number six in 1985 at the ripe young age of sixteen.

Finally, in April 1986, people discovered Graf. She won her first professional tournament at Hilton Head Island, beating no less a formidable opponent than Evert. By year's end, she would win three more titles and climb to number three in the national rankings. Not surprisingly, Graf was named the WTA Tour's Most Improved Player that year.

Long, lean, and athletic, Graf staked her fame on her ability to effortlessly get to balls that seemed nothing shy of unplayable. Add to that a serve that zipped over 100 mph; she was an intimidating force that the tennis world had never seen before.

"Ninety-eight percent of the girls are scared to death to play her," Patty Fendick once said.

The other two percent followed suit by 1987. Graf won her first major tournament that year, beating Navratilova in the French Open final, 6–4, 4–6, 8–6. Navratilova emerged the victor the other two times they met, beating Graf in both the Wimbledon and U.S. Open finals, but they would be Graf's only two losses that year. She won seventy-five of the seventy-seven matches she entered.

"Once I had an aura of invincibility," Navratilova said at the time. "Chris had it for a while. Steffi has it now."

It was an aura that grew exponentially in 1988.

Graf stormed to the Australian Open title, beating Evert, 6–1, 7–6, and then romped over unexpected French Open finalist Natalia Zvereva, 6–0, 6–0. Were it not for a one-hour rain delay, fans wouldn't have had time to get comfortable in their seats. The match lasted only thirty-two minutes.

Graf wasn't foolish to believe her next Slam challenge would be that simple. Navratilova, who would win eight Wimbledon singles crowns before her retirement, had won the previous four titles there going into her finals meeting with Graf.

Early in the second set, it looked as if Navratilova would make it five in a row. She owned a 7–5, 2–0 lead as she started her second service of the set.

And that was the end. Graf broke Navratilova in that game, and the great champion would not win a service game for the rest of the match, bowing to Graf, 5–7, 6–2, 6–1.

"As long as I can focus on enjoying what I'm doing and having fun, I know I'll play well."
—STEFFI GRAF

"There were times last year I didn't know how much I was winning and how tough it was. When you lose a couple of times, it makes you realize how hard winning is," Graf said after the match.

Not that she tasted much more defeat that year.

Graf went on to beat Gabriela Sabatini, 6–3, 3–6, 6–1, at the U.S. Open to complete the Grand Slam.

More relieved than anything, the always-unassuming Graf couldn't quite get her arms around her place in history.

"It's hard to say," she said when asked what it meant to win the Grand

Slam. "It needs some time. The next couple of days will be good."

Actually the next couple of days would merely bring more history. With the Olympics slated to begin in a little more than a week after the U.S. Open, Graf headed to Seoul, Korea, where tennis was being welcomed as an Olympic sport for the first time in sixty-four years.

"Two minutes around Steffi and you forget what she's done in tennis."

—ANDRE AGASSI, GRAF'S HUSBAND

Quite naturally, the inaugural gold medal went to Graf. Only one other player has won all four Grand Slams and a gold medal in his career. Ironically, he happens to share a home with Graf.

While publicly decimating the tennis world that year, Graf quietly embarked on an enterprise that held even deeper meaning to her. Having previously worked with psychiatrists at an outpatient clinic for refugee children, Graf decided to begin her own organization to assist the programs. Children for Tomorrow, which Graf began with her own money, is a nonprofit organization dedicated to helping children and their families who are victims of war, persecution, and violence. With projects in South Africa, Mozambique, Germany, and Kosovo, Graf quietly has helped countless children.

"I've always felt very protective of kids," Graf once said. "Maybe this will be able to change at least some children's lives for the better."

When the 1989 tennis season dawned, it looked as if it would be all Graf, all the time once again. It almost was. Only an upset by seventeen-year-old Arantxa Sanchez-Vicario at the French Open final prevented Graf from winning yet another Grand Slam. She topped Helena Sukova for the Australian Open and then bested Navratilova for Wimbledon, the U.S. Open, and the season-ending Virginia Slims Championships.

"I don't know how much more she can improve," Navratilova said of Graf after Wimbledon that year.

Really, it's possible no one will ever know. Just as Graf's career was starting to hit a stratosphere previously unmatched, she hit her first speed bump. In 1990, her father was falsely accused in a paternity suit, a scandal that weighed heavily on the shy, private Graf. At Wimbledon that year she

"She never allowed the politics of her sport to interfere with her game. I never heard her complain."

—FORMER PLAYER AND TENNIS ANALYST
BETSY NAGELSEN MCCORMACK

broke down in tears during a press conference.

And while Graf struggled with her emotions, a new force snuck up on her. Monica Seles, a grunting teenager from Yugoslavia, blazed onto the scene in 1990, finally providing an equal to Graf. She beat Graf for the French Open title, exposing a vulnerability in Graf's backhand that no one else could. "She hits like she means it," Graf said of her newfound equal.

Between 1990 and 1993, Seles would win three of the four Grand Slam matches the two would play and take over Graf's number one position in 1991.

Critics wondered whether Seles would have been able to mount her charge had Graf not been weakened by a blackmail scandal and a host of chronic injuries. But Graf never blamed her outside problems on her tennis performance. Too much a champion to offer an excuse, she instead insisted that, like the old adage, that which doesn't kill you makes you stronger.

"There is a reason you go through different things in life, and they make you who you are," she once said. "So I don't fight the tough times. I try to understand them, and I try to work through them."

What might have developed of the Graf/Seles rivalry will never be known. In 1993 a deranged fan stabbed Seles during a changeover, later saying he did it to preserve Graf's place as the top tennis player in the world. Seles wouldn't return for two years, leaving Graf again alone at the top.

In the ensuing years, Graf would struggle with nagging back and knee injuries, and though she retained her top status, the injuries limited her tournament appearances and allowed players such as Sanchez-Vicario to push into the limelight.

In 1995 the outside world again collided with Graf's organized tennis world. German authorities accused her of tax evasion, but when it was revealed that her father, Peter, handled her finances, he was jailed for twenty-seven months beginning in 1997. The German tabloids, which rank second perhaps only to London's famous Fleet Street newspapers, had a field day with the downfall of their superstar athlete.

Heartbroken and embarrassed, Graf nonetheless soldiered on.

"I wonder how I manage to survive all of this," Graf told *Sports Illustrated* in 1996. "Sometimes I am an enigma to myself."

Pushing injuries aside, though, wasn't so easy. In 1997, her injured knee twice required surgery. Unable to play, Graf tumbled to number twenty-eight in the rankings and for the first time in ten years, failed to win a single Grand Slam event.

"I always worked hard, and that took a toll at times physically, but other than that, I have to say, what kind of regrets can I have?"

—STEFFI GRAF

For most people, that would have been the end. They would walk proudly off the court and into retirement.

As that one-time tennis prodigy learned, however, Steffi Graf wasn't an ordinary person. Despite missing most of the 1998 season, she fought back to number nine in the world and in 1999 shocked fans, media, and herself. At the French Open, the thirty-two-year-old beat number two Lindsay Davenport in the quarterfinals, number three Monica Seles in the semifinals, and then most impressive, rallied from a set down and down two breaks in the second set to beat number one Martina Hingis for her first Grand Slam title in three years.

"This is the biggest win I've ever had for sure," an emotional Graf told a pro-Steffi crowd after the match. "I've had a lot of unexpected ones, but this is by far the most unexpected. I really came into this tournament without belief. This has been incredible."

She reached the semifinals of Wimbledon, but lost to Davenport. A month later she announced her retirement. At the time she was number three in the world.

"I have done everything I wanted to do in tennis," Graf said.

Some athletes can't walk away. They don't know how to exist without their sport. Graf was just the opposite. Freed from the constraints of a demanding tennis schedule, an almost giddy Graf later recalled leafing through a magazine on the plane home from her final tournament in San Diego, overwhelmed with the excitement that her future life held.

The excitement, much to the delight of the gossip magazines, would quickly include a high-profile romance and marriage to Agassi. Despite their superstar status and careers, the couple somehow managed to avoid the spotlight, with Agassi continuing on in his tennis life until 2006 but leaving his personal life simply that—personal.

During her "Twenty Most Fascinating People" show in 2006, Barbara Walters sat down with Agassi and Graf, telling them they almost seemed to enjoy a sort of fairy-tale romance and life. The pair humbly smiled their assent.

Retirement for the couple, however, does not mean long days on the golf course or idle days on the beach. Together with a Miami-based development company, the couple is designing and developing a mountain resort in Idaho, the Fairmont Tamarack. The luxury condo hotel is scheduled to open in 2008.

Graf also has her foundation to work for, and together, Graf and Agassi continue to spearhead his Andre Agassi Charitable Foundation, the most successful celebrity-run philanthropy in the world. The foundation has raised more than $60 million for at-risk children in Agassi's native Nevada and established a charter school for kids as well.

"I always wanted to see if I could make a difference in someone else's life," Graf said simply once.

On the court and in her life she has.

Indeed, time and again Graf has proven that, unlike the perception of that teenybopping tennis queen at the start of her career, there is no one else like her, not in America, not anywhere.

Steffi Graf's Life Lessons

Rise Above the Fray

For athletes and celebrities, life unfolds on the television and in the pages of gossip magazines. The person who is heralded for his or her climb and accomplishments instantaneously is subject to public scrutiny. Ordinary people may not be able to relate, but Steffi Graf's ability to push the glare of scandal behind her nonetheless holds a message for everyone—that is, to hold your head high regardless of what outsiders are saying and to believe in yourself above all else. "In mental toughness, I'd put her up there with the Michael Jordans, the Wayne Gretzkys, and the John Elways," Tracy Austin told the *Los Angeles Times*.

Work Hard

It sounds simple, but really it is the secret to all successes. Steffi Graf's father practiced her relentlessly, pushing her on the court upward of four hours a day. She was young, perhaps eager to try on the more appetizing role of a normal teenager, but she never let that temptation get in the way of her goals. "It is not amusing to read about how I live only for tennis," Graf told *Sports Illustrated* in 1989. "I have so many other interests. I train for tennis four hours a day, and during a tournament, I practice and play my match. Then that is it. I'd go crazy if I didn't have other things. Only tennis? This is not possible."

Stay Humble

In an era when sports stars celebrate the expected tackle and invent new ways to embarrass their opponents, Steffi Graf was always gracious in victory. More dominant than almost anyone before or after her, she endeared herself to her tennis peers because of her common decency. "She laughs with me. She plays pinball. She is my friend," Patricia Tarabini, a Graf tennis peer told *Sports Illustrated* in 1989. "She is just another player off the court. She is not like, 'I am number one, and you guys get out of here.' She is so plain, so normal."

Remain Focused

Despite personal struggles and outside influences, Steffi Graf never lost sight of what she was striving for, namely to be the best tennis player she could be. As former player Rosie Casals explained, "She was extremely focused . . . big time. All she ever saw was the ball, the court, and being number one."

∽ 12 ∽

Dorothy Hamill:
Gentleness

"Skating is really my first love."

Some athletes and icons age and grow with us. Others are permanently etched in our memories, their lives frozen at the moment of their greatest triumph.

For a generation who grew up in the 1970s, Dorothy Hamill always will be a nineteen-year-old girl wearing a pink skating outfit, with her trademark wedge haircut spinning just so as she finished her routine with a Hamill Camel. Who can forget when she covered her mouth in an "I can't believe I just did that" expression and became America's sweetheart the instant her skates stood still.

It's been more than thirty years since that moment in Innsbruck, Austria. That trademark hair is gray now, and the lines around that nation-capturing smile are outlined in well-earned laugh lines. But Dorothy Hamill still resonates with this country. Other ice skating queens have come and gone, but somehow Hamill remains different, maybe even purer.

She won her gold medal at the 1976 Olympic Games, what many consider the last of the truly innocent Olympics. Politics invaded the next two Games, with the United States refusing to participate in 1980 in Russia, and Russia returning favor by not attending the 1984 Games in Los Angeles. By the time the entire world community gathered again in 1988, the Olympics were a different beast, with more sports and more athletes, with agents and handlers chasing after athletes, and performance-enhancing drugs snaking into the headlines, all of it eroding the purity of amateurism that previously guided the Games.

"We were amateurs," Hamill told the *Dallas Morning News* in 2001. "We didn't have costume designers, agents, publicity representatives, or lawyers. It was so different."

Personifying the simpler times of the Games in which she competed, Hamill was a shy, unassuming champion, a young girl who endeared herself to viewers when she squinted into the television cameras as she tried to see her scores. Genuine and pure, a woman who today still says skating offers her therapy, Hamill was a true sweetheart, not a diva pushed by advertisers to act like a sweetheart.

Her skating performance viewed today seems almost simplistic. She is the last Olympic champion to win a gold medal without completing a triple jump, but what she lacked in athleticism by today's standards, she made up for in grace and beauty. Her spins seemed endless, her form almost poetic as she entranced more than amazed her fans.

"I think her posture, her beautiful straight back, is what I see as her trademark," 1968 Olympic champion Peggy Fleming once said of Hamill. "I wish more skaters today took the time to learn the basics of skating that were the foundation of Dorothy's talent."

Though she was hardly an unknown—Hamill had won three U.S. Championships en route to her Olympic moment—Hamill's Olympic achievement vaulted her to another stratosphere. Instantly famous, she inspired a haircut revolution, with young women and young girls everywhere flocking to their stylists in search of the Hamill wedge.

"The few times I've tried to change my hair, people have sort of said, 'You know, that look isn't good on you,'" Hamill told *People* magazine recently. "It turns out my mother was right."

Pushing fifty now, Hamill still skates with *Broadway on Ice*. She no longer has to. She simply wants to.

"It's my therapy," she told *People*. "I just love putting on the music, going to the ice, and just moving around."

Really, it's always been that way for Hamill.

Raised in Riverside, Connecticut, Hamill enjoyed a perfect childhood, complete with stops at a penny candy store and bicycle rides to school. Her parents, Carol and Chalmers, weren't well off, but the Hamill children—Sandy, Marcia, and Dorothy—didn't know it.

They were happy and content children. As the youngest, Hamill was happy to follow around her big brother and sister. One day, the eight-year-old Hamill followed Marcia and her best friend, Martha, to a backyard pond to skate, grabbing a pair of skates a size too big.

Mesmerized by skating, she raced home to beg for lessons, desperate to learn how to skate backward like her big sister.

"They just completely left me in the dust," Hamill recalled once of that first ice skating adventure. "I wanted to learn how to skate backward, and they wouldn't help me, and they went off and left me on my own. And of course, I went crying home to my mother, up the hill with my skates on my shoulder. I think I must have put on this crying thing for a long time, probably a week or so. And my mom finally said, 'Okay, would you like to take some skating lessons?'"

Painfully shy as a child, Hamill blossomed on the ice. Her mother signed her up for group lessons in nearby Rye, New York, and often Hamill would stay all day, skating around on the public rink until her mother came to fetch her.

"I could be all alone in a big old skating rink, and nobody could get near me, and I didn't have to talk to anybody because of my shyness," Hamill said of her haven on the ice. "It was great. I was in my fantasy world."

She remembered once a competition at the Wollmann Rink in New York City's Central Park, where she noticed the other girls were dressed far fancier than she was. Undaunted, Hamill went on to finish second, realizing then and there that skating brought her something far more important than medals or trophies.

"Skating was where I first learned about winning and losing in life," Hamill said in *It's How You Play the Game.* "For some reason, anywhere else in my life, when people would challenge me or tell me I was not good enough, I would take it personally and more than likely agree that I did not measure up."

It never occurred to Hamill that figure skating could become her life. In the late 1960s, the sport was different. Kids skated on ponds or community rinks. They weren't shuttled off to lessons and ballet sessions in order to get an edge on the competition. Hamill said once she remembered seeing a Holiday on Ice exhibition in New York City, but other than that recalls just one figure skating event on television—Fleming's gold-medal skate in 1968.

"As a Christmas present in 1967, my parents gave me tickets to watch Peggy Fleming at the Olympic qualifiers," Hamill said in *It's How You Play the Game.* "I thought, 'Wow, she is brilliant,' and it was the first time I realized how cool the Olympics would be, without thinking I was Olympic material, of course."

Inspired, Hamill shucked her shyness and began to compete in tournaments. Uninhibited on the ice, she didn't even care that judges were watching her intently or that parents and fans lined the boards to watch her compete. She just skated.

Within a year, Hamill was crowned the U.S. Novice Champion and, in 1970, took the silver medal at junior nationals. Recognizing she could be something special, Hamill and her family that year made the decision to train with Carlo Fassi, the man who guided Peggy Fleming to Olympic gold in 1968, and they moved to Colorado.

Though figure skating wasn't the all-out career it has evolved into today, Hamill's sport nonetheless required sacrifice, for her and her parents. Her mother, she remembered, would wake up every day at 4:00 AM to make breakfast for her daughter and never failed to warm up the car before the pair left for Hamill's early morning practices.

Her father earned chauffeur duties on the weekend, and together, father and daughter would talk music on the way to the rink. Chalmers Hamill was a music buff, a man who spent his spare time at Princeton University composing music and who used his own passion to help pick out music for Hamill's skating routine.

People always ask Hamill if she

"I certainly wasn't more talented than anyone else. Whatever I've done has come through hard work, really, and the love of and the passion for it."

—DOROTHY HAMILL

missed out on her childhood because of skating, but she has never seen it that way. Hers wasn't a traditional girl's life, but she said it was the life she chose.

"My mom sacrificed; I didn't sacrifice anything," she said. "I was just passionate. It was a passion."

"She was a gift to the skating world."
—GORDIE McKELLAN, FORMER SKATING COACH

Hamill's skating career went on a trajectory that even she didn't see coming. Though she dreamed of competing in the Olympics as a kid, she never really considered it a possibility. She skated because she loved it and learned to tolerate the competitive part of the sport. Never able to completely lose her timidity, she suffered before competitions, often finding herself so wracked by nerves before taking the ice that she would become violently ill.

Not to be outdone, her mother, Carol, didn't even come to the arena for Hamill's Olympic skate. Too nervous, she stayed back at the Innsbruck Holiday Inn.

"I often thought it was really like going to your own execution," Hamill said in an interview once. "From the time I got up in the morning, I'd be counting, looking at the clock and saying, 'Okay, I've only got twelve hours until I'm finished,' and 'Nine hours until I'm finished,' and 'Five minutes from now, I'll be finished.' I couldn't wait till it was over. But once I got on the ice and once the music started . . ."

Indeed, once the music started, the beauty began. Hamill looked effortless on the ice, her spins technically perfect but artistically full of grace. She won her third consecutive U.S. championship in 1976 and was a runner-up at the world championship the year before the Olympics, setting the stage for her Olympic moment.

"I certainly wasn't more talented than anybody else," Hamill once said. "I worked as hard as I could. I was always the first one on the ice and the last one off. I'm just one of those people that have to be overtrained and overworked before I can do my best. It was just sheer perseverance. Whatever I've done has just come through hard work really, and the love of and the passion for it."

Hamill went to Innsbruck as America's best chance at a gold in figure skating but still an underdog on the international scene, with the Netherlands' Dianne de Leeuw and East Germany's Christine Errath the favorites.

Nonetheless, back home she was America's biggest hope. Hamill recalled going sightseeing with her mother the day of the long program and returning to her room to find a stack of telegrams. They were from ordinary folks, people Hamill didn't know but who wanted to wish her well.

Momentarily overwhelmed with the responsibility she carried, Hamill cried.

"Dorothy is still America's sweetheart. Nobody skates like her, with those long strides around the ice. She's still exactly the same."

—TOM COLLINS, FOUNDER AND PRESIDENT OF CHAMPIONS ON ICE

But the burden of winning was no match for Hamill's love for skating. Hamill skated flawlessly in her Olympic long program, earning 5.9s from all nine judges for artistic merit to win the gold medal.

"I probably remember most of all the flowers raining down at the end of my performance," Hamill said once. "It was quite a shock and a warm feeling. And of course standing on the podium with that great sense of pride of being an American and having achieved a goal."

When the music stopped, Hamill's anonymity faded with it.

"All the boys wanted to date Dorothy Hamill, and all the girls wanted to be Dorothy Hamill," *USA Today* columnist Christine Brennan said. "Watching her in the Olympics was the highlight of my teen years. Dorothy was the picture of grace and an American icon."

Shortly after, Hamill gave herself a gift. Though everyone in her camp argued against it, Hamill went to Sweden to compete in the world championships. Always a runner-up there, she wanted the chance to win the title.

She did, retiring from amateur competition immediately thereafter.

"In some ways this victory meant more to me than any other," she said. "I won the Olympics for my country. But I won the world championship for myself."

An instant celebrity, the shy Hamill found herself staring from the cover of *Time* magazine, saw her face reflected back in an Ideal Toy Company Dorothy Hamill doll, and her haircut swinging from women across the country. She was on talk shows and morning shows, a guest on the variety show staples of 1970s television, and with her parents tapped out financially (they spent $20,000 a year to fund Hamill's amateur career), Hamill signed a $1 million contract with Ice Capades, the first female athlete to ink a seven-figure deal.

Hamill quickly realized that professional skating was nothing like the skating she had been doing. The grueling schedule of the Ice Capades left little time for training, little time for anything frankly. By now dating Dean Paul Martin (Dean Martin's son), Hamill struggled with the demanding schedule that ferried her from city to city, where she was always the star attraction. She developed a bleeding ulcer from the stress and the pressure.

"I was completely unhappy," Hamill said.

She pushed forward, though, skating as many as thirteen shows a week and also holding up her media responsibilities. She and Martin married in 1982, but with their schedules taking them to opposite coasts, they divorced after just two years. Martin was killed in a plane crash in 1987.

Hamill left the Ice Capades after eight years, signing on instead with the John Curry Skating Company. Run by her '76 Olympic teammate, the troupe was more artistic and less demanding. Revitalized, Hamill skated like her old self, winning four consecutive World Professional Figure Skating crowns.

Hamill remarried in 1987 to Ken Forsythe, a sports physician who was on the Canadian ski team, and had her only child, daughter Alexandra.

In 1993, Forsythe and Hamill bought the floundering Ice Capades, hoping to inject new life into the shows that had been overcome by other skating companies. Along with revitalizing the shows

"[Skating] is therapeutic for me. It's not about the audience. It's the movement. I just work out the cobwebs."

—DOROTHY HAMILL

"It's good to have something that you love in times of trouble. It's carried me through a lot of tough times, skating has. It's my release, my therapy."

—DOROTHY HAMILL

by telling stories, Hamill made it her mission to make life better for the skaters. She did away with the demeaning weigh-ins and set regular practice and training session for the skaters who worked for Ice Capades.

Though their first production, "Cinderella: Frozen in Time," was highly acclaimed, not even Hamill's magic could save the Ice Capades. Three years later she sold it.

Shortly afterward, her partnership with Forsythe ended, too, when the couple divorced.

Clearly, Hamill's life has not been without speed bumps, but asked if she would make changes if her life was given a restart, Hamill declined the chance.

"I've learned so much from the things that I would do differently," she explained once. "I'm not sure I'd have the same perspective if I could go back and change the things that I shouldn't have done. You learn from those mistakes."

What's carried Hamill through, along with her daughter, is skating. She still performs, traveling with *Broadway on Ice*, and recently parlayed her knowledge into a judge's chair for Fox's *Skating with Celebrities*.

Dorothy Hamill's Life Lessons

Don't Be Afraid to Fail

Dorothy Hamill took a risk in 1993, buying the floundering Ice Capades in the hopes of revitalizing the touring ice shows. It didn't work. Within two years, she realized not even her magic could save the show from competitors, and she had to sell. Disappointed that her efforts didn't work, Hamill never regretted taking the chance. "We all fail," she once said. "In this great game of life, you don't know what curve ball is going to be thrown your way. . . . Failures build character."

Trust People

To become a champion, Dorothy Hamill had to have faith in herself, but she also had to put her faith in others. She had to trust the instincts and knowledge of her coaches, had to be certain that all of the people lining up to help her truly had her best interest at heart. "You have to be able to trust people," she once said. "That's a lesson my mother taught me."

Conquer Your Fears

Desperately shy, Dorothy Hamill was beset by a severe case of nerves whenever she skated. Sometimes there would be tears. Always there would be a queasy stomach. But Hamill realized she had a choice. She could sit off to the side and put her passion on a shelf, or she could overcome her shyness and enjoy her skating. She chose the latter. "I'm still working on it," Hamill said of her shyness. "I'm much better than I was, but it was very difficult. Painful."

Embrace Your Passion

From the first time she stepped on the ice, wearing skates so big she had to stuff the toes with socks, Dorothy Hamill felt like the ice was her home. The riches, the celebrity she gained from skating, were all wonderful, but to Hamill, they were never as enriching as the simplicity of just skating. "It's feeling the way a bird would, not having any boundaries, being able to lean and curve, the wind at your face," Hamill once said. "It's magical."

13

Mia Hamm:
Selflessness

"My life proves that anything can happen."

—MIA HAMM

They were the Golden Girls.

Four years earlier, the U.S. Women's National Team in soccer had captured a country's heart, winning a gold medal at the Atlanta Olympics and igniting the women's sports stampede.

Now it was 2000 and the Sydney Games, where everyone anticipated another golden moment.

Only the Golden Girls had turned silver. A heartbreaking overtime loss gave Norway the gold medal and the United States second place.

As they made their way to the medal stand the members of the U.S. team were crushed, reduced to puddles of tears by the disappointment.

All except one. As Mia Hamm walked among her teammates, her eyes were dry, her message clear.

"Heads up," she told them. "Keep your heads up."

As much as Mia Hamm led the charge of women's sports and inspired an entire generation of young women to play soccer, or at the very least play something, her greatest gift to sports was and still is her grace.

A superstar unlike any other before her, she maintained her humility and kindness, teaching young women and boys not only about sport but also about sportsmanship.

"I want my legacy to say, 'She loved what she did and respected the game and respected her teammates, opponents, and the players of the future,'" Hamm said.

Before Mia Hamm, there were great women athletes, plenty of them. Most, however, competed in individual sports: in tennis or golf, track or figure skating. They didn't have the ability to literally jumpstart a team sport movement as Hamm did. They didn't have the opportunity to market themselves and thereby market women as athletes the way Hamm did.

Women's sports needed an identity, a young, vibrant, extremely talented face that offered the refrain, as Hamm did in a legendary Gatorade commercial with Michael Jordan: "Anything you can do, I can do better."

Young girls and women worldwide were simply fortunate that that identity, that face, belonged to a shy young woman who understood she was the star but never acted like it.

"There is no me in Mia," Hamm is fond of saying.

She said nothing pleases her more than when a young fan will ask a seemingly silly question—"What's your favorite color," for example—and simply glows when she learns that she and Hamm share a fondness for green.

"Mia is the epitome of a star and how one should behave," U.S. Women's National Team coach Tony DiCicco said. "She never felt the star role was fair to her teammates. She didn't seek it out, and therefore no other players did either. Mia was the role model to the younger players, and she taught them the importance of being humble and playing unselfishly."

"We always knew there was a bigger cause out there. It was knowing that these young girls in the crowd, when they saw us, they envisioned themselves out there."

—MIA HAMM

That Hamm maintained such humility amid superstardom only a handful of athletes—male and female—ever experience is nothing short of amazing. After winning the World Cup and the gold medal, the U.S. team became a soccer ball-kicking version of the Beatles, with young girls screaming and screeching their names, none louder than "Mia!" Hamm joked that it was because her name was the shortest, but the truth, of course, is because she was the best.

Added to her litany of athletic accomplishments—the two World Cup titles and two gold medals, the all-time leading international goal scorer among men and women, the four NCAA Championships from the University of North Carolina, and the seventeen years as part of the U.S. Women's National Team—are her successes in the more trying world of celebrity marketing. Until her retirement in 2004, Hamm long ranked as the only woman among the top ten most appealing athletes in annual surveys of advertising executives. Gatorade and Nike, the premiere sports product companies in the country, chose Hamm for advertising spots usually reserved for the likes of Michael Jordan and Tiger Woods. Nike even named the largest building on its Oregon campus after her.

"Mia was the perfect soccer icon at the perfect time for women's soccer," her North Carolina coach Anson Dorrance said. "She had a humble personality and didn't want the attention on her, yet was extremely photogenic. People loved that. Here was this attractive, charismatic, and highly talented star with every qualification to sell women's soccer."

And sell it she did. The jump to the soccer pitches by legions of young girls following on the heels of Hamm is legendary. By the 2000–2001 season, after the World Cup, after the gold medal, 292,086 girls were playing high school soccer, according to the National Federation of State High Schools. Five years earlier, there were only 208,287.

Those numbers don't take into account the scores of younger girls who were dragging their parents to soccer fields for youth games on weekend mornings and afternoons and the ones who replaced their movie star posters with those of Mia Hamm.

Hamm didn't necessarily love the spotlight, but if being front and center meant a little girl somewhere might beg her mother for a soccer ball instead of a Barbie, Hamm was more than willing to endure the glare.

"I love being a role model," she said. "I want to inspire young girls to be proud of themselves and do their best. I want to encourage them to celebrate their successes and have fun playing sports."

Growing up, the woman who would become an icon was nothing more than an undersized, painfully shy military brat. Forced to follow her father's itinerant Air Force career, Hamm and her five siblings moved all over the country and the world as children. It made making friends for the shy Hamm even more difficult, but sports were a way in, a place to instantly connect and be part of something.

First spying the game as a toddler while living in Italy, Hamm followed her brother, Garrett, a Thai-American orphan the family adopted when he was eight and Mia was five, onto the soccer fields when the family returned stateside.

The Hamm family first moved to Wichita Falls, Texas, a small town just over the Oklahoma border, that didn't sponsor girls' soccer, so Hamm played with the boys.

"For me, that made a huge impact," Hamm told the *Dallas Morning News* in 2005. "It kind of formed that competitiveness, just from having to prove yourself. I had to be twice as good. It challenged me; it pushed me; it made me be more creative."

Perhaps inheriting the grace from her ballet dancer mother, Stephanie, Hamm proved she wasn't just as good as the boys. She was something special. A force to be reckoned with in Texas, Hamm caught the eye of Dorrance at fourteen when Dorrance heeded the phone call of a local coach who insisted he needed to see this great soccer player named Mia Hamm.

"I didn't want to know who the player was," Dorrance told *Sports Illustrated* about his first encounter with Hamm. "I wanted her to emerge from the game. John's team kicked off, and the girl who received made a pass to her right, and I saw this young kid accelerate like she was shot out of a cannon. Without seeing her touch the ball, I ran around saying, 'Is that Mia Hamm?'"

Dorrance was the U.S. Women's National Team coach at the time, and a year later he added Hamm's name to the roster. She was just fifteen, the youngest team member in the program's history. Previously just a kid who liked to play soccer, Hamm learned how to be an athlete at the first tryout camp. After hours in the weight room, followed by hours more on the practice field, an exhausted Hamm fell into bed, her body and muscles sore like they'd never been before.

But rather than discourage her, the overwhelming training only reinforced her desire to get better.

A year later the family moved to Virginia. By then Hamm already had played a game with the national team in China, but her classmates at Lake Braddock High had no idea who she was. Because she enrolled before her parents officially moved, Hamm couldn't participate in after-school activities, so instead of playing with the girls' team, Hamm trained with the boys' squad.

"I already knew about Mia's abilities," the boys' coach, Jac Cicala, told *Washington Magazine* in 2001. "But I didn't tell the boys much about her. It was funny to watch their faces the first couple of practices, to see their mouths drop when she played. At sixteen, Mia already had that acceleration, that change of pace during dribbling, a willingness to take on defenders. But she never hogged the ball. She was very mature for her age."

Her talent, however, didn't make her popular with the boys. Hamm recalled recently of an encounter after she scored a goal in a boys' game.

"This kid just refused to admit that it was a goal and would not play until I agreed with him," Hamm said in *It's How You Play the Game*. "I wouldn't budge, so he took the ball and was walking away when he shoved me. I shoved him back, so he slugged me right in the face. . . . It was one of the first time I ever stood up for myself. From then on, I've never backed off."

What really separated Hamm from the crowd, aside from her selflessness, was a fear of failure that drove her to become the best. Hamm said her biggest fear is letting down others as well as herself. She used to beat herself up, she said, because she wasn't a vocal leader, but she ultimately came to realize she led by doing other things.

It is that inner drive, the refusal to settle, that made Hamm great even from an early age.

"Mia never felt secure with herself, her game, or her talents. That's what gave her an inner fire to get better."

—TONY DICICCO, U.S. WOMEN'S NATIONAL TEAM COACH

"Mia always wants to do more and not just be good but be great," her longtime teammate Julie Foudy said. "Mia is always learning and thinking, 'Is there something I can be doing?' She has incredible discipline, focus, commitment to conditioning, and respect for her teammates. But then she had this wonderful insecurity that always pushed her to do more. She didn't let the insecurity beat herself up, but let it motivate her."

After graduating from Lake Braddock, Hamm enrolled at North Carolina, where Dorrance was the coach.

He became a mentor.

"My whole time at the University of North Carolina, my parents were living overseas," Hamm said. "Coach took the time to talk with me about life. He was a good listener who helped me celebrate my successes and grow as a person.

"With Mia, it's the process first and the results second. If she does an activity the right way, then she'll know how to repeat it."

—DAN LEVY, HAMM'S LONGTIME AGENT AND FRIEND

"Coach Dorrance created a healthy environment for me, which helped empower me. He pushed me when I needed it and left me alone at the right times. North Carolina was the right school for me even without soccer."

Of course, she didn't fare too badly with soccer, either. The Tar Heels won the NCAA Championship in each of Hamm's four years in Chapel Hill, and Hamm's accomplishments are a laundry list of amazing success. A three-time National Player of the Year, Hamm also twice won the Hermann Award (soccer's Heisman Trophy), as well as the 1993 Honda-Broderick Award, presented to the nation's most outstanding female collegiate athlete. She graduated from North Carolina with a school-record 103 goals and averaged 1.12 goals per game in her tenure there.

But Dorrance knew even before all of that he had something special in Hamm. In the book *It's How You Play the Game,* Hamm recalled a conversation she had with her coach just before her junior year of college, where he explained the difference in being best and just wanting to be the best.

"He asked me if I knew what [being the best] meant," Hamm said. "I didn't. So he walked over to the light switch, flipped it on, and said, 'It's a decision, that's all, a decision. Being the best you means being the best every single day.' For the first time I was learning about true dedication and commitment."

Still, Hamm remained relatively anonymous. She was part of the 1991 U.S. team that won the inaugural Women's World Cup, but those games were played in China and received little attention back home.

"Celebrate what you've accomplished, but raise the bar a little higher each time you succeed."

—MIA HAMM

That changed in 1996 when the summer Olympic Games returned to the United States for the first time in twelve years. By the time Atlanta extinguished the flame, the women's sports movement had begun.

Unlike some of the boorish, brand-conscious behavior of the men's basketball Dream Team, the women's soccer, basketball, and softball teams embraced the Olympic spirit. They lived in the Olympic village and personified the joy we've come to expect our Olympians to possess.

That all three won gold only helped turn Atlanta into the "Women's Games."

The soccer team, heavy favorites in front of the home crowd, hardly disappointed, besting rival China 2–1, for the gold medal in front of 76,481 adoring fans. Troubled all week by a sore ankle, Hamm didn't succumb to the injury until late in the gold medal game when she was taken from the field via a stretcher. Before the final seconds expired, though, she returned to celebrate with her teammates.

Hamm will be the first to say her life has been charmed. Married now to baseball all-star Nomar Garciaparra, the couple has homes in Southern California and Austin, Texas, and recently welcomed twin girls, Grace and Ava.

But she has had her share of heartaches, none worse than the one sandwiched between her two greatest athletic achievements.

Growing up, Garrett Hamm was his sister's champion. When other kids told Hamm she was too tiny to play—she's still only five feet, four inches—

Garrett would pick her for his team, knowing full well she was a pint-sized secret weapon. In 1996, just as Hamm was thriving in Atlanta, Garrett was losing his battle with aplastic anemia, a rare blood disorder. He needed a bone marrow transplant, but because he was adopted and of mixed race, finding a donor was difficult.

During the Olympics, Hamm brought fliers about the disease and urged people to take blood tests for bone-marrow screening whenever she made an appearance.

Finally in February 1997, a donor was found, but as is common with such tricky transplants, Garrett soon developed an infection, and in April he died. He was only twenty-eight.

"The death of my brother Garrett was the most difficult hurdle I faced," Hamm said. "That was so hard to deal with. . . . He was an amazing athlete and a hero to me."

Not surprisingly, Hamm turned her grief to action. She started the Mia Hamm Foundation, which funds bone-marrow research and assists the families of patients.

Hamm, who has said she feels Garrett with her every day, returned to the national team immediately and, in 1999, guided the United States into women's soccer pandemonium when the country hosted the Women's World Cup. Hamm, of course, was the star of the team even if she didn't want to be.

Hamm tried desperately to deflect the attention, declining a chance to pose by herself on the cover of *Newsweek,* but she was the centerpiece of a team that would do extraordinary things.

The women not only won the World Cup title, they won it in front of 90,185 fans, a frenzied crowd that belied the notion that Americans didn't like soccer. When Brandi Chastain memorably tore off her jersey to celebrate the shootout goal that would seal the victory and the title, she turned each of the players into superstars.

None, however, shone as brightly as Hamm. She was in every magazine, endorsing every product, and even the United States' failure to win another gold in Sydney in 2000 did little to damage her aura.

Four years later, of course, the women roared back for a hard-fought gold in Athens, a fitting end for a career. Hamm, along with several of her legendary teammates, roared the national anthem on the medal podium and then hung up her cleats for good.

"Mia walked away from the game of soccer at the peak of her career," her agent and longtime friend Dan Levy said. "I think she's still the best player in the world. What does her future hold? Whatever she wants it to hold. Her opportunities are unlimited."

Hamm is awed and a little overwhelmed at those possibilities. She loves to golf and cook and looks forward to being a great mother, but right now she's still finding her way post-soccer.

"What gets me up in the morning?" she asked. "Coming up with new challenges now that my soccer career is over. I want to find something else to give my life to."

Whatever it is, there's no doubt she will give herself entirely.

I ran into Nomar Garciaparra at a baseball function a while back. I pulled him aside and asked, "Is Mia as impressive as she appears?"

The five-time all-star looked at me and replied simply, "More so."

Mia Hamm's Life Lessons

Respect the Game; Respect Your Opponents, Too

Certainly her desire to achieve personal goals drove Mia Hamm, but just as much was her desire to do right by the sport she loved so much. To take a day off would mean disrespecting soccer, to not play 100 percent would mean snubbing the opponent, and that was something Hamm would never do. "People who accomplish things didn't fall on top of the mountain," she said. "They worked their tails off. Success is not a one-time choice. You have to recommit yourself every day. There are some mornings when I wake up and don't feel very inspired. I don't feel like running wind sprints and working out, but nine out of ten days I'll do it."

Don't Be Afraid to Celebrate Your Successes

When Brandi Chastain tore off her jersey in a spontaneous show of emotion after the United State won the 1999 World Cup, it ignited a maelstrom of controversy. Some deemed such antics inappropriate for a woman, particularly one who served as a role model to young girls. Mia Hamm doesn't understand why there was a problem. "What happens when an NFL player scores a touchdown?" she said. "He starts dancing around and celebrates in the end zone. And what happens when an NBA player dunks a ball? He starts woofing about what he just did. You don't see women doing that very much, and I want to help them understand it's okay to celebrate when you're successful."

Love What You Do

Gifted with natural talent and an innate sense of hard work, Mia Hamm also loved the game of soccer. It was never a burden to play and always a joy. Having that trait, in the end, is as important as the talent and the hard work. "On the field she had an insatiable lust to score goals," Hamm's college and U.S. Women's National Team coach Anson Dorrance said. "There was no one like her. She had this visceral connection with stuffing a soccer ball into the back of a net. Mia had this aggressive goal-scoring personality and wanted to score more than breathe the oxygen in the air."

Be Proud of What You Do

Told she was too small to play soccer competitively and reared at a time when female athletes always took a backseat to their male counterparts, Mia Hamm bucked the odds. Humble and shy about her accomplishments, she nevertheless is rightly proud of what she's done. "I was determined to be the best I could be," she said. "My life proves that anything can happen."

It's Okay to Care

So many athletes and celebrities distance themselves as their popularity grows. The swarms of people and the attention can be overwhelming, but it's easy to forget how one small act of kindness can resonate forever. Mia Hamm never forgets. She tells a story about a visit to a grocery store, where a woman suffering badly from Parkinson's disease was short $3 for her bill. Hamm simply stepped up and paid the difference. "The lady wanted my address so she could mail me a check. I said, 'No, just pass it on. You do something kind for someone and we'll get a movement going.'"

Jackie Joyner-Kersee:
Kindness

"Be true to who you are, and never give up on your dreams."

—JACKIE JOYNER-KERSEE

or months the construction crews, bulldozers, and cement mixers drove up to the corner of 15th and Piggott in East St. Louis, laying a foundation for a massive building just outside of Lincoln Park.

From her vantage point across the street a little girl watched in wonder.

At first Jackie Joyner was sad—sad to see her playground covered up by this monster of a building—but then the precocious child grew curious. Day after day she sat on her porch and watched and wondered. What could it be?

In East St. Louis in the 1960s, progress came slowly, so the beginnings of a building, with all its fresh paint and clean smells, offered hope regardless of its purpose.

Finally Joyner and her friends pestered a security guard enough that he told them what the mystery building was. It was to be a community center, the Mary E. Brown Community Center.

To Jackie Joyner, it was an oasis.

Today the Mary E. Brown Community Center is nothing more than a hulled-out shell.

Not far away, though, sits the Jackie Joyner-Kersee Center, a glistening beacon of hope to a new generation of kids.

"I want to give kids a shot at life and give them hope and inspiration," Joyner-Kersee said about her center. "We offer a wide range of services, but the main thing is to teach them about character. Honesty and integrity are so important."

Honesty, integrity, and grace—those, too, are the words to describe Joyner-Kersee. She was known as the World's Greatest Female Athlete, hardly an embellishment considering her dominance of the heptathlon, the most grueling and demanding track and field event, but really Joyner-Kersee can be considered one of the World's Greatest Citizens.

Chicago Tribune Olympic reporter Philip Hersh shared a story about Joyner-Kersee that more than exemplifies why this woman is as revered as a person as she is as an athlete. In 1991, she pulled a hamstring during the 200-meter event at the world championship, forcing her withdrawal from the heptathlon competition. Emerging on a hospital gurney at the end of the meet, Joyner-Kersee attracted a crowd of reporters. Her husband, Bob, didn't want her to speak, and security guards didn't want her blocking the VIP entrance.

She, however, simply agreed to do the interviews, as well as move to the parking lot where there was more space. Just as a reporter was about to begin his question, Joyner-Kersee turned to Hersh and asked, "How is your son doing?"

"In the midst of disappointment and chaos and pain, Joyner-Kersee thought of someone else instead of herself," Hersh recalled. "She would be selfless to the end."

Indeed, rather than polish her Olympic medals—she has five of them: three gold, a silver, and a bronze—and read the press clippings about her world record in the heptathlon, which still stands eighteen years later, the American record she once held in the long jump, and the barrier-crossing accomplishment of being the first woman to score more than 7,000 points in

> *"Jackie's goal is to be the best person possible."*
>
> —NINO FENOY, JOYNER-KERSEE'S HIGH SCHOOL COACH

the grueling heptathlon, Joyner-Kersee has returned to where it all began for her with the hope that maybe she can provide the spark for another child.

The Jackie Joyner-Kersee Foundation earns its funding and support because of the athletic legacy of the woman for whom it is named, but its heart is from the woman herself.

"I admire Jackie's impeccable character," Bob Kersee, Jackie's husband and coach, said. "She wants to be a good person above being a good athlete. She is genuine, a true person of character."

The children who race through the doors of the Jackie Joyner-Kersee Community Center don't have it easy. They know poverty and hardship from a young age and face a life where the odds generally aren't stacked in their favor.

Joyner-Kersee recognizes those kids well.

She once was one of them.

Mary Joyner was sixteen when she married, her husband, Alfred, only fifteen. Through sheer will they forged a life together, with an expanding family that eventually would include four children. Money was tight, as jobs in the nearby plants grew scarce. In her autobiography, *A Kind of Grace,* Joyner wrote about getting by on mayonnaise sandwiches when times were the toughest.

Like the rest of East St. Louis, the neighborhood where Joyner-Kersee grew up offered little haven. She saw a man murdered when she was eleven, and not long after, she learned that her grandmother, too, had been murdered by a man she was living with.

But as tough as life was for a family headed up by parents barely out of childhood themselves, the Joyner family persevered. Mary Joyner made sure of it, insisting that her children attend church every Sunday and adhere to her strict rules, and that her three daughters behave as young ladies.

"My mother had a big influence on me," Joyner-Kersee said. "She taught me how to be strong and independent and self-reliant. My mother's message was to help yourself first because you can't help others if you aren't a strong person yourself."

Her parents gave her the strong foundation of courage and pride.

"It would have been easy for my parents to lose hope and give in to wayward temptations, the way so many other people did in East St. Louis," Joyner-Kersee wrote in her autobiography. "But they never became dejected or hopeless. . . . Their unwavering commitment to the work ethic and their sound values informed my life from childhood to adulthood."

If her parents gave her the foundation for success, the Mary E. Brown Community Center gave her the windows. It was her place to play, to dream, and eventually to compete. In her autobiography, Joyner-Kersee wrote of waking up early on the weekends during school and every day during the summer. Because her mother wouldn't let her go to the center alone, Joyner-Kersee would coax one of her sisters to accompany her, offering either a candy bar or some change to cement the deal.

Joyner-Kersee enjoyed everything the center had to offer, from arts and crafts to story time to lectures to dance lessons and cheerleading.

In 1972, Joyner-Kersee spied a sign-up sheet at the community center for girls' track. She signed up immediately. At the first practice Joyner-Kersee and the other girls were told they'd have to run a lap around the cinder track behind the center. Most girls whined about the distance or walked halfway around until, after only a handful of days, fewer and fewer girls came to practice. Except Joyner-Kersee. She kept coming and kept finishing her laps.

> *"I maintained my edge*
> *by always being a student.*
> *You will always have ideas,*
> *have something new to learn."*
>
> —JACKIE JOYNER-KERSEE

"In my first race I finished last and said, 'I've got a lot of work to do here,'" Joyner-Kersee said.

Known as "jumping Jackie" during her brief cheerleading stint, Joyner-Kersee thought it would be fun to try the long jump. She didn't have a clue about the intricacies of the sport or technique but the thought of just flying through the air captivated her.

So Joyner-Kersee convinced her sisters to help move some of the sand from the pit at the track back to their house. The three girls filled potato chip bags for days until Joyner-Kersee had her own pit at home; the young girl would climb onto her porch railing, crouch down, and leap into the sand. One day at practice over at the center, Joyner-Kersee couldn't resist. She ran down the long jump runway when she thought no one was watching. Her coach, George Ward, saw her, and the next day she was a long jumper.

"I can still see Jackie as a very young athlete," Nino Fenoy recalled. Joyner-Kersee's age-group and high school coach, Fenoy partnered with Ward to form an AAU track team, the East St. Louis Railers, and guided Joyner-Kersee on the first leg of her athletic path. "She was so excited just to be participating. She always had a big, bright smile on her face and a glowing look in her eyes. When I think of the youthful Jackie, I recall the very congenial, positive person that she still is today," said Fenoy.

By the time Joyner-Kersee was fourteen, Fenoy had persuaded her to try the pentathlon. She wasn't crazy about all five events, but since she already was competing in most of them, the move made sense.

By age fifteen, she won the 1977 Junior Olympics.

"Jackie was coachable as a young athlete," Fenoy told me. "She was able to grasp different concepts, visualize them, and then apply them."

A budding superstar, Joyner-Kersee left her mark all over Lincoln High School, where she starred on the basketball court as well as the track. During her time there, Lincoln won three Illinois state track championships and a basketball state title, while Kersee set state records in the 440-yard dash, the long jump, and the pentathlon.

By 1980 she had earned the right to compete in the Olympic trials, and though her nerves sent her tumbling to an eighth-place finish in the long jump, Joyner-Kersee had emerged on the national stage.

Not surprisingly the college recruiters were winding their way to East St. Louis, and when Joyner-Kersee made her decision, opting for a basketball scholarship to the University of California at Los Angeles (UCLA), it was a media event.

Though Joyner-Kersee had made the decision to relocate to

"Jackie teaches us that you can be a champion without cutting corners and compromising your character."

—BOB KERSEE, JOYNER-KERSEE'S HUSBAND

California, it was a tough adjustment being so far from home, one
made all the more difficult when
the eighteen-year-old freshman
received a horrific phone call. Her
mother, who said she wasn't feeling well when the two spoke the
night before, was in a coma and
brain dead from a rare form of

*"To her, mediocrity is
unacceptable."*

—LECIA RIVES, EXECUTIVE DIRECTOR,
JACKIE JOYNER-KERSEE CENTER

meningitis. Together with her father and older brother, Jackie made the
decision to take Mary Joyner off life support. She was only thirty-seven.

"The loss of my mother was a very difficult time in my life," Joyner-
Kersee said. "It was so hard because she didn't get to realize the goals and
dreams we shared together."

With a heavy heart, Joyner-Kersee returned to Los Angeles and continued her college career. She played for three years before taking a little hiatus.

She had business to take care of at the 1984 Olympic Games.

By now under the watchful eye of her future husband, Bob Kersee, who
was an assistant on the UCLA track team when Joyner-Kersee competed
there, Joyner-Kersee was a force on the track. Bob Kersee, a former Marine
sergeant, fell in love with his protégé, but that didn't buy her any breaks at
practice. He pushed his soon-to-be wife (the two wed in 1986) to achieve
more than she ever thought she could.

At the Los Angeles Olympic Games, Joyner-Kersee, who was fifth in the
long jump, struggled through the 800-meter event because of a pulled
hamstring, and she had to settle for a silver medal in the heptathlon.

"Jackie played three years as a starter for me and then took a year off for
the Olympics," former UCLA Coach Billie Moore said. "I told her that
many doors would open for her, and she was not obligated to come back
for her fourth year. She looked at me as if I had lost it. She wouldn't hear
of it. She came back and finished her fourth season at UCLA."

Equally important, Joyner-Kersee graduated in 1986, receiving her
degree in history, something she told me she is every bit as proud of as her
Olympic achievements.

Between the 1984 Games and the 1988 Games, Joyner-Kersee became the overwhelming heptathlon favorite. The owner of nine consecutive victories in the event that includes the 100-meter hurdles, high jump, shot put, 200 meters, long jump, javelin, and 800 meters, Joyner-Kersee also became the first woman to break the 7,000-point barrier at the 1986 Goodwill Games.

To no one's surprise, she blew away the competition in Seoul in 1988, winning an Olympic gold by a new world record of 7,291 points, a record that remains standing eighteen years later, and five days later, she long-jumped her way to another gold medal and an Olympic record.

Four years later in Barcelona, Joyner-Kersee dashed off with another gold in the heptathlon, giving her more than enough credence to call herself the World's Greatest Female Athlete. She earned a bronze in the long jump.

"She's the greatest multi-event athlete ever, man or woman," Bruce Jenner, a man who knows a thing or two about that, said once.

That she did all this while hiding a health secret is even more amazing. Diagnosed in 1983 with asthma, Joyner-Kersee ignored the disease for years, wishing it would just go away. For a long time that worked, but as she grew older the asthma, coupled with severe allergies to nuts, shellfish, fruit, dust, grass, pollen, ragweed, feathers, and animal hair, wreaked havoc on her system. Her husband, Bobby, learned to look for the signs of an asthma attack and would literally pull her off the track if he thought she was in danger.

Eventually Joyner-Kersee started wearing a surgical mask when she raced, but even that couldn't stem the tide. An attack landed her in the hospital in 1991, followed by two terrifying scares in 1995 where Bobby had to call 911 as Joyner-Kersee's breathing became frighteningly limited.

"My greatest fear has always been about being asthmatic," she said. "The possibility of dying crossed my mind, and I had a deadly fear of collapsing on the track. I denied being asthmatic for a while, but later I accepted it as fact and did what the doctors told me to do."

"I view myself as a servant to other people."

—JACKIE JOYNER-KERSEE

In 1996, Joyner-Kersee, the defending U.S. champion on the

heptathlon, planned to go out in style, competing in her final Olympics in her home country. But the Atlanta Games provided more tears than joy for Joyner-Kersee, who was forced to withdraw from the heptathlon because of a hamstring injury. She did, however, win a bronze medal in the long jump, a medal her husband called "a medal of courage."

Joyner-Kersee attempted to make the 2000 Olympics, but failed to qualify, and a year later at the age of thirty-eight, she retired.

Well, retired isn't exactly accurate. Joyner-Kersee no longer races competitively, but to say she's leading the luxurious life of retirement is a bit of an overstatement. In 1988 she had formed the Jackie Joyner-Kersee Foundation and has made it her life's work.

"After the 1988 Olympics, Jackie took 103 kids from East St. Louis to the Macy's Thanksgiving Day Parade in New York," remembered Lecia Rives, the executive director of the Jackie Joyner-Kersee Foundation, who introduced Joyner-Kersee at a ceremony at Lincoln High School when Rives was a high school senior there. "I was among that group. That was my first plane trip and my first trip to a really big city.

"People ask me all the time, 'Is she really that nice?' and I say, 'Yes, she's really that nice.'"

Thanks to Joyner-Kersee's name and hard work, the foundation raised more than $12 million to open the Jackie Joyner-Kersee Community Center in 2000. Like the community center that helped forge her life, Joyner-Kersee's namesake offers myriad opportunities and experiences for children, ranging from tutoring and educational programs to sports, dance, and arts.

In addition, Joyner-Kersee hosts a race in East St. Louis every year, a meet that annually includes a motivational program Joyner-Kersee calls Winning in Life.

Of course, the topic winning in life is something Joyner-Kersee knows well. A champion on the track and a star on the basketball court, she endures as a woman who overcame so much to become even more.

"We all have obstacles in our path," Joyner-Kersee said. "But you can't use them as an excuse. When you have setbacks, face them, set your agenda, and keep going forward."

Jackie Joyner-Kersee's Life Lessons

Be True to Who You Are

If there is a mantra that Jackie Joyner-Kersee lives by, this is it. She says it over and over as she talks about her life, her accomplishments, and her challenges. She has never been swayed by public opinion or the media, never stopped being the woman she's wanted to be. "My strength and inspiration come from within," she said. "I'm always talking to myself and saying, 'I can do it.'"

Stay Humble

Jackie Joyner-Kersee's humility and kindness is almost as legendary as her athletic career. Blessed with so much, she nonetheless considers everyone her equal. When she was a high school senior, Lecia Rives was given the honor of introducing Lincoln High School's most famous graduate. After she graduated, Rives decided to write the woman who had impressed her so much, really just to tell Jackie Joyner-Kersee how much she admired her. "I'd write her, and she'd answer me," Rives said. "It's amazing that she did that." Even more amazing, today that high school girl is the executive director of Joyner-Kersee's foundation.

Be Kind to Your Neighbor

The Olympic trials are a place where dreams are realized or dashed. It is a competition that is fierce and frantic, with so much on the line. Yet Bob Kersee, Jackie's husband, remembers the 1988 Olympic trials as much for his wife's generosity as the world record she set there in the heptathlon. "She seemed more concerned about others' needs than her own," he said. "Still, she wanted to win, proving that you can compete hard but still be sensitive to the needs of others."

Remember Your Beginnings; Never Forget Where You Came From

On the West Coast since she left for college, Jackie Joyner-Kersee easily could have turned her back on East St. Louis. She made it. She was out. Instead, once she was financially able, she immediately set out to help her old neighborhood. "I admire Jackie for her commitment and dedication to the children of East St. Louis," Valerie Foster, Joyner-Kersee's executive assistant of sixteen years, said. "She's always giving back to them, and to see her interact with the kids is an amazing sight."

∽ 15 ∽

Billie Jean King:
Vision

*"I always performed my best when
the confrontation was the most heightened."*

—BILLIE JEAN KING

lbert Einstein. Ernest Hemingway. Jonas Salk. Eleanor Roosevelt. The Wright Brothers. Henry Ford. Walt Disney. Martin Luther King Jr.

Life magazine's 1990 list of the one hundred most important Americans of the twentieth century was wide in scope, juxtaposing political figures next to entertainers, authors in line with scientists.

Only four athletes made that list.

Three of them were men.

Billie Jean King was the fourth.

Alongside the groundbreaking Jackie Robinson, the country's first sports superstar Babe Ruth, and the world's most recognizable athlete, Muhammad Ali, stood King, a woman who is nothing less than a present-day trailblazer.

King's legacy today is wrapped up in the "Battle of the Sexes," her 1973 upset of Bobby Riggs that made King the poster child for women's equality and women's rights. Really, though, King's handprint on women's athletics extends far beyond one made-for-television match against an aged tennis hustler.

She is nothing less than a pioneer, a woman who shepherded women's sports into the Title IX era and an incredible champion who risked her own stardom and paycheck for the greater good. Female tennis players and golfers, ice skating queens, soccer stars, WNBAers, and swimming champions really all owe a debt of gratitude to King.

"Without Billie Jean King, we wouldn't have sports for women," New York–based sportscaster Ann Liguori said. "I've seen her at banquets, and she goes to every table, meets people, shakes hands and never stops promoting women's athletics."

Without her, the women's sports movement might have found its way, but with her, it bulldozed toward the door of equality, using her voice and her influence to knock down hurdles along the way.

"She is a true visionary," tennis analyst Betsy Nagelsen McCormack said. "Any time some issue appears on the horizon, Billie Jean thinks, 'Is there a cause here?' . . . Every woman athlete in the world today owes Billie Jean a big thank you. She is one of those rare individuals in a lifetime that comes along to impact society through her passion and intensity."

An incredible serve-and-volleyer, King won a record twenty Wimbledon titles (in singles, doubles, and mixed doubles) and thirty-nine Grand Slam trophies in all, held the number one ranking for four years, and in 1972, became just the fifth woman and only American to win all four Grand Slam titles when she completed the round-robin by winning the French Open.

As exhaustive as her tennis resume is, King's off-court accomplishments are more important. When women's tennis was overshadowed by the men, King championed the Virginia Slims Tour. When the Grand Slam tournaments refused to pay women equal prize money to the men, she threatened to boycott the U.S. Open, making that tournament the first to up the ante for women. Realizing that women needed a unified voice, she helped establish the Women's Tennis Association (WTA) as a player's union and served as the WTA's first president. Together with her ex-husband Larry King, she financed and founded World

"I see the big picture first and then go backwards to execute it."

—BILLIE JEAN KING

Team Tennis (WTT), bringing a team element and more fun-filled game to fans everywhere.

"I call her 'Mother Freedom,'" tennis analyst and longtime *Boston Globe* columnist Bud Collins said. "From 1968 on, she led the way for the women's pro tour in tennis. She played like a champion, but preached equality like a champion, too. She's still doing it today."

"Victory is fleeting but losing is forever and that makes all the difference. Defeat is something I just can't seem to get rid of. It never leaves my insides."

— BILLIE JEAN KING

"She was a crusader for us all," Martina Navratilova once said of King. "She was carrying the flag."

Billie Jean Moffitt wasn't born to be a crusader. The daughter of a fireman and a homemaker from Long Beach, California, she was a tomboy—a term King despises but best explains her love for sports. An expert shortstop, she joined the fifteen-and-under softball team, and as a ten-year-old played football with the boys outside of her house on 36th Street. She lived for the after-dinner dashes down the street, timed by her father.

Though Betty Moffitt never discouraged her daughter from her athletic endeavors, she drew the line at raising a female football player, suggesting to her daughter that perhaps she find a more "ladylike" sport. Flummoxed, King went to her father, who suggested swimming, golf, or tennis. Not a big fan of the water, King quickly nixed swimming and decided golf was too slow to contain her energy. She didn't know much about tennis, but when her father explained, "Well you run a lot and hit a ball," she thought it was worth a try.

King started to take lessons at Houghton Park in Long Beach, tutored by Clyde Wexler, an employee of the recreation department who gave up on coaching kids at the area country clubs, tiring of kids who were there only because their parents forced them. After showing King how to hold the racket, drop the ball, and swing through, Wexler gave one simple instruction. "All right, Billie Jean, now you get to try it," and she was smitten.

"I actually hit it, and it even went over the net," King wrote in her 1972 autobiography *Billie Jean.* "You can believe this or not, but that first day I really fell in love with tennis."

Nine months later, the eleven-year-old King competed in the Southern California Junior Championships. She didn't win the championship, but the experience left a burning impression on King anyway. After the tournament was over, all of the kids were asked to pose for a picture, but King was excluded. Rules at the posh Los Angeles Tennis Club said that girls must wear tennis dresses, and King, from a modest background, was wearing a blouse and pair of shorts that her mother had made.

"I guess I should have been stunned and embarrassed when they kept me out of the picture . . . but mainly I remember feeling just the opposite, that what they had done was so petty that it wasn't even worth getting embarrassed about," King wrote in her book. "I think I sensed without ever really being able to say it that if I ever got the chance I was going to change tennis, if I could, and try to get away from that kind of nonsense."

People couldn't keep King out for long. By 1958 she won that same tournament, and in 1961, the seventeen-year-old and her doubles partner, Karen Hantze, won at Wimbledon.

Tennis always had come fairly easily to King, as her quick rise will attest, but when she did hit a speed bump, it didn't stop her. It inspired her. In 1965, King faced the legendary Margaret Court in Forest Hills. Three years earlier the upstart King had upset Court at Wimbledon, but since then went 0–14 against the veteran. But in the finals of 1965, King looked to be in charge. She lost the first set 8–6 after leading 5–3, but rallied to take another 5–3 lead and hold a 40–15 double set point in the second. Showing her poise, though, Court rallied to win the set and match, 8–6, 7–5.

"For the first time in a major championship I began to understand what it took to win one of those things," King wrote. "I began to sense what it meant to have that killer instinct, to be able to go for the jugular."

> *"I don't think it's a stretch to say that Billie Jean King is the single most important person in the history of women's sports."*
>
> —TENNIS GREAT JOHN MCENROE

Tennis in the late 1960s and early 1970s, wasn't the sport we are accustomed to now, particularly for women. Fractured by different associations, the game was mired in political infighting, with talented players caught in the crosshairs. The Grand Slams until 1968 forbade professional players to compete, and talented players like King, paid little in prize money, took jobs outside of tennis. King, for example, served as a coach at Los Angeles State College and a playground instructor, earning $100 a week.

What few people realized, though, was that the Slams were enticing players to their tournaments with under-the-table payments, a practice that roiled the equality-minded King. By then ranked number one in the country, she started to blast the tennis establishment for what she called "shamateurism" in her post-match press conferences.

"If you're number one and still complaining, I felt, maybe people will realize that something really is wrong," King wrote in her book.

By 1970, tennis had sorted itself out, paying players aboveboard and welcoming professionals into the Slams.

That didn't include women, though. Many tournaments didn't pay women at all until they reached the quarterfinals, and the champions' pay was considerably less than their male peers. King wrote of the Italian Open where she earned $600 for a trophy while the men's singles winner took home $3,500.

The frustration for King reached a boiling point at Forest Hills that year, where the men's champion was to receive $20,000, and the women would divvy up an entire pot worth just $7,500.

To King, it wasn't about the money but what the money represented.

"There had to be some way of letting young women know there was a way to make a living playing sports, that their desire to compete and excel wasn't abnormal," King once said. "There had to be some vehicle for women who were interested in athletics to find out what was happening for women in all sports."

A group including King decided to do something about it. They declared they would boycott the Pacific Southwest Open in Los Angeles because of its 8-to-1 ratio in prize money in favor of the men and instead accepted $1 contracts to compete in an unsanctioned tournament in Houston sponsored by Virginia Slims cigarettes.

Thus was born the Virginia Slims Tour, which would grow into a $23 million enterprise with the famous slogan, "You've come a long way, baby," before segueing into the WTA Tour. A grassroots effort, the Slims Tour relied heavily on its players to make things happen, and none rose to the challenge more than King. She

"A champion has got to say to themselves, 'I want the ball no matter what,' and be willing to be at high risk. You just gotta do it."

—Billie Jean King

pestered promoters when crowds weren't as large as she wanted, granted countless interviews to promote the Tour, and even sold tickets. In between, she played tennis, winning eight of the fourteen Slims tournaments offered in its first full year, 1971.

She also amassed $117,000 in prize money, making King the first woman athlete in any sport to eclipse the $100,000 barrier.

Recognizing her accomplishments, *Sports Illustrated* put King on its cover alongside basketball legend John Wooden as its sportsmen of the year.

"She has prominently affected the way 50 percent of society thinks and feels about itself in the vast area of physical exercise," sportswriter Frank Deford wrote about King in *Sports Illustrated*. "Moreover, like Arnold Palmer, she has made a whole sports boom because of the singular force of her presence."

A household name by then, King exploded into the national consciousness for a match that had nothing to do with tennis and everything to do with women's rights. Bobby Riggs, the 1939 Wimbledon champion, for years had crowed that women's tennis was no match for men's, that they didn't deserve equal prize money, and in May 1973, he challenged Margaret Court to a match. Court lost handily, 6–2, 6–1. When King saw the result, she knew that after years of dodging Riggs, she had to play him.

This was 1973, the year after Title IX went into effect but a full decade before the federal ruling impacted athletics. Women athletes were hardly the norm, and young girls who dreamed of becoming a champion had few posters to hang on their walls.

Billed the Battle of the Sexes and played in the cavernous Houston Astrodome, the match captured a nation. The week before the match, the

Stanford marching band spelled out "BJK" during its halftime rendition of "I Am Woman," and more than thirty-thousand bought tickets for the five-setter in Houston.

King knew that to Riggs this was nothing more than a show, the latest hustle for a guy who used his "male chauvinist pig" image to his benefit. She also knew, however, that for women this was no show.

"Billie Jean is a visionary who sees beyond others because she's focused on the big picture."

—FORMER PROFESSIONAL TENNIS PLAYER ROSIE CASALS

"I thought it would set us back fifty years if I didn't win that match," she said. "It would ruin the women's tour and affect all women's self-esteem."

Rather than slugging out base-line shots as Court did, King made it a point to get to the net, challenging Riggs head on. She won easily, 6–4, 6–3, 6–3, in what the *London Sunday Times* called "the drop shot and volley heard round the world."

"It wasn't about tennis; it was about social change," King would say later. "It was about changing a way of thinking, about getting women athletes accepted."

To this day, King said people come up to her and talk to her about the match, offering her glimpses into the inspiration she provided.

"A lot of women who had never had the courage to ask for a raise, who had never followed their dreams, they went ahead and just did it," King told *USA Today* columnist Christine Brennan. "And I meet a lot of men in their forties, and they say it changed their life because they started to believe in girls and women, and now they have daughters, and they insist that their daughters have equal opportunity."

John McEnroe was one of them.

The legendary tennis player told *Investor's Business Daily* that his opinion has changed with fatherhood.

"I was a fourteen-year-old male-chauvinist kid who hoped that Bobby Riggs would kick her butt," McEnroe said. "But now that I am the father of four little girls, I have to say for the record that I'm glad Billie Jean won."

To most people, the Riggs match was the culmination of King's career.

Really, it was just the midway point. King played for ten more years, winning another U.S. Open and Wimbledon singles title, and in 1983, she became the oldest player to win a professional tour title when, at the age of thirty-nine years, seven months, and twenty-three days, she took home the hardware in Birmingham.

Off the court, she barely slowed down. King and her husband, Larry, founded World Team Tennis, and in 1974, she became the first woman to coach a professional team when she led the Philadelphia Freedoms in their inaugural year.

Considered at first a passing fad, the WTT instead has survived for more than twenty years, giving fans a more relaxed atmosphere to enjoy tennis and players the pleasure of being part of a team. Pete Sampras rolled out of retirement to play World Team Tennis, and active players such as Maria Sharapova and Andy Roddick still compete as well.

"Billie Jean is one of those rare individuals who comes along in a lifetime to impact society through her passion and intensity."

—Tennis analyst
Betsy Nagelsen McCormack

"We think it's very important for people to see tennis in their own backyards," King once said.

Time has proven that King hardly was tilting at windmills. Today the WTA Tour is every bit as strong and compelling as the men's ATP Tour. Women champions at every Grand Slam receive the same pay as men (Wimbledon finally changed its policy in 2007), and female athletes finally are embraced, not just accepted.

Not that King is satisfied. As outspoken as she was when the barriers to be broken down were higher, King continues as a crusader for women, women's sports, and other causes that she deems important. The director of the Women's Sports Foundation (which she founded in 1974) board, King also serves as the director of the Elton John AIDS Foundation board.

"Billie's outreach is beyond tennis," former professional tennis player Rosie Casals said. "She has impacted the world as a champion for women's causes. She's bigger than life and is one of the most recognizable sports figures in the world. She transcends the world of sports with all that she has done."

Tennis player turned analyst Pam Shriver told me she remembers attending King's sixtieth birthday party, a swanky Los Angeles affair hosted by Elton John that brought together people from all walks of life. Shriver was amazed at King's energy and that the same woman who awed her when she was only sixteen awed her even more as an adult.

"Billie's favorite line is 'Go for it,' and I think that's a great life lesson," Shriver said. "If you want something, then go for it. Don't be afraid of failing; just go full speed ahead while keeping your eye on the ball."

Accepted and lauded where once she was denounced as a radical, King enjoys a place today as a living pioneer, a woman whose efforts and work are universally appreciated. An International Tennis Hall of Fame member since 1987, King in 1995 received the Sarah Palfrey Danzig Award, the United States' highest honor for sportsmanship and contribution to tennis. In 1998, the WTA Tour chose to name its season-ending tournament trophy after her, and in 2003, she became one of the first inductees into the U.S. Open Court of Champions.

And in 2006, the United States Tennis Association (USTA) announced that the National Tennis Center in Flushing Meadows, New York, where King won one of her Grand Slam titles, will be named in her honor. The forty-five-court complex, which hosts the U.S. Open each year, is believed to be the largest sporting facility named for a woman.

"You're talking about coming up with something that measured up to the impact Billie Jean has had on tennis and society," USTA CEO Arlen Kantarian told the *New York Times*.

Using those standards to measure by, perhaps Kantarian is right. Maybe the world's largest public tennis facility isn't quite grand enough.

Billie Jean King's Life Lessons

Think Beyond Yourself

Had she desired it, Billie Jean King could have enjoyed a quiet, lucrative tennis career and peacefully faded into the twilight. Instead, she used her career and her celebrity as a platform, setting the stage for change and improvements that she herself would never see as a player. Women tennis players today enjoy equal attention and equal pay, thanks to King. "She is a true visionary," tennis analyst Betsy Nagelsen McCormack said. "Any time some issue appears on the horizon, Billie Jean thinks, 'Is there a cause here?' . . . Every woman athlete in the world today owes Billie Jean a big thank you. She is one of those rare individuals in a lifetime that comes along to impact society through her passion and intensity."

Take Chances

Billie Jean King's entire life is about taking risks. She played sports at a time when girls simply didn't play sports. She fought for women's rights in sports when few others did, but the biggest risk she took was taking on a challenge from Bobby Riggs. She knew how much was at stake, fearful to the point that she was literally sick before the match, but she also knew that to back down from the challenge was worse than losing the match and that living a life without risks was barely living at all. "Be bold," she said. "If you're going to make an error, make it a doozy."

Don't Be Afraid to Fight

When Billie Jean King fought for equal prize money in women's tennis and equality for all women, it wasn't a popular topic. Women were barely considered athletes, let alone on par with men. Publicly criticized if not vilified, King didn't back down. Hers was a cause as much as a commonsense expectation, and regardless of the opposition, she refused to let the topic rest. "It wasn't about tennis; it was about social change," King would say of her lifelong battle. "It was about changing a way of thinking, about getting women athletes accepted."

Never Stop Fighting

Donna Lopiano, CEO of the Women's Sports Foundation, once said, "Billie Jean King was a true visionary. She knew what she wanted tomorrow to look like." King got a peek at her tomorrow in 2007, when Wimbledon finally changed its policy, becoming the last Grand Slam to offer equal prize money to women and men. "It's not about the money," King said. "It's about the message we're sending to women and girls around the world."

❧ 16 ❧

Julie Krone:
Courageousness

"You have a responsibility to channel your gifts."

—Julie Krone

Too weak, too small, too female.

That mantra pulsated like a staccato beat timed to the horse's hooves as Julie Krone began to ride.

Too weak, too small, too female.

It followed her into a professional jockey career.

Too weak, too small, too female.

It whispered in her ear as she blazed down the track and around the turn to victory.

Too weak, too small, too female.

It teased and tormented her as she recovered from gruesome spills and painful injuries.

And then it finally stopped.

In 2000, Julie Krone was inducted into the National Thoroughbred Racing Assocation Hall of Fame, silencing the mantra for her and every woman after her.

"The nicest tributes from my fellow jockeys came when they said, 'She rides like a man. Never take your guard down out there on the track. She's good. She's cool. I trust her,'" Krone said. "That's a big compliment from your competitors."

Today, we tend to think there are no trails left to blaze, that our pioneers came from another generation and the current generation need only carry the torch.

Julie Krone proved otherwise. Still only forty-three years old, she pushed through the barriers of her sport, taking gender out of the equation in horse racing for good.

Her life teaches us so much, not just about determination, but also about grit and spunk, about how a sweet-looking blonde pixie less than five-feet tall can change perceptions and expectations simply because she believed she could.

In the annals of horse racing, other jockeys have won more races and claimed more prize money, but none have affected their sport quite like Krone. In an eighteen-year career she won 3,545 races, more than $81 million in purses, and became the first (and still only) woman to win a Triple Crown race.

None of that measures her success accurately.

Krone was successful simply because she was there.

"When I think of Julie Krone, I think of one word: nerve," said long-time horse racing reporter Dick Jerardi of the *Philadelphia Daily News.* "She was really tough, but she had to compete in the ultimate masculine sport. Think of this ninety-pound woman on a thousand-pound thorough-bred with tons of horseflesh around her."

Not long after Krone was born, other women jockeys tried to enter the fraternity. In 1968, Kathy Kusner sued for the right to ride, while Penny Ann Early couldn't even get a mount at Churchill Downs. A year later, Barbara Jo Rubin's trailer was stoned. Women were considered sideshows, circus acts who might make for good publicity stunts but lacked the strength, ability, and frankly the stomach for any real staying power.

"To me, success is a self-propelled desire that comes from inside you."
—JULIE KRONE

And then along came a girl, a free spirit raised by equally free-spirited parents, who changed everything.

Don and Judi Krone, he an art teacher and she a riding instructor, didn't believe much in rules. Their children ate what they wanted and when they wanted, went to school if the mood struck them, or stayed home if that suited them. It was more strange than idyllic, but it helped form the personality Krone needed to succeed.

Thanks to her mother, horses were always a big part of Krone's life. She sat astride her first mount at the tender age of two, when Judi Krone, trying to prove a horse she was trying to sell was docile, plopped her toddler on its back. The horse trotted away for a stretch, but then the diapered baby reached down and grabbed the reins and the horse turned around.

"Julie teaches us to hold tight to your dreams in spite of the setbacks you'll have."

—JOHN FORBES, KRONE'S TRAINER

Three years later, Krone owned her first ribbon, winning a competition at a county fair.

Enamored of gymnastics, Krone thought for a while about combining that passion with her love for horses and joining the circus as a stunt rider. Most parents would put a kibosh on that dream in a hurry.

Though their childrearing may not have followed the textbook definition, Don and Judi Krone never extinguished their children's dreams. Where other parents saw danger or frivolousness, the Krones saw a chance for their children to spread their wings and try new things.

"Every day was a missile launch," Don Krone told *Sports Illustrated* in 1989. "Yes, there was always the element of possible disaster, but it was just like a missile—if it goes, good, there's going to be that moment of glory. You can't tell a kid to go for it, to be whatever they want to be, and also tell them to be careful. If we all ride the safe road, who will we look up to? Who will be on the high road? No, we didn't worry about the little things."

And so for a while little Julie didn't just ride horses.

She learned to do backflips off of them.

"When I was about ten, every word to my mother was, 'I can do that,'"

Krone said. "If I saw a circus trick or gymnastics move or a softball game, I'd blurt out, 'I can do that!' My mother's answer to me was, 'And you could.'"

Circus tricks didn't feed her passion. In 1978, Krone watched eighteen-year-old Steve Cauthen ride Affirmed to the Triple Crown, and the young teenager knew then and there what she wanted to do.

Once more, it was her parents who helped make it happen.

When her daughter said she wanted to be a jockey, Judi Krone figured there was only one place to learn—Churchill Downs. So Judi Krone packed a forged birth certificate (one that said the fifteen-year-old was sixteen and therefore eligible to work) and Krone in the car and drove to Louisville. Krone's brother, Donnie, remembers the image well, of mother and daughter packed up in the family's '71 GMC pickup, heading for Kentucky.

"They slept in a camper, and when they got to the track, mom boosted Julie over the fence," Don explained. "She had her boots and helmet with her and got a job galloping horses until school started again."

Krone made $50 a week that summer as a groom and realized she had found her dream.

The following year she entered her first races, competing in Michigan, Ohio, and Illinois.

Krone was only a high school junior.

Unfortunately, Krone's horse racing fever wouldn't wait for her diploma. Smitten with the world she had entered, Krone decided to quit high school midway through her senior year and move to Florida, where she could live with her grandparents and compete in better races.

"She put it all on the line to do what she loved," Donnie Krone said of his sister.

In 1981, the seventeen-year-old won her first race, riding Lord Farkle to victory at Tampa Bay Downs.

ᐧᑯ ᣞ ᑯᐧ

"You can rest and take a break, but then you've got to start over and keep trying."

—JULIE KRONE

It never dawned on Krone that, as a young woman, she shouldn't be doing what she was doing, wasn't welcomed in the man's world. Her parents didn't believe in limitations, and so the pie-in-the-sky Krone didn't either.

Not everyone else saw it that way.

"It was like a girl playing shortstop for the Yankees," Krone's one-time agent Larry Cooper told a London newspaper in 1990.

She met resistance at every turn. The casual observer knows the horse racing we see on television, the wide-brimmed hats at the Kentucky Derby every year, where refined folks enjoy their mint juleps.

The real horse racing world is much edgier, filled with hard-nosed characters and grueling training. It is not a place for the timid.

Krone certainly didn't look like she could survive, what with the tussle of blonde hair, the singsong voice, and the tiny frame. But she carved her own path, oftentimes turning the old adage—you get more with honey than vinegar—to her favor.

"There was an old-time trainer, Harry Wells, who swore he'd never use a girl jockey," her New Jersey–based trainer John Forbes said. "Julie kept going to his stable, but he'd pay no attention. Finally one day he said to her, 'Don't even come by.' The next morning Julie showed up wearing a mustache. She said, 'Now can I ride?' She had a sense of humor and a lot of doggedness."

Krone also wasn't afraid to stand her ground. She endured more than her share of scuffles with other jockeys, earning their respect even at the expense of a few fines.

"She combines high personal standards of performance and dedication to her craft, along with deep and almost spiritual gratitude for the gift of her natural abilities."

—JAY HOVDEY, KRONE'S HUSBAND

Even later in her career, when her legacy was solidified, and she didn't need to fight the good fight any more, Krone stood up for what she believed in.

Her husband, Jay Hovdey, the respected columnist for the *Daily Racing Form,* recalled a rogue rider who was tormenting other jockeys during the 2003 season in California, but officials were reluctant to punish him. At Del Mar one day, Hovdey said, this jockey made an especially dangerous move that affected Krone and others.

Realizing quickly that nothing would be done unless drastic measures were taken, Krone made her statement.

"After dismounting, she sought him out and, in full view of the public and officials, threw a water bucket in his direction and used language normally reserved for sailors on shore leave," Hovdey said. "It was a shock to see a Hall of Fame athlete, especially the cool, even-tempered Julie Krone, behave in such a manner, but in essence, she was temporarily sacrificing her good nature and reputation for greater purposes."

None of this would have mattered, of course, if Krone didn't have talent—but from a young age, she was spookily gifted.

"When I was racing, the whole thing was so easy and natural for me," Krone said. "I'd be up at 4:00 AM to go about my duties as a jockey. I'd watch the sun come up, but that was never hard for me. I was just so driven from within."

By 1982, she was the top jockey in Atlantic City, and in 1987, Krone became the first woman to win a riding title at a major track when, at Monmouth Park in New Jersey, she led all riders with 130 wins.

She repeated the feat the next two years before moving on to the Meadowlands, where she took riding titles in 1989 and 1990.

Grudgingly accepted by her male peers who couldn't argue with her success, Krone rode straight into history. In 1992, she won seventy-three races at Belmont Park and $9.2 million in prize money, placing her ninth in money earned that year.

That same year Krone became the first woman to ride in the Kentucky Derby, and on one glorious day in 1993, her legacy was cemented.

Aboard long-shot Colonial Affair, who went off at 13:1, Krone won the 125th running of the Belmont Stakes, becoming the first female rider to win that race or any other leg of the Triple Crown. As she rode toward the winner's circle, *Sports Illustrated* described the scene: Krone looked down at George Martens, a longtime jockey and Colonial Affairs' exercise rider and said, "How do you stop crying?" He replied simply, "You don't."

Named ABC News Person of the Week and honored with an ESPY award as the top female athlete of the year, Krone appeared on the cover of *Sports Illustrated* and quickly became a household name.

She loved it. Some people might demure when asked about the bright lights of fame. Not Krone.

"Do I like being famous?" Krone said. "Oh, come on. We all love that stuff."

The spotlight for Krone, however, was short lived. On August 30, 1993, just two months after reaching the summit of her career, Krone was in a hospital. On the last day of racing at Saratoga Springs, New York, Krone's horse, Seattle Way, got tangled up with another horse, throwing Krone onto the ground. She landed on her feet and then bounced, as one reporter described it, "grotesquely," and ended up sitting on the track, facing the rest of the horses. One of the horses, Two Is Trouble, couldn't avoid the helpless Krone, kicking her in the chest.

"Pow! I got hit in the heart," Krone recalled of the fall to *People* magazine that year. "My arm was cut so you could see the elbow socket. My ankle hurt so bad I kept thinking, "Pass out. Please pass out.' But I didn't."

By the grace of God and the advice of legendary jockey Jerry Bailey, Krone was wearing a protective vest—akin to a bulletproof vest—that day, and so instead of what likely might have been a fatal blow, Krone suffered only a cardiac contusion.

Nothing, including a heavy dose of painkillers in the hospital, could take the pain away from an ankle shattered in eleven places. Days later she was flown to Staten Island University's trauma hospital, where a doctor likened her ankle injury to those he'd only seen from parachutists landing improperly. Ultimately, Krone would need two surgeries, two steel plates, and fourteen screws to repair the damage to her leg. Hospitalized for three weeks, she was out of racing for nine months.

It was awful for her, not just because of the physical pain but the emotional pain.

But if Krone's life had told her anything, it was that nothing comes easily. She fought through the pain and the emotional walls, toiling in physical therapy and casually riding horses without a finish line in sight.

"Facing death is a big issue in my sport because it's so dangerous," Krone said. "Jockeys do get killed, and some are paralyzed. I never feared this because I am a Christian and know I'm going to heaven."

That said, her faith and grit certainly were tested when, less than a year after her return, she fell again. At Florida's Gulfstream Park, Krone took a spill that fractured her wrist and hands.

This time the physical toll wasn't nearly as difficult as the emotional one. For the first time in her life, Krone was nervous, afraid even, and when she got back to racing, longtime trainers thought she seemed timid.

She returned, but she couldn't coax back her confidence. She retired in 1999.

She mounted a brief comeback, and this being Krone, of course it was a successful one. She won one of the Breeders Cup races in 2003 before walking away for good.

Leaving, she admits, wasn't easy. Krone likens life with horse racing to "HD television" and life without it to "black and white."

"The biggest hurdle in my life is not racing," Krone said. "I want to race every day. I still have the physique for it, but I broke vertebrae in my neck and two ribs. I've had too much wear and tear on my body. God gave me a talent, and I can't use it anymore, so the empty feeling never leaves. It's a torture for me to watch any horse race on TV because I always want to be out there. On the big racing days, the feeling really rears it head."

But Krone has found peace in her life. She and Hovdey recently welcomed their first child, a daughter, Lorelei Judith. Her middle name honors Krone's mother, Judi, who passed away in 1999 from cancer.

And like that mother, Krone now looks at her daughter as a treasure, not just to feed and nurture but a treasure to encourage and inspire.

"I want her to look at me and say, 'I want to do this so bad,' and I don't care what the activity is," Krone said. "I want to see this passion burning within her. I want her to get excited like I was as a jockey and see this activity really drive her. There's nothing greater than the pleasure of talent and the drive to go along with it."

Julie Krone's Life Lessons

Always Persevere

At so many crossroads in her life, Julie Krone could have quit. Outsiders and critics told her time and again that women couldn't succeed as jockeys. Krone didn't listen. Two nasty spills easily could have ended her career, and no one would have blamed her. Krone didn't quit. Every time, she literally got back in the saddle. "To be successful, you must have persistence because it overcomes everything else," Krone said. "You can rest and take a break, but then you've got to start over and keep trying."

You Don't Have to Be Perfect; You Will Have Bad Days

Society today is consumed with the endless pursuit of perfection, and athletes are leading the charge. It is no longer acceptable to learn from mistakes because mistakes and failures are viewed as weaknesses. Yet a woman who enjoyed more success than failure, who demanded of herself more than anyone could demand of her, says that it's okay to slip a little. If her lengthy career taught Julie Krone anything it was that she couldn't win every race, but in her mishaps and her own personal flaws were the nuggets of her future success. "I want it said that I matured with my sport and its challenges," Krone said. "I didn't need to overreact all the time, and if there was a better way to do something, I went for it."

Slow Down and Appreciate the Times You Are By Yourself

As a world-class athlete, Julie Krone was hounded by the press, lauded by her fans, and revered by her peers. She loved it all, admitting to me that being famous was never a burden. None of that, however, could have come her way if Krone wasn't at peace with herself. As she grew and matured, she quickly realized that the down times, the early mornings when she would rise at dawn and be alone with her horses, were the most precious. "I'm never bored," Krone said. "I could have fun watching ants on the sidewalk. I enjoy life's simplest things. I see fun everywhere and get a big kick out of life. How don't I have fun?"

Savor Your Successes

No one ever sees the end of their career, the day that the fans stop clamoring and the glories stop coming. That Julie Krone can no longer compete, her body too beaten up by her demanding sport to continue, is her greatest disappointment. What stops Krone from languishing in that, though, is that while she was atop the world she lived in the moment. She soaked up her successes and remembered every moment so that today, retired from the sport she loved so much, she can say she didn't waste a minute. "Savor those times as an athlete, like the roar of the crowd that just runs through you," Krone said. "When you're a civilian, you'll savor those special moments."

∽ 17 ∽

Michelle Kwan:
Flawlessness

"The bigger the challenge, the harder I work."

—MICHELLE KWAN

To outsiders, people who judge solely on first-place finishes and medal collections, Michelle Kwan's career will always be incomplete.

There is a hole in her trophy case where an Olympic medal should lie, a spot reserved for her sport's most prestigious award that Kwan never was able to achieve.

And so the critics and naysayers will argue about Kwan's place in figure skating history and define her not by the championships she's won but by the one she didn't.

Michelle Kwan knows better. She knows it is not the missing Olympic gold or even the world championship and U.S. national titles that make her who she is.

It is much, much more.

"To have people talk about how I carried myself, that's as good as gold to me," Kwan told the *Chicago Tribune's* longtime Olympics reporter Philip Hersh after finishing as a runner-up to Tara Lipinski at the 1998 Games in Nagano. "That's where I am as a person—no matter how a competition goes or where it turns, to set an example for other people that if you tried your best, life goes on, and it's okay. . . .

"I see other skaters who have defined their lives by those minutes on the ice. There is so much more, so many other opportunities out there. Even if I won, I didn't want it to be everything about me. . . . I don't want a medal defining who I am as a person."

No, the words that should define Kwan are grace, beauty, and poise. She displayed all three not only on the ice, where her delicate ballet lines moved spectators and even grizzled judges to tears, but off of it, where she never failed to compliment her competitors and stood tall and dignified when the questions came at her about the Olympics.

In an era of figure skating where the only thing that seemed to matter was landing on two feet after executing ever more powerful jumps, Kwan was once called a jumping bean because of her ability to land triple jumps. She reinvented herself as an artist, proving that a woman could showcase the necessary power but retain the beauty that long has defined the sport.

And Olympic gold or not, it is hard to argue that Kwan is arguably one of the best women or men in figure skating history. She is the United States' most decorated figure skater, with five world championships and nine U.S. championships on her resume, including an unprecedented eight consecutive U.S. crowns. A silver medalist in 1998 and a bronze medalist in 2002, Kwan received fifty-seven perfect scores of 6.0 in world and national competition, a record that will never be equaled because of the change in scoring.

"She brought a sense of grace to the sport," *Los Angeles Times* sportswriter Helene Elliott said. "She is tiny but powerful. She's an athlete and has a strength to her you can see."

More than that, though, Kwan should be lauded for her staying power. In its recent inception, figure skating has been done in by champions who have come and gone, skating to the top of the podium and then off into the Ice Capades sunset. They were one-hit wonders, teenyboppers and kids who put together one flawless evening for instant celebrity and let that lone image last forever.

"I'm here to promote America. This is a place where anything is possible."

—Michelle Kwan

Kwan stayed, competing long after she could have retired to a normal life, going up against kids when she was fully a woman.

"Michelle teaches us don't do what's expected of you," Hersh said. "For years she was expected to retire, but Michelle discovered that figure skating is who she is. She loved to skate. She was not willing to do her time and step aside. She didn't, and no one could beat her. She beat more good people over a longer period of time than anyone else, all because she followed her own compass."

Some would argue Kwan stayed because she couldn't capture that Olympic gold, that she, too, felt incomplete.

She would answer that she stayed because she simply loved it too much to leave.

"It's not about the gold. It's about the spirit of the Olympics."

—Michelle Kwan

"Just to be able to skate, I was lucky," Kwan once said. "At the first competition [my sister and I] won, when we were seven and nine, we already thought, 'Everything that comes now is extra.'"

Danny and Estella Kwan were never wealthy. Chinese immigrants from Hong Kong, they toiled to find their American dream. The couple, who met in the fifth grade, arrived in the United States in 1971. Danny took a job as a busboy to make ends meet, then taught himself to cook before joining a partner to open the Golden Phoenix Restaurant in Torrance, California. Estella ran the restaurant while Danny worked at Pacific Bell.

The Kwan's three children, Ron, Karen, and Michelle, started biweekly skating lessons as toddlers, with Ron eventually choosing hockey. The girls continued with their lessons, with the number per week varying depending on the family finances. Both girls were talented, but Michelle was particularly smitten with the sport, sometimes sleeping in her skating clothing so she would be ready for the 3:00 AM wake-up call that got her on the ice before school.

"I remember thinking all I wanted to be was a famous ice skater," Kwan told Hersh in 1997. "I don't think there would ever be a day when I would say, 'I don't want to be famous.' I always liked the spotlight."

Both Karen and Michelle excelled to the point that the Kwans were spending upward of $100,000 a year for lessons, costumes, and competitions. It was more than the restaurant could handle, so the Kwans sold their house and moved in with Danny's parents. Still, when an eleven-year-old Michelle was set to compete for her first junior nationals, the family could no longer afford to pay her longtime coach, Terrance James. Instead, Danny coached Michelle at juniors, where she finished ninth.

Kwan's performance caught the eye of the Lake Arrowhead Foundation, which, with the financial assistance of others at the Los Angeles Figure Skating Club, offered the Kwan girls a place for the family to live, along with training at the prestigious Ice Castle International Training Center and a coach.

The coach was named Frank Carroll, one of the most successful yet most demanding coaches in the sport.

"Michelle, when she first came to Ice Castle, had a lot of energy, a lot of spin in her legs, but had totally no sophistication whatsoever," Carroll told CNN.

However, Kwan also had spunk. In 1993, Carroll was training Kwan for another run at the junior nationals when a business trip took him away to Canada. While he was gone—and against his wishes—Kwan took the test required to move up to senior competition.

She passed.

In 1993, Kwan, only twelve, became the youngest competitor at senior nationals in more than twenty years.

"I remember she had a little ponytail and a pink dress on, and she had no makeup at all . . . and I just thought she was so cute," former Olympic champion Brian Boitano told CNN. "She reminded me of a little chick because she was so green."

Green but good. Kwan finished sixth at those nationals, a place that is all the more astonishing considering figure skaters often are pre-judged based on their reputation. The twelve-year-old Kwan had none.

"Michelle teaches us to never, ever give up."

—Tom Collins, founder and president of Champions on Ice

Not long after, she started to earn one. Kwan won the 1993

Olympic Festival in San Antonio, putting everyone on notice that she was worth watching.

"Today, she became a star," Carol Heiss, the 1956 Olympic champion at the age of sixteen, said at the time.

The irony of Kwan's life is that she might have been one of those teenaged one-hit wonders. In 1994, Kwan finished second at U.S. nationals in the figure skating competition that forever changed the sport. That was the year that Nancy Kerrigan was clubbed on the knee by associates of U.S. champion Tonya Harding. Were it not for the commotion, people might have noticed Kwan even more that year—even if Kerrigan had competed—but amid the hubbub she became the answer to a trivia question.

Though Kerrigan wasn't able to compete at nationals and earn her spot, the U.S. Figure Skating Association granted her a place on the 1994 Olympic team. Because the United States had just two spots that year, Kwan, thirteen, went to Lillehammer, Norway, as an alternate. Had she competed, who knows what would have happened?

After Lillehammer, Kwan continued to push into the mix, finishing second to Nicole Bobek at the 1995 U.S. championships.

Unsatisfied with all the runner-up finishes, Kwan and Carroll decided they needed to change to make Kwan a champion. In her early years as a skater, Kwan was called a "jumping bean," a girl who made the required triple jumps—she landed seven at the 1995 nationals—look like nothing.

"Michelle is a tremendous champion and has been a great ambassador to the sport."

—DAVID RAITH, EXECUTIVE DIRECTOR OF U.S. FIGURE SKATING ASSOCIATION

Carroll wanted more than jumps. He wanted an artist.

Together with choreographer Lori Nichol, Carroll recreated Kwan in a year. The pair ditched Kwan's girlish music and instead put together a long program that told the tale of Salome, a biblical seductress.

And in 1996, Kwan seduced the figure skating world. She won the U.S. nationals with ease and then stunned the world by upsetting China's Chen Lu at the world championships. Only fifteen, Kwan became the third youngest woman to win a world title and the youngest American.

Beset by a stress fracture, Kwan suffered through 1997 but reemerged in 1998 as a skater unlike any other the sport had ever seen. At the U.S. nationals that year in Philadelphia, Kwan's performances still are considered among the best in skating history. Fifteen of the eighteen judges gave Kwan a perfect score for artistic impression in her long and short programs, and one judge, Joe Inman, was moved to tears.

But after such a high came the disappointments. She finished second to a once-in-a-lifetime skate from Tara Lipinski at the 1998 Olympics by the narrowest of margins. Overcome with understandable emotion, Kwan broke into tears after her long program was over, but remained graceful in defeat, earning her even more fans.

"She's the kind of young woman you'd want your daughter to be or your son to marry."

—CHICAGO TRIBUNE
OLYMPICS WRITER PHILIP HERSH

"Michelle teaches us how to accept defeat graciously," *USA Today* columnist Christine Brennan said. "Her losses in the Olympics had to be devastating to her, but she was able to handle those disappointments in a remarkable fashion."

In the *Los Angeles Times* Mike Penner wrote, "Of all the losing locker rooms I have visited in two decades as a sportswriter, listening to grown men rationalize ninth-inning errors and air balls at the buzzer, I have never seen anyone cope with crushing defeat with more poise, dignity, and maturity than a teenage girl named Michelle Kwan."

In the rivalry-inducing world of figure skating, where divas rule the roost and are born overnight, Kwan was beloved not just for her skating, but also for her personality. Always gracious and engaging, she knew she was talented but made sure never to flaunt that knowledge.

"She has always conducted herself in such a way that she has earned the respect of her peers and anyone who has ever watched figure skating," former men's champion Todd Eldredge once said.

Much of the credit for Kwan's decency goes to her parents. Raised with solid morals and taught to work for what she wanted, Kwan has not changed, although her pocketbook has. The young girl whose father had to scrape to pay for her lessons now is worth an estimated $20 million.

She brushes elbows with celebrities, many of whom are as starstruck by her as she is by them, but she still considers herself nothing special.

"My dad once told me, 'If you had $20 shoes but now you're wearing $200 shoes, you better be able to wear $20 shoes again," Kwan told Hersh once. "The one thing I've learned is to never take it for granted."

Certainly, defeat keeps a person humble, and the disappointment of 1998 would not be Kwan's last.

At the 2002 Olympics in Salt Lake City, Kwan led after the short program but two-footed one landing and fell on another, opening the door for yet another unknown American teenager to steal the show. Sarah Hughes surprised everyone to win the gold, with Russia's Irina Slutskaya taking the silver. Kwan went home with bronze.

Suddenly the news no longer was about what Kwan can and had done, but what she hadn't.

"It all happens at once, and it hits you like a rock," Kwan once told Hersh. "I remember counting backward, thinking, 'Three years, two years, one year.' Before you know it, it's over, and it's only four minutes of your life. As a kid I never thought, 'How would it feel not having it come true?'"

Others might have buckled under the weight of disappointment, withdrawing from competitions to begin a so-called normal life. Kwan didn't.

She pushed on, training full bore with an eye toward the 2006 Olympics in Turin, Italy, even though she would be twenty-five, ancient by figure skating standards.

Though Kwan likely would never buy into it, she does seem cursed when it comes to Olympic competition. In 2005, the warm-up year for the next Olympics, a painfully injured knee made it difficult for Kwan to complete the jumps she once landed with ease. The injury certainly frustrated her, but never one to harp on what she can't control, Kwan soldiered on.

"Worry—you have to kind of push that aside," Kwan told the *New York Times* that year. "This is what I have. This is it. I can't change anything that's happening. It's the best I can do. I have to push and see what the limitations are. I do have to make a decision on my body. When it says no, you have to stop."

Her body said no at the U.S. championships, the pain in the hip just too much for her to compete in the event that serves as the Olympic qualifier.

In a twist that brought her full circle to her first Olympic experience, where Kerrigan took Kwan's spot on the Olympic team despite not competing at nationals, Kwan petitioned the U.S. Figure Skating Association and, after proving her mettle during a private skate, earned a spot on the Turin team.

Fate, however, continued its cruel Olympic assault on Kwan. After just one day of practice in Italy, she tearfully announced she was withdrawing from competition because of a groin injury.

Though Kwan hasn't officially retired from figure skating, it appears doubtful she will return. She took off the 2006–2007 season to recover from hip surgery, and at the age of twenty-six, enrolled at the University of Denver, where she plans to study political science.

Recently tabbed as the first American public diplomacy envoy, she's quickly put her studies to use. In 2006, Kwan went to China to meet with students, women's groups, and government officials. Far from political, her message was about the life she lived, one of empowerment despite struggles.

"In the reality of life, it's not always smooth sailing, and you have to pick yourself up and keep on going," Kwan said of her message during a press conference in 2006.

Should she never return to the ice competitively, the debate will rage as to where to place a figure skater who has never won the sport's most prized possession. Certainly no one wishes Kwan won a gold more than Kwan herself.

But the woman who brought grace back to the ice long ago learned that fulfillment doesn't come from one event.

It comes from a life.

"It has always been a dream to win the Olympics," Kwan said upon announcing her withdrawal from the 2006 Olympics. "My parents arrived last night and want me to be happy and for their baby to win gold, have her dreams come true. I have tried my hardest. If I don't win the gold, it's okay. I've had a great career. I've been very lucky."

Michelle Kwan's Life Lessons

It's Not Whether You Win or Lose

Winning with dignity is easy. It is how a person behaves when things don't go their way that is the most telling. At her worst, when yet another Olympic Games ended without a gold medal around her neck, Michelle Kwan showed what she was really made of. Endlessly gracious and never once blaming outsiders for her losses, Kwan reminded everyone of that elementary school adage—it's not whether you win or lose, it is how you play the game—that somehow has gotten lost in a world so desperate for first-place finishers. "To have people talk about how I carried myself, that's as good as gold to me," Kwan told *Chicago Tribune* reporter Philip Hersh in 1998. "That's where I am as a person—no matter how a competition goes or where it turns, to set an example for other people that if you tried your best, life goes on, and it's okay."

Don't Back Down from a Challenge

Rare is the figure skater who competes in more than two Olympic Games. Not unlike gymnastics, the sport is dominated by young girls who peak as teenagers before heading off to lucrative careers in ice shows. Michelle Kwan stuck around for four Olympic experiences. Some would argue she stayed to pursue the elusive gold medal, which certainly has some truth to it, but Kwan stayed simply because she wanted to. "What I like is that she has always been a fighter," two-time Olympic champion Katarina Witt once said of Kwan. "There have been so many young skaters coming and going, winning the Olympics and leaving. She kept defending her titles and still setting goals for herself, which I think is great. She always could have taken the easy way, and she never did."

Stay Grounded

So many times we hear of athletes and celebrities who insist they remember their roots and who they were, but who live a life that proves otherwise. Michelle Kwan could simply go on right now being Michelle Kwan, celebrity figure skater worth millions of dollars. Instead she has enrolled in college, hoping that in retirement she can rediscover a normal life. "My dad once told me, 'If you had $20 shoes but now you're wearing $200 shoes, you better be able to wear $20 shoes again," Kwan once said. "The one thing I've learned is to never take it for granted." It is a lesson many of us forget as we climb whatever ladder to success we lay out for ourselves.

18

Lisa Leslie:
Exquisiteness

"When preparation and opportunities meet, you will have success."

—Lisa Leslie

he tears came easily and frequently. Stuck at home in California with a live-in housekeeper or at the house of yet another relative willing to take on the task of tending to three young girls, Lisa Leslie would simply cry.

She missed her mother.

Christine Leslie, a single mother of three, decided when her children were young that putting money in the bank and food on the table was the most important thing, no matter what the sacrifice. So when Lisa was just eleven, her mother took a job as a truck driver. For three years, Christine Leslie crisscrossed the country, leaving her girls for days and weeks at a time.

All the while, Lisa Leslie was growing. Already taller than her teacher in the second grade, she sprouted to six feet, two inches in the ninth grade, suffering the torments and taunts of children who disliked nothing more than someone who was different.

Somewhere along the line, Leslie decided to dry her tears. When she did, the girl who her family lovingly called "the Shadow" because she stuck so closely to her mother realized something amazing.

"My mother taught me not to wait for others to do something for you. She taught me to be a go-getter," Lisa Leslie said. "She'd tell me to think positive and made me believe I could do it. That impacted me and made me think, 'Why not me?'"

Indeed, why not Lisa Leslie? Why couldn't Lisa Leslie be the one to dominate a sport like no one before her? Why couldn't Lisa Leslie be the one to give women's basketball a much-needed identity? And why couldn't Lisa Leslie do it on her own terms?

No reason she couldn't, and so she did.

Fueled by her mother's passion, Leslie became the best female basketball player in the world, a three-time Olympic gold medalist, a three-time Women's National Basketball Association (WNBA) Most Valuable Player (MVP) and all-star, and a three-time collegiate all-American.

But it is how Leslie played that really changed women's sports. The same woman who possessed the "eyes of an assassin" according to her WNBA coach Michael Cooper, emerged postgame looking every inch the lady. She brought women athletes full circle. Once considered too delicate to compete, women were later forced to hide their femininity in order to prove their athletic prowess.

Leslie, however, proved a woman could be both. She showed women that it was okay to be fierce, competitive, sweaty, and strong when the game is on, and then bask in their femininity when it was over.

"I always want to be a lady first and an athlete second," she said. "Girls don't have to look like boys in order to be athletes. It's okay for a girl to sweat, but I always have my hair combed when I play, my nails are done, and sometimes I wear ribbons in my hair."

Indeed, in Leslie, there was beauty in the person and beauty in the game.

"Lisa has a calm personality and, in the middle of the storm, can come up with the answer."

—CHRISTINE LESLIE, LESLIE'S MOTHER

Before Leslie, women's basketball was defined by its guards. Teresa Edwards, Dawn Staley, and Cheryl Miller were the superstars, feisty speedsters who commanded the court by commanding the ball. Leslie was a center, a position rarely defined by nimbleness or grace, yet Leslie brought both to the court.

"Most women that tall played next to the basket," WNBA executive Renee Brown said. "But Lisa has so many skills, she went on the floor and started doing things no big player had ever done before."

Taught at a young age to rejoice in her height, Leslie used it to its full advantage but never let her size detract from her determination to improve the other parts of her game.

"Lisa's mother instilled in her an awareness of her physical stature," Leslie's University of Southern California (USC) coach Marianne Stanley said. "Christine Leslie's message was, 'Lisa, be proud of your height and don't walk around hunched over.' Lisa got that, while society gives a mixed message to tall girls. Some tall ones view themselves as freakish, but Christine Leslie taught Lisa to celebrate her height, to be proud of it and utilize it."

"Lisa never sat back and took her skills for granted."

—Van Chancellor, former WNBA coach

And utilize it Leslie did. A record-setter in high school who once scored 101 points—in a half—Leslie would become the most dominant player in women's basketball. A three-time USA Basketball Player of the Year, Leslie ranks as the U.S. women's all-time leading scorer, rebounder, and shot blocker in Olympic Game history.

That Leslie could play with such ferocity but retain such grace away from the game made her more than an athlete. A fashion model and product endorser, Leslie became the face of women's basketball and defined the game for a generation.

"Lisa is incredibly regal," said Donna Orender, the president of the WNBA. "She has a majesty about her and a purity of heart to go with it. Lisa will leave an unmatchable legacy of outward grace and inner toughness and competitiveness."

Ask Leslie about those gifts, and she doesn't hesitate to point to their source.

It all stemmed from Christine Leslie.

Stranded by her husband before Lisa was out of diapers, Christine Leslie never let her daughters' circumstances dictate their lot in life. They grew up in Compton, California, a notoriously rough-and-tumble neighborhood. But in the Leslie household, the girls were given etiquette lessons and taught proper posture and good table manners.

A woman of six feet, three inches herself, Christine never apologized for her height, nor did she expect her girls to. When a second-grade teacher reported that little Lisa already was taller than her, Christine Leslie saw that as a reason to celebrate.

"The closer I got to my mother's height," Lisa Leslie told *People* in 1997, "the more beautiful I felt."

For a time Christine worked as a postal worker, but when the opportunity and the paycheck from truck driving came along, she jumped at it. She bought an eighteen-wheel rig and hit the road. It meant sacrifice for everyone—summer vacations would find the three girls stuffed in the back of the truck for rides with their mother—but raised to believe that struggle was good, the girls endured.

During one of her mother's absences, Lisa first picked up a basketball. Up until middle school, Leslie was perfectly content playing neighborhood games: kickball and Double Dutch were favorites. But when Leslie was in the seventh grade, a friend named Sharon Hargrove encouraged the willowy Leslie to try the game. Though gifted, the sweet-natured Leslie didn't immediately have the ferocity to make her a star.

"The passion, the heart, and fight it takes to play basketball didn't come naturally to me," she said. "I had to learn to do that, because off the court I'm a passive person. I don't like conflict and arguing. I've always been the peacemaker in the family."

Inspired by Los Angeles Laker James Worthy, nicknamed Big Game James because of his willingness to take the ball in the clutch, Leslie slowly developed the on-court mentality to make her a winner.

"I've seen her start out as a shy, humble girl and become a strong, confident athlete."

—TERESA EDWARDS, OLYMPIC TEAMMATE

By ninth grade, the already six-foot, two-inch Leslie was turning heads, and at the age of seventeen, was named to the junior national team. Popular at Morningside High School, Leslie still maintained an honor-roll grade point average while serving as class president and, of course, dominating on the basketball court.

"I saw Lisa play in high school, and I knew she was good," Christine Leslie said. "However, at the USA trials at Stanford, I realized she was different. At the trials, she was up and down the floor in drills ahead of everyone else. She had baby oil on her legs, and they were so shiny and muscular in the light. I was in tears watching her and realizing this is my daughter, and she's become a world-class athlete right before my eyes."

Widely considered the most talented player in the country by her senior season in high school, Leslie made national news when she scored 101 points against South Torrance.

Not everyone was thrilled with Leslie, with columnists and sports reporters lining up nationally to chastise her and her team for poor sportsmanship. Each year, Morningside coach Frank Scott gave one of his seniors the chance to break Cheryl Miller's longstanding national scoring record of 105 points. No one else had come close.

But South Torrance, saddled with injured players, was no match for Leslie. By the end of the first quarter, she had scored all of her team's points—forty-nine in all— and at the half, the score was Morningside 102 (Lisa Leslie 101), South Torrance 24. The South Torrance coach, down to four players because of foul trouble, had enough, and pulled his team off the court. Leslie finished four points shy of the record

"Billie Jean King was a hero to me," Leslie said. "I remember seeing her play tennis on television, the only woman I can recall playing sports."

—LISA LESLIE

"It wasn't personal," Leslie said at the time to *Sports Illustrated.* "They knew I was going for the record. I thought knowing that would take some of the hurt away."

Though the temporary criticism may have stung Leslie, it did nothing to hurt her appeal. Lured by every college in the country, she eventually settled at the University of Southern California. As a freshman she had what any other player would consider a monster year—averaging 19.4 points, 10 rebounds, 2.6 blocked shots, and earning Pacific 10 Conference Freshman of the Year.

But Leslie was fully aware that the comparisons for her were different.

"People expected so much more and felt I'd underachieved," Leslie said. "That was a difficult time for me because I felt I hadn't reached my goals."

Fueled to do better, Leslie went on to become the national Player of the Year, the Pac-10 Conference Player of the Year, and the first player in the Pac 10 to earn all-conference honors in each of her four years at college. With Leslie on board, USC went to four NCAA tournaments, and she graduated as the third all-time leading scorer, the fourth all-time leading rebounder, and the career leader in blocked shots.

Though long able to dunk, Leslie never allowed herself to become a sideshow. She was a basketball player, not a one-trick pony.

"Lisa's life teaches us to walk through the world cutting our own path. Go your own unique way, and be yourself."

—MARIANNE STANLEY, LESLIE'S COACH AT USC

"Lisa was a dream to coach," Stanley, her USC coach, said. "She would listen to others who had the experience and be willing to learn from them. She didn't argue and act like a big shot. That was her mother's impact."

A towering presence in women's basketball, Leslie remained somewhat anonymous as her sport looked to explode in the mainstream. Two years later, that happened. In 1996, the United States women's basketball team strode into the Olympic Games with a streak of fifty-two consecutive victories. With Leslie serving as the team's leading scorer, the United States ran the mark to 60-0, capturing the gold medal and the imaginations of a generation desperate for women to idolize.

Leslie, young, vibrant, and beautiful, gladly stepped into the void. The woman who never even heard of Cheryl Miller until she got to high school, who never thought of playing college basketball until middle school, understood perfectly how desperately young girls were yearning for female role models.

In Leslie, young girls had found a woman who said she could be as tough and competitive and strong as the men but keep her feminine spirit, a combination previously unheard of.

"Lisa is an incredibly classy athlete and a great ambassador for women's sports," former WNBA president Val Ackerman said. "She's smart and very funny. You can put Lisa with anyone of any age, and she'll be at ease with them. She knows exactly what to say. Lisa is the complete package and a great salesperson for women's athletics."

Sparked by the success of the Atlanta Games, women's basketball finally put together a pro league. In partnership with the NBA, the WNBA opened its doors with its 1997 draft. Leslie was the first pick for the Los Angeles Sparks. Dominant in the league from the outset, Leslie and her teammates, however, remained stymied in their attempts to win a championship. From its inception, the WNBA was dominated by one team—the Houston Comets, starring Sheryl Swoopes. The Comets won each of the league's first four championships, twice eliminating Leslie along the way.

> "I want to be remembered as a class act."
>
> —LISA LESLIE

Dismantled again by Houston in the 2000 season, Leslie decided to do what she does best. She set a goal.

"I'm a big believer in writing down your goals," Leslie said. "I put mine on a mirror at home and stay focused on them. That's helped me reach my goals in life."

In the summer of 2000, her goals were simple. In the same year she would lead the United States to yet another gold medal, this time in Sydney, Leslie aimed for the WNBA championship and the league's MVP trophy. She hired a personal trainer to get in even better shape and spent countless hours working with her Sparks coach, Michael Cooper, a one-time NBA top defensive player.

At the end of the 2001 season, the Sparks hoisted the championship trophy, and Leslie, who averaged 22.3 points, 12.3 rebounds, and 4.4 blocked shots in the playoffs, became not only the league MVP, but the MVP of the WNBA finals and the all-star game, the first woman to sweep all three league honors.

"Lisa has tremendous talent, but really works hard to get better," Houston Comets coach Van Chancellor said. Buoyed by their superstar's ignited passion, the Sparks went on to win another WNBA title in 2002 and finish as runners-up in 2003.

"Lisa helped make the WNBA a successful league," *New York Daily News* basketball writer Dick Weiss said.

Leslie, who became the first player to dunk in the WNBA when she threw down a slam in 2002, went on to capture her third Olympic gold medal, leading the United States' charge in Athens. And she's not finished yet. Leslie said she'd like to try for the Beijing Games in 2008.

A dominant player still today, Leslie now finds herself the veteran, challenged by younger players. To improve her game, the WNBA superstar left her new husband, Michael Lockwood, to play in Russia in 2006, hoping to focus on her game away from the bright lights of the WNBA

In 2006, the Sparks named the Staples Center Court in her honor, but instead of starring on that court, Leslie came off the bench to do her damage. She took the substitute role with grace, but no one expects her to stop pushing.

"She's an amazing talent with great versatility," former WNBA coach Ronnie Rothstein said. "And she'll take your head off. She's a tough competitor."

Not even the toughest competitor can fight with biology. Leslie took off the entire 2007 season to await the birth of her first child.

"I thought I owed it to my fans to let them know," she explained in December.

Leslie also has made a difference off the court. In 1998, she opened the Lisa Leslie Sports Complex at her high school alma mater. The 42,000-square-foot center offers twelve basketball hoops for kids at Morningside High to practice on, and in 1999, the Big Sisters of Los Angeles honored Leslie with its Young Heroes Award, thanking her for her generous work with foster children.

A celebrity who counts Shaquille O'Neal and Justin Timberlake as her friends, Leslie nonetheless has stayed true to the graceful young woman her mother raised. Proud that she made the right choices as a young girl—she didn't smoke, drink, or party—Leslie is today even more proud that she has grown into the woman her mother envisioned.

"Whenever someone would tell me, 'You can't do it,' I'd remember my mom who told me I could do whatever I set my mind to," Leslie said. "There was never a time I didn't think I could do it. If you study successful people, they have intensity and discipline in some area of life. They've decided, 'I'm going to do this,' and then they did it."

Lisa Leslie's Life Lessons

Be Specific in Goal Setting

It is one thing to say you want to be a great basketball player or pianist or writer. It is another to have the courage to say exactly what you want to achieve. In the summer of 2000, Lisa Leslie could have said she wanted to be a better basketball player. Instead she said she wanted to win a WNBA championship and capture the MVP trophy, lofty goals but only attainable because Leslie aimed for them. "Every dream must have a goal first," Leslie said. "I am a goal setter, both short-term and long-term goals. When preparation and opportunities meet, you'll have success."

Work to Get Better

Blessed with height and gifted with natural ability, Lisa Leslie may have become a very good basketball player just by showing up to practice. She became a great basketball player, though, because she never settled for mediocrity. Rather than play the low-post game assigned to most centers, she improved her footwork and her jump shots to expand her repertoire unlike anyone before her. "She's a very determined person who never wants to finish second to anyone," Dawn Staley said about Leslie. "She doesn't like to lose."

There's Always Room for Improvement

A force in high school basketball, Lisa Leslie learned as a college freshman that she had hardly reached her peak. Though she put together a fine rookie season, Leslie knew that others expected more, that she frankly expected more of herself. "I think it was a revelation to Lisa that there were weaknesses in her game that other people could exploit," Marianne Stanley, her coach at the University of Southern California, said to *Sports Illustrated* in 1991. "There's a lot that she's still learning. She's like the colt who wants to get up and go and isn't real secure with all the skills yet."

Treat People the Way You Want to Be Treated

She has appeared on the pages of *Vogue* and guest starred on various television sitcoms, but Lisa Leslie is anything but an aloof star. Warm, personable, and always willing to stop for an autograph or picture, Leslie is thrilled to have the chance to touch people. "I am most proud of being a positive role model to young women," she said. "I enjoy being a motivational speaker and challenging girls to live up to their full potential."

∽ 19 ∽

Nancy Lopez:
Joyful

"The first thing I do after losing is forget it."

—NANCY LOPEZ

Nancy Lopez walked off the green during a tournament in High Point, North Carolina, and was stopped by a young man with his mother.

For Lopez, that was nothing unusual. Popular and friendly with a smile as well known as her game, she had been greeted by fans for as long as she could remember.

This, however, was different.

The mother was blind.

"She told me, 'Nancy, I came to *hear* you hit the ball,'" Lopez recalled. "That day I realized why I am here and why I have this gift."

Athletic greatness can be a selfish place. To become a gifted athlete requires hard work and single-mindedness, a tunnel vision of purpose that focuses primarily on oneself. So often we hear of athletes who have "forgotten where they came from" or "forgotten who helped them become who they are." It's understandable. The inward thinking and focus required to reach for the brass ring would make it easy for any world-class athlete to lose sight of the ladder that's already been climbed.

Nancy Lopez never had that problem. As remarkable as her golf career was, as amazing as her game was, what always has been most impressive about Lopez is the person she has remained.

"Nancy gets great personal peace by bringing joy to others," said Lopez's husband, former World Series MVP Ray Knight. "She is such a giver, and she proves that you don't have to be selfish to be successful. Nancy loves to give of herself and her time."

It is her human nature as much as her superhuman talent that has made Lopez perhaps the most beloved personality in her sport. "Nancy's Navy," the spin-off of Arnold Palmer's "Arnie's Army" of fans, followed her from hole to hole because they knew they'd see greatness and also because they knew they'd experience warmth and good feeling.

"She's got the greatest amount of humility of any great athlete I've ever known," longtime Cincinnati Reds radio announcer Marty Brennaman said. "She is classy and graceful and puts people at ease. She is to the LPGA what Arnold Palmer was to the PGA."

Her successes, the almost fifty titles, the four Player of the Year awards, belonged to the fans as much as to Lopez. She embraced them all, and they embraced her back, watching when in 1987 she became the youngest golfer ever inducted into the Ladies Professional Golf Association (LPGA) Hall of Fame and following her step by step in 2002, her final season on the tour.

During a twenty-five-year career, Lopez won a case full of trophies, but the one she is most proud of had nothing to do with a final score. In 1998, the U.S. Golf Association presented Lopez with the Bob Jones Award for distinguished sportsmanship.

"I want to be remembered as one of the best golfers who ever played, but more important, I want to be remembered as one of the nicest golfers ever," Lopez said. "It makes me proud to be recalled as a nicer person than I was a golfer."

"Believe you can do anything, and then take a stab at it."

—NANCY LOPEZ

Rather than forget where she came from, Lopez allowed her roots to define her career. Raised in Roswell, New Mexico, Lopez didn't come from a wealthy background. Her father, Domingo, worked at an auto body shop, but from him she learned invaluable lessons about working hard and doing a job right.

"If his customers weren't satisfied with his work, he'd do it all over again until he'd done the job right," Lopez said. "That left a huge impression on me that I remember to this day."

What her parents lacked in finances, they made up for in love. Though Lopez's mother, Marina, was strict, she was a warm and loving presence. It was Marina's chest pains that actually turned the family onto golf. Domingo thought the game would help alleviate her discomfort, and when a young Nancy showed interest in the game, her father sawed off a four wood for her to play with.

That was when Lopez was eight.

When she was nine, she won her first tournament—by 110 strokes.

Certainly, some of her talent was God-given, but a great deal of it came from hard work. Lopez once said that as a kid, she hit balls until her hands bled from the blisters and putted until her feet hurt from standing.

"In golf, you win some and you lose some. In life it can be the other way around. You can lose some and then win some."

—Nancy Lopez

"I think all the top-notch athletes have a lot of God-given talent, but you have to run with it and do something with it," Lopez said. "As a young girl I had a feeling deep inside that I was created to be a golfer."

Convinced his daughter was gifted, Domingo Lopez excused Nancy from household chores so as not to injure her hands. But he was no drill sergeant of a father. Domingo Lopez was the first to console his daughter after a tough day and insisted from the get-go that she keep the game fun. He told her that she'd lose more often than she'd win, a lesson Lopez told me she's kept with her forever.

"After I lost, he'd have a big hug for me," Lopez said. "He always supported me and never criticized me. After a tough outing, I'd hear, 'Honey, it's okay.' He was always encouraging me and never used negative words. In 1976, I missed the cut at the U.S. Open in Philadelphia, and as I came off the last green, I was crying. Dad said, 'Nancy, I'm sorry.' And then he started to joke with me and made me laugh."

Golf has been long considered a game for the elite, and in the early 1970s as Lopez was learning her way, it was by no means typical to see a young Mexican-American woman on the greens. The subtle discriminations Lopez experienced would have been enough to turn many people bitter. That never happened with Lopez.

Unable to join a country club, Lopez plodded along on her own, but despite the financial challenges, her parents never let her suffer. Her mother made sure she had a new outfit for every tournament, and her father sacrificed precious money to give his daughter braces, convinced that she'd be famous one day and would need a perfect smile.

Though her parents made exceptions for Lopez, the examples they set in their daily life stayed with their daughter. She told me that her parents never expected her to work as a kid, allowing her to use her free time to work on her golf game, but at the age of sixteen, she took a job at a C.R. Anthony's store in New Mexico.

"I was wrapping presents for $2.25 an hour," she said. "I made $100 and bought my own Christmas presents. I gave my dad a pair of boots and got Mom some lingerie. I'm so proud I did that."

Domingo, however, had good instincts about his daughter's abilities. Naturally gifted, Lopez won the New Mexico Women's Amateur as a twelve-year-old and followed that with two U.S. Golf Association Junior Golf Championship titles as a teenager. In high school Lopez played on the boys' team, helping Goddard High School to state titles in 1973 and 1974.

ఴ **.** ౿

"She is a better person than golfer."

—Donna Caponi,
LPGA player and TV analyst

In 1976, Lopez became the first woman to receive a full golf scholarship to the University of Tulsa, an investment she quickly returned when, as a freshman, she won the AIAW national championship and the school's Female Athlete of the Year honors.

A year later, she turned pro.

"When Nancy came on the LPGA Tour at age nineteen, she had the game and maturity of a thirty-five-year-old," former LPGA star and golf analyst Donna Caponi said. "She was just a young girl, but she had a style that's hard to describe, and she kept working at it. Nancy had a fire in her stomach and heart and loved to compete."

She finished second in two of the six tournaments she played in but later lamented that she played it too safe, avoiding bogeys rather than going for birdies.

Her outlook changed drastically in September 1977 when her mother died unexpectedly after an appendectomy.

"She had poured her whole life into mine, and she never saw me win," Lopez said. "She sacrificed so much for me, and I couldn't pay her back while she was still alive."

Fueled by her mother's passing, Lopez stormed through the 1978 season. She played in twenty-six tournaments and won nine of them, winning her first professional title in Sarasota, Florida, when she birdied the seventy-first hole. From May to June, she won five consecutive tournaments, including the LPGA championship, a feat not replicated until Annika Sorenstam came along in 2005.

Lopez told me that growing up, her hero had been Joanne Carner. But Lopez's respect for Carner had nothing to do with her actual golf game.

"She always seemed to be having so much fun," Lopez said. "She never lost her temper and didn't curse. She was a classy lady."

Fans and golf aficionados soon

"From her performance on the course to the way Nancy has lived her life, she has taught us that no matter how great the adoration from the world or how much success one achieves, it is our friends and family that enrich us."

—CAROLYN BIVENS, LPGA COMMISSIONER

were saying the same about Lopez. With her winning ways and even more winning personality, she stole headlines in a sport usually reserved for the men, even appearing on the cover of *Sports Illustrated.*

"She was to women's golf what the Beatles were to popular music," *Golf Digest* once said of Lopez.

By the end of 1978, Lopez had won all of the LPGA's major awards, capturing Rookie of the Year and Player of the Year honors as well as the Vare Trophy, given to the player with the lowest scoring average.

Not much changed in 1979. Lopez repeated as Player of the Year and Vare Trophy winner, capturing eight titles to become the tour's leading money winner.

Though her numbers dropped a little in 1981 and 1982, she still managed to win an impressive twenty-five titles out of the 115 tournaments she played from 1978 to 1982.

Lopez has said that what made her great really was the same personality that won over her fans. She loved the game, so even when it tortured her with its difficulties and intricacies, she was enjoying herself. She learned at an early age to trust her instincts and so always was able to bring a singular focus to her game.

"Do your best one shot at a time," she once said. "And then move on. Remember that golf is just a game."

In 1982, Lopez married Knight, forging a sort of athletic dynasty. Buoyed by his support and understanding of her life, Lopez continued to play even after she had one, then two, and eventually three, daughters.

"As women we always feel guilty about not doing something for our kids—and then we end up not doing anything for ourselves," Lopez once said. "I've realized I can do both."

Indeed, despite being pregnant with her first daughter, Ashley, Lopez won two tournaments and exceeded the $1 million mark in earnings.

In 1985, Lopez again won five more tournaments and returned to the number one ranking and, a year later, welcomed her second daughter, Erinn Shea.

Lopez continued to play well through the 1980s, but struggled in the 1990s because of knee and gallbladder surgeries. She still managed to astound people when in 1991, the four-months-pregnant Lopez won the Sara Lee Classic.

No matter her results, the fans were always there.

"Nancy Lopez was a hard worker and an awesome player and competitor," said Blaine Cornwell, who, along with his twin brother, Boyd, caddied on the tour from 1985 to 1992. "She always took time for her fans because she genuinely cares about people. I'll never forget her beautiful smile."

Equally impressive, Lopez was every bit as well-liked by her peers.

"My friendships from golf have lasted and carried over into real life," Lopez said. "Loyalty is very important to me. When I tell a friend I'll do something, I'll do it. That's a big part of character, and really that's all you have."

Certainly, Lopez had her struggles. She retired having failed to win a U.S. Open, finishing second four times. The worst, she told me, was in 1997. At forty she became the first woman to post four rounds in the sixties, but despite such amazing numbers she still lost by one stroke to Alison Nicholas.

"That killed me because I played so well and just knew I was going to win," Lopez said. "I was devastated and still crying six and seven months later."

Recognized as one of the game's greatest contributors in 2000, Lopez decided in 2002 that she would retire. The Nancy Lopez Retirement Tour, which included fourteen tournaments and a rousing ovation at the U.S. Open, sadly coincided with Domingo's passing early that year.

Since leaving the game, Lopez has remained extremely active. After Ray Knight suffered a heart attack in 2004, the couple launched a Back in Full Swing campaign to promote life after heart disease, and Lopez also is an avid supporter of AIM, a nonprofit organization that uses music and movement to help handicapped people.

"Nancy cares, and that makes all the difference," Lopez's good friend Jo Geiger said. "She cares about playing golf; she cares about people; she cares about her charity work."

Lopez has been further invigorated by her own health scare. In 2006, she suffered bouts of vertigo. Tests showed early signs of hypertension, news that pushed Lopez to can the junk food diet and start working out again. She shed twenty-eight pounds and felt good enough to compete in the Jamie Farr Owens Corning Classic, and she is now embarking on a sort of comeback tour, playing six tournaments in 2007, each time with designs "to make the cut."

"Although Nancy has become a legend who is revered around the world, she has never lost her roots," Bivens said. "Nancy's values, which include humility, empathy, compassion, and dedication, are evident in everything she does. Family is her first priority, and contributing her time to charitable causes and helping others is paramount for her in life. That is who Nancy is. And the fact that she combines all of this with a wonderful sense of humor makes her even more endearing to friends and fans worldwide."

Mostly, though, her life is about her family. She said her favorite day is when she gets to make a nice lunch and ride her four-wheeler with her husband and kids. She's most proud of her three daughters, all respectful young ladies who talk to her and trust her.

Of course, Lopez remains a fan favorite.

The current generation of golf fans may be more enamored of Sorenstam and Michelle Wie, but Nancy Lopez's name still resonates.

She told me a story about some of her daughters' classmates at Auburn University.

"Some of the boys found out I was their mother," she said. "The boys said, 'Can we play golf with her?' I went over and played, and we had lots of fun that day."

Nancy Lopez's Life Lessons

Being Loyal to Friends Is Important

When Nancy Lopez is asked to describe herself in one word, she doesn't hesitate: "loyal." Others agree wholeheartedly. Longtime friend Jo Geiger paid Lopez the highest compliment. She says, "Here's how I describe my relationship with Nancy: she's a real friend."

Success Is Not Winning and Losing;
It's Giving 100 Percent All the Time

As a young girl, Nancy Lopez received sage advice from her father, Domingo. He told her she may become, a great golfer one day, but no matter how great she became, she would lose more often than she would win. Accepting that has allowed Lopez to enjoy her success. "When my girls were younger they'd lose a game in youth soccer," Lopez said. "One of them would say, 'I hate it that we lost.' I'd say, 'Did you give 100 percent?' And they'd say, 'Yes, Mom.' That's all you can do."

If You Love Everything You Do, You Will Be Successful

So often the secret to success is too simple for people to recognize. It lies not just in talent, but in joy. Nancy Lopez took joy in her golf game, just as she now takes joy in her retirement. "The most important personality trait to be successful is to always be positive," Lopez said. "That'll make good things happen."

Be the Best You Can Be

"I want to be the best wife, mother, golfer, and businessperson I can be," Nancy Lopez said. That's a tall order, and perhaps one not easily reached, but without reaching for the pinnacle, Lopez never would have challenged herself and never would have achieved greatness. "She is a warrior and a dove, and it's legitimate," Nancy's husband, Ray Knight, said. "Very few people have both of these sides to them."

Treat Everyone the Same

More than her golf titles and trophies, Nancy Lopez's legacy is her kindness. Everyone who has met her, from casual fan to golfing legend, says that Lopez is a wonderful person. There is nothing better that can be said about a person. "She's a nicer person than a golfer," former LPGA star and golf analyst Donna Caponi said. "Nancy is loved by the public because she has never slighted her fans. She's very giving of her time."

Family Counts Most of All

How many professional athletes and businesspeople work and work and work, only to lament that they missed their children growing up? Nancy Lopez will never have that worry. She balanced her life, mixing her love for golf with her love for family. It wasn't always easy, but it always was worth it. "From her performances on the golf course to the way Nancy has lived her life, she has taught us that no matter how great the adoration from the world or how much success one achieves, it is our friends and our family that enrich us," Carolyn Bivens, LPGA commissioner, said.

20

Shannon Miller
Determination

*"I knew that if I wanted to be successful,
I was going to have to stop dreaming and start doing."*

—SHANNON MILLER

Commentators called her ethereal, waxing eloquent about her captivating grace and elegant style. She was a tiny slip of a thing and painfully shy, more interested in counting floor tile or contemplating the knots on her shoelaces than smiling into the bright lights of the television cameras.

It all made Shannon Miller seem somehow fragile, like some sort of delicate bird that needed protecting.

American gymnastic fans had an image of great gymnasts. They were supposed to look like Mary Lou Retton, a spark plug of power who attacked her apparatus with the same ferocity as an offensive lineman tackled a sledding dummy.

Shannon Miller didn't fit the image.

By the end of the 1996 Olympic Games, however, John Q. Public had to rethink its standard. Miller showed that image isn't substance and that power comes in all sorts of packages. She proved that sport could be about beauty, and that beauty could still result in excellence.

Miller also showed that behind that placid face and unassuming demeanor lurked a competitor as fierce as a snarling beast, a young woman who wouldn't settle for anything less than perfection from herself and, in the end, brought gold to her country.

"She had a determination to succeed like no one else," Miller's longtime coach, Steve Nunno, said. "Her goal was always to do her best and hit her routine. Then at a meet she could turn it on like nobody else."

The smiling Retton was the impetus for a mad rush of pixies who discovered the joys of a four-inch-wide balance beam and learned not only what a punch front is, but how much fun it can be to do on that little apparatus.

Miller is the by-product of Retton's greatness. She is the face of the generation that took Retton's inspiration and made it reality. The United States had never won a gold medal in gymnastic team competition until Miller and her peers did in Atlanta in 1996. No American woman had ever won back-to-back world championships until Miller won in 1993 and 1994.

And as great as Retton was, it is Miller who lays claim to the addendum, "the most decorated American gymnast in history." She owns seven Olympic medals.

It says everything about the person that Miller is, though, that when asked about her legacy she doesn't talk about milestones and history, or really even athletic accomplishments.

"I would like my legacy to be about the person I am and not the things I have done," she said. "I would hope that people would look back and remember me as someone who was a reliable, dependable, and compassionate person, someone who strived to be positive and live each day to the fullest. Someone who wasn't afraid to make mistakes but would learn from those mistakes when they happened. And I would hope that people would think of me as someone who helped motivate and encourage others to always do their best in any situation."

In 1992, Shannon Miller became a fifteen-year-old rock star. After capturing a silver medal in the all-around competition at the Barcelona Games and helping Team USA to a bronze, she was greeted with the teenybopper screams and autograph requests usually reserved for a boy band.

It was all a little strange to a young girl who still hung posters on her own bedroom wall back home in Edmond, Oklahoma. Miller never set out to win Olympic gold or even compete in the Olympics. She just wanted to be like her big sister.

"When I was five years old, I didn't even know what the sport was, and I had never even seen the Olympic Games," Miller said. "But I knew that I wanted to be just like my big sister [Tessa], and if that meant following her into gymnastics, then that was what I was going to do."

Miller's parents, Ron and Claudia, had no idea they had a born gymnast until one Christmas they acceded to their girls' wishes and bought a trampoline. Little Shannon hopped on with Tessa, and within two weeks, figured out how to do a front flip. Her parents, Miller admitted to the *St. Louis Post Dispatch* in 1993, were a little "freaked out" and decided maybe putting her in gymnastics lessons with Tessa would be a safer outlet.

Miller and gymnastics was love at first sight. She said she remembers walking in the gym, feeling like a kid in a candy store as she tried to decide whether to swing around the bars, flip into the big foam pits, or bounce on the trampoline.

She didn't have any grand plans, nor did her parents, but Miller was exceptional, and in 1986, she traveled to the Soviet Union for training. There, Nunno, a renowned Oklahoma City–area coach, saw her work out and asked Miller to join his team, the Dynamos. Gymnastics, though still a passion, became more than just a hobby. She quickly moved through the elite gymnastics ranks, and in 1991, she won the balance beam and floor at the U.S. championships.

That same year the fourteen-year-old Miller helped the United States to a silver medal at the world championships, slotted right behind the powerful Russians and impressively ahead of the Romanians. Miller finished fourth in the all-around, the highest among all U.S. competitors.

She was no longer a sweet little girl from Oklahoma. She was on the cusp of becoming an Olympic star.

She had no idea. Miller still was a kid.

Fortunate to train near her hometown, she came home each night for dinner—though the family would have to wait until as late as 9:00 PM for Shannon to wrap up the last of her six hours per day at the gym. There was no tutor to teach her. She went to public school. She liked movies, collected teddy bears, and visited the mall on the weekends.

In other words, she was a teenager, a regular kid who happened to be one of the greatest gymnasts in the world. It was a strange dichotomy, but one Miller's parents made sure to keep intact.

"My parents went out of their way to make sure that I knew that there was more to life than gymnastics," Miller said. "My parents understood that I needed a good balance in my life so that gymnastics didn't consume me."

Miller told me the story of her parents' annual trip into Nunno's office, where they'd explain that Shannon would be taking off four days around the holidays in order to visit her grandparents in San Antonio.

"My coach didn't like it, but he would send a list of conditioning and stretching I needed to do and let me go," Miller said.

Certainly, Miller's parents helped keep her grounded, but her sense of responsibility and her determination also are innate. Her parents never had to harp on her to do her schoolwork. Miller worked as hard in the classroom as she did in the gym, maintaining a 4.0 grade point average throughout high school despite the rigorous demands of her sport.

Her mother, Claudia, said that in 1992, when Miller was only fifteen, a clothing company called Elite Sportswear wanted to design a line of Shannon Miller gymnastics clothing.

"Basically, they just wanted to put Shannon's name on the clothing," her mother recalled. "Shannon called Reading, Pennsylvania, and wanted to know all the details. She ended up designing the leotards and was involved in all of the production."

Ultimately, her sense of responsibility set her apart from her peers in the gym. She worked tirelessly, methodically doing her routines over and over again until there wasn't a toe left unpointed.

ᘯ ᐧ◆ᐧ ᘰ

"Life is full of mistakes, but you have to decide if you want to learn from a mistake or let it bog you down and hold you back."

—SHANNON MILLER

ᐧ◆ᐧ

"I call her 'The Drive Machine' because she was so unbelievable in her practice sessions every day," famed gymnastics coach Bela Karolyi said.

That Miller's specialty was the most disciplined of the six apparatus—the balance beam—really says it all. The beam is not for the faint of heart. A mere four inches wide, it swallows up even the most seasoned competitor. To be a champion on beam isn't just to be able to flip and stick landings. It takes extreme focus.

"Shannon has always been able to stay calm in every situation," her mother, Claudia, said. "It didn't matter if there were thirty thousand people watching her in competition or being out of action for six months with an injury. Shannon took it all in and never went crazy."

By the end of the Barcelona games, of course, everyone was crazy about Miller. She came home with five medals: a silver in the all-around and beam, a bronze in the vault and floor exercise, as well as a bronze team medal. In thirteen of sixteen routines, Miller scored a 9.90 or better. Her lowest mark of the entire Olympiad was a 9.75.

An instant media darling, Miller made the talk show circuit and was fêted at the White House as well as in her hometown. She took part in two post-Olympic tours, where fans screamed her name and young girls held up her poster.

It all caught the quiet Miller a little off guard.

"Shannon was always there and never complained."

—RITA BROWN, FORMER U.S. OLYMPIC COACH

"In 1992, when we came home with a bronze medal as a team, it was still . . . I don't know," Miller told *Inside Gymnastics* in 2004. "Maybe I was young, maybe I had just been in so many competitions. I mean, it's not that we weren't excited and ecstatic about winning a bronze medal, but I look back now and think, 'How could you not know how big that was?'"

Success in any walk of life is fleeting. Gymnastics is particularly cruel. It is a sport that requires discipline and hard work and talent, all the things a person can control. It also is a sport where discipline, hard work, and talent can be undone by the uncontrollable: biology.

The summer after winning the 1993 world championships, Miller said she came home from practice crying every night. The sport that had always come so easily suddenly was difficult. Her back ached, and she had painful shin splints in each leg.

She was going through a growth spurt.

"I came home one afternoon and told my parents I wanted to quit gymnastics," Miller said. "I wanted to be normal. I had no idea what that meant, but I just knew I wasn't happy. My parents wanted me to be sure and just asked that I sit down with my coach and talk about it before making a final decision."

So Miller did just that, sitting down one evening with Nunno. The coach offered a deal. He told his star pupil that if she came into the gym for just three hours a day over the next three weeks instead of the normal six-hour regimen, worked only on things that didn't hurt her back or her shins and still wanted to quit, he would understand.

Miller took the deal.

Three weeks later, Miller's back and shins felt great, she had learned four new skills and, most important, after talking at length with Nunno, got to the crux of her troubles.

"Shannon was very precise in her goals and then outworked her competition to make them happen."

—BELA KAROLYI, LEGENDARY GYMNASTICS COACH

"I realized that the problem wasn't burn out or injuries," she said. "My problem was that I had never been without goals. I had always had something to work toward, and all of a sudden, there seemed to be nothing left. But that's where I was wrong. There is always another challenge, another goal.

"We discussed international competitions, including the 1994 world championships and even the 1996 Olympic Games. I started to think about how wonderful it would be to compete in front of a home audience in Atlanta. All of a sudden I had that spark back, and gymnastics became interesting and fun again."

The road back wasn't easy. Her comeback trail endured speed bumps, but true to form Miller remained determined and focused and, in 1996, despite nagging tendonitis in her wrist, won the U.S. championship all-around title.

The win, however, took its toll. The wrist injury prevented her from competing at the U.S. Olympic trials, and Miller had to petition to make the 1996 Olympic team.

Naysayers thought she was well past her prime. Gymnasts, after all, didn't enjoy return engagements to the Olympics. Four years equates to a lifetime in that sport, and usually veteran performers are quickly replaced by the next ponytailed teenage sensation.

The naysayers really didn't take into account that Miller wasn't just a gymnast. She was a competitor and a fighter.

"I believe the most important tool to be successful is to believe in yourself," Miller said. "It's not always as easy as it sounds."

Backed by a hometown crowd, some thirty-two thousand strong, chanting "U-S-A, U-S-A" as soon as the women took the floor at the Georgia Dome, the American contingent rolled through the competition, and when a valiant Kerri Strug stuck her dramatic vault despite a severely injured ankle, the United States women became the first to capture team gold at an Olympic Games.

"When the lights went on, no one could touch her."

—STEVE NUNNO, MILLER'S LONGTIME COACH

Miller was the mark of consistency, putting up solid scores one right after the other.

After a disappointing all-around competition—Miller would finish eighth—she regrouped to capture her first individual gold, winning the balance beam competition.

This time the fanfare for the team dubbed the Magnificent Seven was near pandemonium. Miller and her teammates were on magazine covers and talk shows, welcomed by screaming young girls who all dreamed of being them. In Oklahoma, the town of Edmond erected an eighteen-foot bronze statue of their hometown girl, and a park and part of a freeway now bear her name.

Miller retired in 1998, went to college, and lived that "normal" life she had longed for.

"I had a blast," she once said of her two-year break.

But while training for a gymnastics tour in 2000, the familiar bug bit her again, and at the age of twenty-three, she set her sights on the 2000 Games in Sydney. She figured why not. She had nothing but her own sweat and aches to lose.

In January, Miller returned to the gym in earnest with Nunno, who endorsed her effort entirely. "I think Shannon Miller can do anything she puts her mind to," he told *USA Today* in 2000.

Her body, however, she couldn't control. Miller suffered a hairline fracture in her leg in July 2000. She recovered enough to try to stake her claim during the Olympic trials in August, but in her first event—the vault—her knees buckled as she landed, and a tearful Miller had to be helped to the training room and withdrew from the competition. When Karolyi, then the U.S. team coach, elected not to name her to the 2000 team, many were disappointed, but no one was surprised.

"The one thing I know for sure," Miller said, "is nothing in life is for sure."

She retired for good afterward and turned her attention to that "normal life" she always craved. Of course "normal" is a bit of a stretch for a woman who's so used to balancing so much.

"I can see Shannon serving the public through a life in politics," her friend and agent Sheryl Shade said. "She touches people, so a life of public service is in the cards. We definitely have not heard the last of Shannon Miller."

The once shy young girl is now a television commentator and motivational speaker, but of course Miller could never be content resting on her Olympic laurels. Miller is currently pursuing her law degree at Boston College. She takes classes Monday through Thursday, purposefully leaving her weekends open so she can travel to cover various meets.

Still in top shape, Miller said she has been known to do back handsprings down a hotel hallway and is a frequent visitor to the fitness centers.

It is a full life, filled with exhaustive studies and travel and business meetings and commitments.

Miller would have it no other way. Long ago this sprite of a woman revealed her inner dynamo, and it is still pushing her today.

"Success is not just about gold medals," she said. "It's about continually moving forward, learning, and improving yourself and the world around you. It means making mistakes but treating those mistakes as opportunities instead of obstacles. But most of all success means being able to be happy and at peace with yourself."

Shannon Miller's Life Lessons

Set Goals

At the biggest crossroads of her career, Shannon Miller considered walking away from gymnastics. She was enduring a growth spurt following the 1992 Olympic Games and was convinced she was burned out. Thanks to a little time off, she realized her problem. She hadn't set any goals for herself. "One of the best lessons I learned from my coaches was how to set goals," Shannon said. "Once I set those goals, they taught me how to create a plan of attack, so I could see a logical way of achieving those goals."

Don't Set Limits on Yourself or Allow Others to Do So

Conventional wisdom said that in 1996 Shannon Miller was too old and past her prime to compete in another Olympic Games. After all, gymnasts usually competed in one Olympics and were done. Fortunately, Shannon ignored conventional wisdom and its limitations, not only competing in the 1996 Games, but helping the United States to its only team gold medal in gymnastics. "I like that gymnastics is open-ended," Shannon said. "There is never a time when you can learn every skill there is because there are just too many. And even if you do, you can just start making up new ones."

Hard Work Pays Off

What set Shannon Miller apart from her peers was her willingness to strive for perfection. In the gym, her coaches said, she would work on a routine over and over again until she got it exactly right. She refused to take a day off, never took her foot off the gas pedal, and always looked to improve. "Shannon was always there and never complained," gymnastics coach and gym owner Rita Brown said. "She kept doing it until she did it right."

Believe in Yourself

Like any superstar athlete, Shannon Miller's career was full of crossroads, rife with doubters. Though she always could count on her parents, Claudia and Ron, for support, as well as her coach, Steve Nunno, ultimately what kept Shannon working and improving was Shannon herself. She wasn't pushing to win medals, necessarily, but pushing to be her best. "I believe the most important tool is to believe in yourself," Shannon explained. "It's not always as easy as it sounds."

Don't Be Afraid to Fail

Gymnastics is a sport fraught with failure. No one sticks every landing. No one goes through a career without stumbling off the balance beam. Shannon Miller's career was no different. After winning team gold at the 1996 Games, she started her all-around competition by stepping out of bounds on the floor exercise, all but eliminating herself from medal contention. Though devastated, she rebounded to win a gold medal on the balance beam. "I know that life is full of mistakes, in sport and every other part," Shannon said. "Things are going to happen that I don't like, but just like in gymnastics, I have to pick myself up and decide whether I want to learn from my mistake or let it bog me down and hold me back."

Be Helpful and Kind to Others

As distinguished as her gymnastics career was, Shannon Miller is most remembered for her demeanor. She was—and is—a humble and decent person. Never rude, never snobby, she made time for her fans, treated her competitors with respect, and shouldered the responsibility as a U.S. athlete with honor. "I hope that people would think of me as someone who helped motivate or encourage others to always do and be their best in any situation," Shannon said.

Wake Up Each Day Happy for What You Have

There are always two options in life—the half-full glass option and the half-empty glass option. No matter how successful a person might appear to others, he or she always can find reason to choose the half-empty glass. Shannon Miller could do the same; she could pine for the medals she doesn't own or lament an injury that kept her out of the 2000 Olympics. Instead she chooses to revel in her successes and move forward with her life, to challenge new ventures in law school and plan for her future rather than dwell on her past. "Most of all," Shannon said, "success means being happy and at peace with yourself."

~ 21 ~

Martina Navratilova:
Daring

"Whatever your limitations might be, don't let them define you."
—MARTINA NAVRATILOVA

*M*artina Navratilova left Athens without a gold medal.

The oldest Olympic tennis player in the history of the Games, she realized in the midst of her comeback trail that she finally might be able to compete in the one tennis competition that had eluded her for her entire career—the Olympics. Relying on her inner strength, commitment to fitness, and desire to play, Navratilova became one of the top four American doubles, players in 2004, thus earning a spot on the Athens roster.

Like every other time she stepped on a tennis court, Navratilova went to Greece to win. It didn't happen. The forty-seven-year-old Navratilova and her doubles partner, Lisa Raymond, were beaten in the quarterfinals.

The question, then, was an easy one: Was it worth it?

In her newest book, *Shape Your Self,* Navratilova answered simply, "The way I see it, you never regret new experiences, only the ones you've missed."

Martina Navratilova is a woman of few regrets. Athletically, she achieved her dreams, and personally she lived the life she wanted. She embraced

challenges and stood tall in the face of criticism, never once allowing anything or anyone to deny her from being her true self.

Once the hated rival of the adored Chris Evert, the left-handed
Navratilova became instead a beloved champion. Her fierce competitiveness once made her the perfect villain. Now it is lauded. The woman once
considered stoic now is appreciated as warm, funny, and engaging. She is
Czechoslovakian by birth, but she is an American treasure.

"The body of work is what I'm proud of and the passion that I brought,"
Navratilova said in a ceremony in her honor as the newest member of the
U.S. Open Court of Champions in 2006. "And probably as far as more per-
sonal, it is just being true to myself and speaking my truth and living it."

No tennis player, male or female, has won more than Navratilova's 168
singles titles, a run that includes a record nine Wimbledon championships,
four U.S. Open crowns, three Australian Open titles, and two French
Open trophies. The number one player in the world for 331 weeks,
Navratilova was no worse than number four from 1975 to 1991, an unbelievable run of almost two decades. Her on-court rivalry with Evert remains
one of the sport's greatest, and her consecutive match win streak of seventy-
four is almost DiMaggio-esque in its domination.

And her longevity—she won her final doubles title at the age of forty-
nine—is nothing shy of mind-boggling.

"Keep in mind, Martina has been competing for over thirty years as a
professional," former pro tennis player turned television analyst Betsy
Nagelsen McCormack said. "That is almost impossible to imagine."

But her career was not without bumps in the road, and her rise from
teenage sensation to middle-aged marvel had more than a few rough spots.
Shunned by her home country after she defected, Navratilova then endured
the stinging criticism of her new home, America, when she appeared to
enjoy the good life a little too much.

That she stayed the course, never apologizing for who she was, and
trusted her gut to do what she believed best, reveals what truly is inside a
champion.

"Martina is probably the most daring player in the history of the game,"
TV analyst Bud Collins once said of Navratilova. "She dared to play a
style antithetical to her heritage without worrying about making a fool

of herself. She dared to remake herself physically, setting new horizons for women in sports. And she dared to live her life as she chose, without worrying what other people thought of her."

Perhaps it has to do with watching your country succumb to oppressors or living for so long without. Whatever fueled her, once given the opportunity to achieve, Navratilova would not be denied. Born in 1956, Navratilova was at a tournament in Pilsen when Russian troops invaded her country. At first angry that her tournament had been cancelled, Navratilova quickly recognized the gravity of the situation. Tanks rumbled down the streets and soldiers turned machine guns at heckling natives to quiet them. Navratilova endured a four-hour ride with her father on a motorbike to get home, stopped frequently by soldiers who wanted to know where they were going.

"When I was twelve or thirteen, I saw my country lose its verve, lose its productivity, lose its soul," Navratilova wrote in her autobiography, *Martina.*

Navratilova never lost hers. A tennis player since she was four, she loved nothing more than spending hours with her stepfather, Mirek Navratil (though she called him her "second father"), on the practice court. Eventually Mirek brought his daughter to George Parma, a former Czech champion, for lessons.

Impressed by his young protégé, Parma quickly set about changing Navratilova's game, getting rid of her two-handed backhand and working tirelessly on her mastery of shots, strategy, and psychology, sowing the seeds of a legendary serve-and-volley attack. The invasion, however, left more than an impression on Navratilova. It affected her personally. Parma had been in Austria when the Russians invaded. He never returned.

> *"I think we know when we are letting ourselves off the hook. If you look in the mirror and you really look yourself in the eye, the image you see forces you to be honest with yourself."*
>
> —MARTINA NAVRATILOVA

"I understood completely why my coach was not coming back," Navratilova wrote.

Left with little recourse, Navratilova continued to play and continued to win, showing her spunk whenever she could. After a Russian competitor refused to shake her hand following a match, Navratilova retorted, "You need a tank to beat me."

By the time she was fifteen, Navratilova was the reigning Czech champion and a year later turned pro, enabling her to compete for the first time in the United States. She spent eight weeks touring the country, amazed at everything she saw and, more important, finally feeling at home.

"I didn't feel I belonged anywhere until I came to America for the first time when I was sixteen," Navratilova wrote. "This country was waiting for me. It would give me the friends and the space and the freedom and the courts and the sneakers and the weight machines and the right food for me to become a tennis champion, to play the best tennis any woman ever played."

"Martina goes about athletics with such joy. She doesn't work at tennis; she plays it."

—MARY CARILLO, TENNIS ANALYST

Agog at what she experienced, Navratilova returned to the United States in 1974, winning her first professional tournament in Orlando that year. Though pleased with her victory, Czech tennis authorities were none too happy about the player they believed was becoming "too Americanized." They tried to shorten her tennis leash, hoping to curb her enthusiasm for America.

It was too late. By then Navratilova knew that in order to really achieve her dream, she would have to leave her home country.

During the U.S. Open in 1975, Navratilova spent practically the entire tournament in her hotel room, meeting with FBI agents and lawyers. After she lost to Evert in the semifinals, she crossed the river to Manhattan's Lower West Side to meet with Immigration and Naturalization Service personnel, beginning the process of seeking asylum.

Navratilova's beef with the Czech government was personal not political. She was angry that they tried to control her career, miffed that they wanted her to finish high school instead of playing tennis, and overwhelmed by the sadness that she thought permeated her country.

The night before she left for the Open, her father took Navratilova aside.

"Well, if you're going to do it, stay there. Don't let us talk you into coming back. Just stay."

Navratilova never told her mother her plans, though Jana certainly knew. She didn't return home again until 1986.

"Once you leave your family behind and don't know when you will see them again, everything else is peanuts," Navratilova said recently of the pain of leaving her family for so long.

Though number two at the time of her defection, the transition to America was hardly easy for Navratilova. Overwhelmed by her sudden tennis fame and status, lonely for her family, and criticized by the press for selfishly leaving her family behind, Navratilova was hardly a champion. She was a mess. She had gained thirty pounds, a fact the press had a field day with, criticizing her love for all things American, particularly fast food.

At the U.S. Open, the site where she had planned her defection a year earlier, Navratilova led 6–1 over virtual unknown Janet Newberry before collapsing in a four-set disaster. Unable to move, Navratilova stood on the baseline sobbing until Newberry shepherded her off the court.

"Martina doesn't just talk. She goes out and gets things done."

—Mary Carillo, tennis analyst

The next day, a press account labeled Navratilova as a "washed-up tennis player grown gluttonously fat on American greed and fame and pizza." Even her friend Billie Jean King took jabs, quoted in a *New York Times* Sunday magazine piece as saying, "It would help the women's game if Martina lived up to her potential and started beating Chris regularly, but I don't know how hard she'll push herself. She likes to enjoy herself. She has a tendency to goof off, get distracted, you know, buying things, not practicing enough."

A person has two choices when the pain of rock bottom smacks at them: to wallow in the freefall or wipe off the dirt and start over.

Not surprising, Navratilova chose the latter. Days after her debacle at Forest Hills, she bought a house in Texas, a home that provided her sanctuary. "The house was the first thing I owned in America that meant anything to me," Navratilova told *Sport* magazine in 1978. "Finally I had roots and security. It was what I had been searching for."

Energized by her new home, Navratilova rededicated herself to tennis.

She worked out feverishly, dropping from her ballooned weight of 167 pounds to a competitive 144. With input from golf champion Sandra Haynie, Navratilova also learned to relax, to not lose focus but to also not beat herself up after every mistake.

Rejuvenated, Navratilova blasted onto the tennis circuit in 1978, winning thirty-seven consecutive tournaments, the exclamation point coming at Wimbledon where she beat Evert for her first major title.

"She is one gifted, terrific athlete who could've been a star in any sport."

—ROSIE CASALS, FORMER PROFESSIONAL TENNIS PLAYER

Her career, however, ebbed and flowed in the late 1970s, instead of following an upward trajectory. She won her second Wimbledon title in 1979, but also lost to Evert, 6–0, 6–0, in 1981.

That year she met Nancy Lieberman, then still a competitive professional basketball player. She credits Lieberman with turning her tennis career on its ear.

"She began her career in 1973 as a physically unfit player, but then launched a tremendous fitness kick that she still employs," Collins said. "All the other players have followed her."

Navratilova dropped her body fat to 8.8 percent, began cross training, incorporating basketball as well as other sports into her exercise regimen, and consulted with a dietician, a norm nowadays but unique in the 1980s.

"Martina would have excelled at any sport she took up," television analyst Mary Carillo said. "She has incredible desire and is totally dedicated to getting the most out of her body. She is a physical animal, like an attacking tiger or a great race horse."

Finally, Navratilova found herself on the path she envisioned. In 1982, she ascended to the number one ranking for the first time in her career and didn't cede the top position until 1987, a run of 156 consecutive weeks. Along the way she won Wimbledon six years running, from 1982 to 1987, and took along two Australian (1983, 1985), two French (1982, 1984), and four U.S. Open (1983, 1984, 1986, and 1987) crowns.

The epic battles between Evert and Navratilova finally started to shift toward Navratilova, a sure sign of her dominance. After losing twenty-one of their first twenty-five matches, Navratilova finished with a 43–37 edge over Evert.

"Martina revolutionized the game by her superb athleticism and aggressiveness, not to mention her outspokenness and her candor," Evert told *Women's Sports and Fitness* magazine once. "She brought athleticism to a whole new level with her training techniques. She had everything down to a science, including her diet, and that was an inspiration to me. I really think she helped me to be a better athlete. And then I always admired her maturity, her wisdom, and her ability to transcend the sport. You could ask her about her forehand or about world peace and she always had an answer. She really is a world figure, not just a sports figure."

"Lead by example and you'll be able to achieve a lot more and make a difference in people's lives that way."

—MARTINA NAVRATILOVA

The world that once disliked Navratilova intensely slowly warmed to her. She allowed herself to smile on the court and to cry when she received her trophies, opening what previously had been perceived as a cold demeanor. That she earned her embrace while becoming one of the first athletes to admit she was a homosexual only makes her sense of self even more impressive.

Not long after she finally earned her U.S. citizenship in 1981, Navratilova admitted that she had a relationship with author Rita Mae Brown, and though her honesty likely cost her millions in endorsements, it liberated her, as well as countless others.

At the U.S. Open final that year, Navratilova was upset by eighteen-year-old Tracy Austin. Devastated, she went to receive her runner-up trophy with tears on her face.

"But then something marvelous happened—the crowd started applauding and cheering," Navratilova wrote in her autobiography. "Their ovation lasted for more than a minute, and I stood there and finally started to cry, but I cried tears of appreciation, not sadness. . . . It was really strange, not like tennis at all. . . . They were cheering for me. I had never felt anything like it in my life: acceptance, respect, maybe even love."

"I enjoy the process, and that's what separates the champions from the rest of the crowd."

—MARTINA NAVRATILOVA

In 1986, Navratilova made her first trip to Czechoslovakia, leading the U.S. Federation Cup team to victory there.

Toppled from her number one perch in 1987 by Steffi Graf, she nonetheless continued to win titles. In 1990, Navratilova beat Zina Garrison to win her ninth Wimbledon title, beating the record of eight set by Helen Wills Moody.

"You can do great things regardless of your age if you just believe and, you know, go for it," she once said. "Don't get limited by people that say, 'No, you can't do that because you're too old or because you're heavy or you're not an athlete.' Whatever your limitations might be, don't let them define you. I didn't let it define me."

She officially retired in 1995, but bored and missing the game, came back as a doubles player in 2000, and in 2004, she won a first-round match as a singles player at Wimbledon.

"Her devotion to fitness and nutrition changed the way women looked at these topics," former player Mary Joe Fernandez said. "She's 100 percent professional all the time."

Inspired again, she continued to compete in doubles matches, both mixed and women's, showing she hadn't lost a step.

"It's about her personal battle with the sport," her coach Michael de Jongh told *USA Today* in 2006. "It's not about proving to other people anything. That's why most people completely misunderstand why she came back."

Finally, at the 2006 U.S. Open, Navratilova stopped toying with retiring and called it quits. Only days shy of her fiftieth birthday, she teamed with

Bob Bryan to win the Open's mixed doubles title, her fifty-ninth Grand Slam championship, and then gracefully said good-bye.

"I just wanted to keep inspiring people the way they inspired me and sort of show people you can do great things regardless of your age if you just believe and go for it," Navratilova told *USA Today* in 2006.

In her 1985 autobiography, *Martina,* Navratilova opened her book with a story about apples. Once a grand family in Czechoslovakia, Navratilova's mother and grandparents found their thirty-acre property diminished to one red-clay tennis court and a cement home after the Russian invasion. From her window, Navratilova looked over a grove of fruit trees that no longer belonged to her family. Defiant and angry, she would sneak into the grove and take apples for herself and her friends.

When she moved to America, Navratilova, who just recently was named a sports legend of the Czech Republic, helped her family buy a property in a village called Revnice. It would be years before she could see the place for herself, but she made sure of one thing. The property included forty apple trees.

"I have never believed in playing it safe in life," Navratilova wrote in *Shape Your Self.* "I like to create. I like to make things happen. In other words, I come to the net. That is where all the fun happens. I try to find an opening, then I go for it. This is how I play tennis; this is how I live my life."

Martina Navratilova's Life Lessons

Don't Worry What Others Think

Martina Navratilova mastered perhaps the most difficult life lesson of all. She stood tall in the face of criticism, never once letting outsiders dictate who she would be. "You can do great things regardless of your age if you just believe and, you know, go for it," she once said. "Don't get limited by people who say, 'No, you can't do that because you're too old or because you're heavy or you're not an athlete.' Whatever your limitations might be, don't let them define you. I didn't let it define me."

Take Risks

Had she stayed in her native country, Czechoslovakia, Martina Navratilova would have been a national hero. Frustrated by the limitations her government was putting on her, she defected to the United States, leaving behind the security of her family and walking into a country that already had its tennis darling in Chris Evert. "You set your goals and then break it down and try to figure out how to get there," Navratilova once said. "Then it becomes a palatable, doable daily routine."

Push Yourself

On God-given talent, Martina Navratilova could have been a good tennis player. By reaching deeper, she became a great one. Overwhelmed by her new country, Navratilova's once overpowering game faltered as her weight escalated. Critics, including Billie Jean King, started to write Navratilova off. Her response? A training regimen unlike anything women's athletics had ever seen that reshaped her body and helped her to reclaim her dominance. "There are lots of great athletes who don't live up to their gifts," tennis analyst Mary Carillo said. "Martina is just the opposite. Once she is committed to something, she is in it all the way."

Lead by Example

In a world dominated by boorish behavior, Martina Navratilova managed to stand her ground without ever embarrassing herself. As important as it was for her to defend herself, it was equally important that she handled herself with class because she knew others were always watching. "There are few things more satisfying in life than being a good role model, someone who sets an example and motivates other people toward positive change," Navratilova wrote in *Shape Your Self*.

22

Mary Lou Retton:
Power

"Even though it may seem counterintuitive, a comfort zone is a dangerous place to be."

—Mary Lou Retton

Were it not for an injured hip, the world might never have heard of Mary Lou Retton. That megawatt smile beaming from the cover of Wheaties boxes and magazines in the summer of 1984 might have gone unshared; the glorious moment of Retton, arms thrust into the air as if signaling a touchdown after her vault to perfection, may never have occurred.

Of course, that simplifies things a little too much. It gives a little too much credit to fate and happenstance and not enough to hard work. If there's one thing Retton's life personifies, it's hard work.

So, really, the accurate way to explain it is to say that Dianne Durham's injured hip opened the door, allowing Retton to compete in the 1983 American Cup, a worldwide tournament that serves as the precursor for the Olympic Games.

Retton's hard work blasted the door off its hinges and made her a star.

"In a perfect world there would be no such thing as pressure, but unfortunately for most of us, there's no escaping it," Retton wrote in her book *Mary Lou Retton's Gateways to Happiness*. "The good news is that if you are truly prepared, you will be ready to meet that pressure head-on. When you've been incredibly disciplined in working toward your goal and building the skills you need, the confidence you'll have as a result will give you a significant mental edge in any situation."

Really, Mary Lou Retton never should have become a gymnastics star. She was built all wrong for her sport, a stocky spitfire in an era when gymnasts were lithe as ballerinas. Hers was the figure of power, muscle-toned legs that seemed to serve almost as trampolines for her compact body.

With fans still picturing pixie-ish Nadia Comaneci daintily flitting across the floor during the 1976 Games, here came Retton bulling her way down a vault ramp.

But as one sports columnist wrote during the 1984 Olympic Games, "Of her ninety-four pounds, sixty-five are heart."

"She lived out a dream of a lifetime," Retton's father, Ronnie, said. "Mary Lou was in the right place at the right time. God has a way of making things happen, and he blessed Mary Lou in a special way. As a result, she has become a role model for all of us."

The granddaughter of a West Virginia coal miner, Retton knew early about hard work and discipline, about making things better for yourself instead of counting on someone else to do it for you. Enduring workouts that would bring men twice her age and size to tears, absorbing the sometimes harsh criticism of coach Bela Karolyi without batting an eye, and living two years apart from her family in order to experience the best training, Retton made herself a champion.

The first American woman to win an Olympic gold medal in gymnastics, Retton earned her jewelry in fine style, scoring perfect tens on both the vault and the floor exercise. She left Los Angeles with five Olympic medals in all (one in the all-around, three individual event medals, and a team medal), a haul unmatched by any of her American peers that year.

"Mary Lou teaches us to follow your dreams," former Olympic coach Rita Brown said. "She was so passionate and wanted to succeed so badly. She had the fire within her and loved her sport. You could see it all over her face with that big smile."

Blessed with that winning smile and an exuberant personality, Retton certainly had her down days, but she refused to let them last. Teased as a kid because of her tiny size (she topped out at four feet, nine inches), Retton learned to turn the cutting remarks into jokes and to this day believes strongly in the sedative power of laughter.

It is that energy, that joie de vivre more even than the gold medal, that made Retton truly America's sweetheart.

"The big smile people see on the outside comes from a place deep within me that isn't affected by any of those day-to-day matters," Retton wrote in *Gateways*. "True joy and contentment are within reach for all of us, no matter how bad our circumstances may seem."

That's a lesson Retton learned as a child. The youngest of five children raised in Fairmont, West Virginia, Retton and her family certainly didn't live in the lap of luxury. Ronnie co-captained West Virginia's 1959 national runner-up basketball team alongside Jerry West and spent five years in the Yankees farm system as a shortstop. Unable to cut through the political ceilings of Double-A ball, Ronnie finally called it quits and returned to Fairmont, where he started his own company that repaired transportation cables for the coal-mining companies that dot the Fairmont landscape.

All five kids were active and athletic. Retton's older brothers, Ronnie, Donnie, and Jerry, all played collegiate baseball, and her older sister, Shari, was an all-American gymnast at West Virginia University.

But before those organized sports days, the kids made do with running around the West Virginia hills, playing whatever games they could put together. As the youngest, Retton was shuttled to all of her siblings' practices, trying a few sports out for herself. She ran track, swam, and competed as a cheerleader.

"Achieving that goal is a good feeling, but to get there you have to also get through the failures."

—MARY LOU RETTON

When Retton was seven, her mother enrolled her in Aerial-port, a new gymnastics school in Fairmont. Young and fearless, Retton loved the three nights she spent at the gym, eagerly attempting tricks that others wouldn't dare to try.

"Mary Lou was extremely active as a little girl," Ronnie said. "We got her into a tumbling class, and she would practice at home. We were always picking up broken lamps after some of her routines."

Obviously talented, Retton started winning events as a youngster, and after spying Comaneci on television during the 1976 Games, decided at the age of eight that she, too, would be an Olympic gymnast. Her parents did little to discourage her dream, even letting her abandon her other activities and concentrate solely on gymnastics at the age of twelve. Really no one knew exactly what sort of talent they had on their hands.

That changed when Retton turned fourteen. By then Retton realized that to become the sort of gymnast she dreamed of being, she'd have to leave West Virginia. Competition there was limited, and Retton was left to push herself. Though a hard worker, she struggled without anyone to challenge her to do yet one more set on the balance beam or one more vault on her blistered hands.

"She was the sunshine of my coaching career."

—BELA KAROLYI, LEGENDARY OLYMPIC GYMNASTICS COACH

On December 23, 1982, Retton met Karolyi following a meet in Reno, Nevada. The Transylvanian, who had mentored Comaneci and defected to the United States in 1981, already had a reputation for being a tireless taskmaster but a groomer of great gymnasts. He told Retton's parents that if she seriously wanted to point her sights to the 1984 Games, she would have to come train with him immediately.

In Houston.

"Once they heard me voice my hopes they recognized that, by saying no, they might very well be standing in the way of what could turn out to be the greatest opportunity of my life," Retton wrote in *Gateways*. "Only now, looking back, do I fully realize what an incredible gift my parents gave me. . . . My parents' love for me was the reason I made it to the Olympics, pure and simple."

Her parents were equally impressed with their daughter's will and desire.

"It takes a unique little girl to leave home at fourteen and move a thousand miles away, live with a family you don't know, and train eight hours a day," Ronnie Retton said. "That's something special. Mary Lou had a dream to be in the Olympics and had the determination and will to get there."

Though training with Karolyi was a dream come true, in some respects it was also a nightmare. Retton went from one three-hour practice in West Virginia to two four-hour sessions in Houston, grueling workouts that left Retton's body sore and her spirit sometimes battered.

"She had extraordinary determination and believed in her coaches and herself," Karolyi said. "That combination made her very successful. She bought into everything we taught her about being a great champion. She was highly motivated and worked so hard in practice, which enabled her to progress so quickly."

Karolyi took Retton's raw talent and refined it. A gymnast once chided for inconsistency became so familiar with her routines that she was like an autopilot. A woman who never could summon the patience needed to be successful on the four-inch balance beam became, with the help of Karolyi's wife, Marta, near perfection.

"Each of us has a fire in our heart for something. It's our goal in life to find it and keep it lit."

—MARY LOU RETTON

It wasn't easy. Far from it. Retton heard criticism far more often than praise, finishing a routine she believed was quite good only to hear, "No, no, no," in Karolyi's thickly accented English.

Toss in the fact that she was living more or less away from home, and Retton admits to having more than her share of doubting moments.

"I was living with a strange family by myself, in a new school, and working out eight hours a day after being used to training just three hours back home," Retton said in *It's How You Play the Game.* "But after four months, I started getting better, and the voice in my head was saying, 'I can do this.'"

Pushed by Karolyi, as well as the presence of Durham in the same gym, Retton forced herself to complete routine after routine after routing, turning those "no's" into "not bads" and eventually into the bear hugs that Karolyi is famous for.

But more than Karolyi, more than Durham, Retton pushed herself. She had made the decision to come to Houston because she dreamed of becoming an elite gymnast, and so she worked through painful injuries and sleepless nights, pushing herself and her body to extremes she didn't know she could realize.

"You can always avoid taking risks and meeting new challenges," Retton wrote in *Gateways*. "Avoiding them is, without question, the easy way out. But it's only by taking those risks and meeting those challenges head-on that you can ever break out of your personal comfort zone and reach new levels of happiness and personal satisfaction. . . . Even though it may seem counterintuitive, a comfort zone is a dangerous place to be."

Retton was easily among the country's, if not the world's, best gymnasts in 1983, but gymnastics is a funny sport. Rarely do athletes come out of nowhere to win gold medals. They need a reputation, a familiar name so that the judges will be aware of them as soon as they begin to compete. No one knew that little political game better than Karolyi, and so the coach tried every avenue to get Retton into the 1983 American Cup.

He couldn't. That meet was reserved for men and women who had established their supremacy at the previous world championships. Retton went to the event in New York's Madison Square Garden as an alternate.

On the eve of competition, Karolyi told her she was competing, that Durham's sore hip would keep her out of the competition. He begged Retton to "not let me down."

No worries there. She scored a meet record 9.95 on the vault, won that event as well as the floor, tied for first on bars, and won the all-around title, landing herself into the gymnastics' consciousness and onto the cover of *International Gymnast*.

By the time the Olympics rolled around the following summer, Retton had put together an unbeaten streak of meets and was clearly the favorite for the gold.

Paths to glory rarely come without potholes, and Retton's road was no different. Six weeks before the Olympics were to begin, Retton was competing in an exhibition meet with her teammates in Louisville, Kentucky. After finishing up an autograph session following the meet, Retton couldn't stand up. Her knee had locked and she couldn't straighten it. Frightened, she slept that night with a bag of ice on her knee, but when she woke up, the ice was melted and her knee was swollen beyond belief.

No matter how many doctors Retton visited, they all offered the same diagnosis. Retton had torn cartilage, needed surgery, and the rehab would take at least three months. Momentarily devastated, Retton soon summoned the confidence and personality that millions across the world would come to recognize at the Olympics.

She simply said no—not to the surgery since that really wasn't an option, but to the lengthy rehab. If the calendar said she had six weeks to get ready for the Olympics, then she'd be ready in six weeks.

"The day after we get back [from Richmond, Virginia, where Retton had the surgery], Mary Lou returned to the gym, and we began the nightmare of rehabilitation," Karolyi said in *Creating an Olympic Champion.* "She was trying to walk with tears in her eyes, but Mary Lou showed a tremendous will to recover. Very few athletes in similar situations, knowing the short time frame, would even try to get in shape."

Retton wouldn't be dissuaded, and three days postsurgery she was already jogging. When it was time to march in for the opening day ceremonies, Retton was ready.

"No matter what anybody tells you, never stop believing in yourself," Retton wrote in *Gateways.* "It sounds so easy, yet often we're the first ones to sell ourselves short. But when your confidence remains unshakable, even in the face of people telling you that you're bound to fail, you'll eventually find a way to succeed."

With such strong belief in herself and such intense training, it's not really surprising that Retton left Los Angeles with a gold medal around her neck. Remembering the days she spent lying on the floor watching Comaneci in 1976, Retton seized her moment. A ten on the floor exercise kept her on pace with Romanian Ecaterina Szabo in the all-around competition, but even with that notch of perfection, Retton would need a 9.95 to tie and a ten on vault to win the gold.

Packing every bit of energy into her compact frame, Retton ran with gusto, banging the springboard for her vault, twisting and turning to plant her feet as if they were bonded with cement. "A vault without fault," *Sports Illustrated* appropriately pegged it.

The vault gave Retton the gold and quite literally catapulted her into instant celebrity. There was Retton, shaking hands with the president, chatting up the host of *The Tonight Show,* and becoming the first female athlete to grace a Wheaties box. She was only sixteen.

"I won my medal for the Olympics on Friday night, and on Saturday, the morning headlines said, 'A star is born overnight,'" Retton said once. "I kind of chuckled because I thought, 'Where did the nine years go that I put into this?' A good friend, Michael Jordan, once said to me, 'Fame doesn't change you. It changes the people around you.' It's really true."

Retton competed in the American Cup one more time, becoming the first woman to win three titles there, but by age eighteen, she retired from competitive gymnastics.

"I knew I was going to be okay in the world after I retired because of what I had learned in sports," Retton said in *It's How You Play the Game.* "I knew that the sacrifice, focus, and discipline would help me in my life and in any career I would choose."

Retton enrolled at the University of Texas, but uncomfortable with the recognition she received on campus and frankly unsure of herself in a classroom setting after a life of tutoring, Retton left after two years to marry former Longhorn quarterback Shannon Kelley.

The couple have four children, and motherhood has hardly slowed Retton down. Along with raising her children, Retton has appeared in various television shows and movies, works as a motivational speaker, and is a spokeswoman with the Children's Miracle Network.

Like every working mother, Retton struggles to balance the challenges of her life. She limits her travels to weekdays, insisting that weekends are for the family, and tries to never leave her children for more than one night.

"Mary Lou is a good mother," Rita Brown said. "Her daughters go to my gym in Houston. Mary Lou sits in the stands with the rest of the parents. She's just another mother, although the other little girls like to be in the same classes with her daughters. They get a big kick out of that."

A devout Christian, Retton has grown more comfortable sharing her beliefs as she's grown older. Where she once shied away from anything too political or too personal, Retton now embraces her faith.

Taped to her desk at home is a piece of paper that reads, "Good morning! This is God. I will be handling all of your problems today. I will not need your help, so have a good day!"

"Isn't that great?" Retton asked author Christin Ditchfield. "I love it. That's what I try to live my day by, not stressing over the little things, the things that are out of our control. We can worry ourselves sick."

Retton also has put both her personality and her talents to work, starting her own children's show, "Mary Lou's Flip-Flop Shop." Getting the show on the air wasn't easy. A labor of love created and funded by Retton and her husband, the show took seven years before landing on PBS, a torturous process that would have discouraged most people.

Mary Lou Retton, though, is not most people. Using the same determination, perseverance, and inner strength, Retton fought and worked on behalf of her television show.

"All that I learned in my athletic experience, in my gymnastics training, the perseverance, the determination, the sacrifice, the hard work ethic," Retton once said, "it helps me every day."

Mary Lou Retton's Life Lessons

Avoid Comfort Zones

Already a talented gymnast, Mary Lou Retton exchanged the workout sessions she had mastered in West Virginia for grueling four-hour torture rounds with Bela Karolyi in Houston. Only by turning her personal and athletic life on its ear did Retton believe she could realize her full potential. "Even though it may seem counterintuitive, a comfort zone is a dangerous place to be," she wrote in her book *Mary Lou Retton's Gateways to Happiness.*

Don't Sell Yourself Short

Six weeks before the Olympics, Mary Lou Retton underwent knee surgery. The prognosis included a rehab that ordinarily would last three months. Everyone assumed her Olympic experience was over before it started—everyone but Retton, that is. "No matter what anybody tells you, never stop believing in yourself," Retton wrote in *Gateways*. "It sounds so easy, yet often we're the first ones to sell ourselves short. But when your confidence remains unshakable, even in the face of people telling you that you're bound to fail, you'll eventually find a way to succeed."

Embrace Joy

The big smile is what the world remembers about Mary Lou Retton. It made everything she did seem so effortless, so fun. The real beauty of that smile, though, is that it was never forced. Hers was a genuine joy, one that had nothing to do with sticking landings on difficult tumbling passes or earning perfect tens. "The big smile people see on the outside comes from a place deep within me that isn't affected by any of those day-to-day matters," Retton wrote in her book. "True joy and contentment are within reach for all of us, no matter how bad our circumstances may seem."

Success Is Never Easy

The day after Mary Lou Retton vaulted into the public's consciousness, scoring a perfect ten at the 1984 Olympics to win the all-around competition, newspapers and magazines heralded America's new sweetheart. She came, it seemed, from obscurity to superstardom in an instant. Retton knew better. "I won my medal for the Olympics on Friday night, and on Saturday, the morning headlines said, 'A star is born overnight,'" Retton said once. "I kind of chuckled because I thought, 'Where did the nine years go that I put into this?'"

23

Dot Richardson:
Spirit

"Ultimate success is making a difference in the lives of other people."
—DOT RICHARDSON

The ten-year-old girl just wanted to play baseball. Growing up, she tried the stereotypical girlie things, like ballet and tap dancing. She was pretty good, too, so good in fact that while living in England she was chosen to perform for the Queen.

But her heart had always been in sports, and at an early age she zeroed in on baseball. Unfortunately, little girls weren't allowed to play organized baseball, so she watched her brothers play Little League from the bleachers. She could only dream of the chance to one day be out on the playing field.

Her heart broke time and time again when she thought that she'd never get the chance to play the game she loved.

One day she was pitching to her brother before one of his Little League games, and a coach spotted her. He asked if she wanted to be on his Little League team. She couldn't believe it. Her prayers had been answered.

But then the coach said, "We'll cut your hair short and give you a boy's name. We'll call you Bob."

Dorothy Richardson said, "Sir, thank you, but no thank you. If I have to hide who I am, I just don't feel it is right."

She went by Dot. She wasn't going to be a Bob for anyone. She was a young girl and proud to be one, a young athlete and even prouder about that.

Sadly, she was also an athlete without a team.

"I knew God had given me a gift of being athletic because I loved being physically active, and sports came so easy and with so much joy," Richardson said. "The biggest problem was that I wondered why I was given so much talent with no opportunities to express that talent."

The reason, it turns out, was because Richardson wasn't meant to be lost in the shuffle with a bunch of boys. She was to be a pioneer, a trailblazer, a woman who would become such an ideal of what young girls could become that a company called Girls Explore would choose her, alongside such historical notables as Harriet Tubman and Amelia Earhart, as one of its "women who follow their dreams to make a better world" and make a Dot Richardson doll.

Known universally as Dr. Dot, Richardson is a double-whammy of impressive success. While training for the first of her two Olympic gold medals, Richardson also went to medical school and attended an orthopedic surgery residency program. Instead of wilting in the face of such overwhelming pressure, Richardson turned that workload into a daily shot of adrenaline.

The pepper pot is the one we remember from those 1996 Olympic Games, the first to include softball as an Olympic sport. Her fist-pumping, upbeat attitude, her catchphrase "Max out!" and her zest for life personified what turned into a sports movement for women.

What can girls, women, anyone, learn from her? What can't they? How about perseverance in the face of incredible odds, that the word "sacrifice" parallels the word "dream," and that the greatest gift of all is to believe in oneself?

"Even when there appears to be no doors of opportunity open, continue to believe in the gifts you've been given, and know your talents are meant to be shared to touch the lives of others," Richardson offers as her personal life lesson.

Sports, softball in particular, have made Richardson famous, but for this incredible woman, sports have merely been her vehicle, her way to achieve what she calls "ultimate success."

"Success is not being at least one run or one point ahead of another athlete or team," she explained. "True success is giving it everything you have to be the best you can in everything you do. Ultimate success is making a difference in the lives of other people, making them feel as special as they are.

"My greatest success is seeing the joy in the eyes of others when I meet them, hearing the silence from their attentiveness when I speak to them, and feeling that I have touched someone's life and made them feel special."

Special—that's how Richardson always felt as a kid. Her father, Ken, was in the U.S. Air Force, so the family moved around a lot, but Richardson and her four brothers and sisters thrived in the exotic locales, including Guam and England, as well as the stateside addresses that included New Mexico and Kansas.

Exposed to a world of culture, Richardson gravitated to sports. She was always active—too active, her parents might say. Her father told *Sports Illustrated* that when Richardson was nine months old, back in the days before car seats, the family got so weary of little Dot scrambling around the car during a cross-country trip from California to Orlando that they found a box for her to call home.

"We put her in a box in the backseat," Ken told *Sports Illustrated.* "That's how she got across country—in a box."

No matter where she went, though, Richardson always ran into the same cement wall when it came to athletics.

Sports weren't for girls.

"The message was loud and clear that a girl being good at athletics was a 'freak,' and something had to be wrong with her," Richardson said.

"In the huge scope of things, sport is just a game that prepares us for the real challenges of life."

—DOT RICHARDSON

Lots of kids would have found another outlet. Richardson wasn't so easily deterred. Blessed with fierce determination, she also had a set of parents who didn't believe their daughters should be treated any differently from their sons. They encouraged Richardson's passions and told her if a door was shut, it was up to her to open it.

Richardson remembers clearly that day when the Little League coach asked her to cut her hair and change her name. She went to her mother, Joyce, and asked why.

Her mother didn't sugarcoat her response.

"Because the parents will be upset when you strike out the boys," Richardson remembered her mother saying.

Fate, though, has a funny way of walking in the door when you least expect it.

Not thirty minutes later on that awful day, a fast-pitch softball coach spied Richardson playing catch and asked her to join her team.

"She has this unshakable belief that everything is going to work out great."

—Sue Enquist, one of Richardson's UCLA coaches

Many of the players in the Women's Fast Pitch Class A Division were in their twenties and thirties. Richardson was all of ten. Her parents, however, showed their support by giving her permission to compete with and against the older players. They believed in her talents.

Two years later, Richardson became the youngest player to compete at the highest level of fast pitch softball when she was asked to join the Orlando Rebels.

Her coach, Marge Ricker, didn't care. She treated Richardson just like she treated the other women on her team, imparting to the teenager lessons that were about softball but really were about much more than a game.

"She taught me that the day you think you have learned all there is to learn is the day to hang up your cleats," Richardson said.

Buoyed by Ricker's support, Richardson blossomed. By seventeen she was a gold medalist at the Pan American Games.

As her talents grew, Richardson had countless opportunities to capitalize on her abilities. A handful of professional leagues that sprouted up over the years offered Richardson a place and, better yet, a salary, but she had bigger dreams.

She imagined a day when she would wear red, white, and blue and play for her country in the Olympic Games.

That softball wasn't an Olympic sport didn't deter her dream.

"All the way back when I was fifteen, I had it in my mind," Richardson told the *Los Angeles Times*.

So instead of playing professionally, Richardson went to college, transferring from Western Illinois to the University of California at Los Angeles (UCLA). In her three years in Westwood, the shortstop led the Bruins in hitting and earned all-American honors every year. When her career ended, the NCAA tabbed her as its 1980s Player of the Decade.

Toss in four more Pan Am Games gold medals and four world championships and Richardson's athletic life would make for a remarkable tale to tell.

"Dot took her talent and maxed it out. Dot never went on cruise control. Not many people do that."

—MICHELE SMITH,
OLYMPIC SOFTBALL PITCHER

Except like most extraordinary people, Richardson isn't fueled by one passion, and in her case, her second love is perhaps even more grueling than her first.

Richardson loves medicine, an irony considering she hated hospitals as a kid. At UCLA she was a premed major, a young woman who would dash off the softball field in her Bruin blue and gold and into a lab, where she'd toil for hours to complete a biology, chemistry, or physics assignment.

She completed her undergraduate degree, but missed most of her medical school application deadlines and initially was accepted nowhere.

For the next four years she juggled softball with her pursuit of a career in medicine, brushing up on her bat speed while trying to simultaneously build a medical resume. She worked as an emergency medical technician, then went on to earn her master's degree in health and exercise physiology from Adelphi University, all while serving as an assistant coach on the softball team.

Of course, she also competed at the highest level softball had to offer.

Finally, in 1988, she reapplied to medical school and was accepted at the University of Louisville School of Medicine in Kentucky.

As if the rigors of medicine weren't enough, Richardson kept her softball dreams afloat as well. She played for the Raybestos Brakettes, a fast pitch team considered one of the best organizations in the country.

Only problem: the Brakettes were based in Connecticut, a bit of a commute from Kentucky.

But Richardson would cram her medical school work into a five-day week and on Fridays fly to New York, limo over to Connecticut, change in the car, and play a weekend of softball. When it was over, it was back to Louisville and the all-consuming class work.

When the International Olympic Committee (IOC) dropped softball from consideration for the 1992 Barcelona Games, a devastated Richardson figured it was time to go full-throttle into medicine. In 1994, she began her five-year orthopedic residency at USC University Hospital–Los Angeles.

"Opportunity presents itself when the timing is right for your dream to start taking on consciousness," Richardson said of her philosophy.

Indeed, along came fate once again to throw a wrench, albeit a good one, into Richardson's plans.

The IOC added softball to the menu for the 1996 Atlanta Games, and not as a demonstration sport, but as a medal sport.

Already thirty-four, Richardson probably should have done the logical thing. She should have smiled wanly and forged ahead in her residency.

This, however, is the same woman who needed a box to contain her enthusiasm before she could even speak.

Instead, she took a year off from her orthopedic surgery residency and trained for the Olympic Games, staying sharp in medicine by assisting on two surgeries while at training camp in Columbus, Ohio.

"There were a lot of moments when I said, 'What am I doing?'" Richardson told the *Los Angeles Times* in 1996. "A lot of my friends said, 'What are you doing?' Because I only had enough time in my life for medicine and softball. I'd maybe find some time to go to a movie once a month."

Some people might think that

"I do believe in the power of the dream. I have learned to have the courage to dream, and I hope others have been empowered because of it."

—Dot Richardson

it is a huge sacrifice, but Richardson hates the word sacrifice. She prefers to consider her life a quest for a dream.

The catch with those sorts of dreams, of course, is they don't always come true.

Richardson's did on July 30, 1996. In the gold-medal game against China, Richardson launched a two-run home run in the third inning. It would stand as the game-winning run in a 3–1 victory, earning Team USA the first Olympic gold medal in softball.

The lasting image of that history-making moment is of Richardson, smiling through her prideful tears as the national anthem played.

"Dot's energy is contagious and can motivate a whole team," Olympic softball pitcher Michele Smith said. "She was a great leader from that short-stop position."

Four years later Richardson returned, earning a spot at the Sydney Games at the age of thirty-eight. Her on-field role changed. She selflessly moved from shortstop to second base to make room for an up-and-coming rookie, but her off-field leadership was vital for a team that had a little more work to do than in 1996.

"Why did I move forward to 2000?" she told the *Detroit Free Press.* "I love this sport."

Officially, Richardson is retired from softball. That just means she doesn't play competitively. Her role in the game is as big and as important as it was when she prowled the infield in Atlanta and Sydney.

Richardson is an ambassador of her sport, a woman who somehow carves out time from her real job as the director and medical director of the National Training Center in Clermont, Florida, to give motivational speeches as well as lead her own grassroots league, the Dot Richardson Softball Association, an instructional nonprofit organization designed to improve technique as well as safety and health issues related to the sport. Richardson also is an integral part of organizing the professional fast pitch softball tour.

"There is no such thing as a free lunch."

—DOT RICHARDSON

She's also the vice chairman of the President's Council on Physical Fitness and Sports, designed to encourage Americans to be more physically active and live healthier lives.

Softball is the hook. It is not the message.

Richardson's story appeals to all people, whether or not they can hit a curveball or turn a double play.

Her lessons are about commitment and inner motivation, about hard work and humility. The first woman awarded a Rawlings Gold Glove, Richardson also is breaking barriers in her profession. Of the twenty-four thousand board-certified orthopedic surgeons in the United States, only 3 percent are women.

"It's amazing how we're given everything we need to overcome obstacles," Richardson said. "It is not an easy road, but a road worth traveling."

Asked to explain how softball has impacted her life, what sport has taught her, Richardson offers up a lengthy list that she says only scratches the surface.

"I have learned through sports that when I fail, I am not a failure, and when I succeed, I am not perfect," she said. "I have learned to remove all doubt even when others are doubtful. . . . I have learned that there is no such thing as a free lunch.

"I have learned through sport that the greatest gift of all is life, that we must live each moment with focus and purpose to be the best person we can be."

Dot Richardson's Life Lessons

Believe in Your Abilities

Through so many closed doors and seemingly insurmountable obstacles, Dot Richardson never gave up. Most people would have quit, thrown up their hands, and chosen a new, easier passion. Richardson never did because she trusted her gut. "The most important ingredient young athletes must possess to be successful is an inner drive and a belief that their talents are gifts that are meant to be shared," she said. "It is that recognition that removes all doubt and inhibitions."

Trust in God

Asked for one word to describe her career, Dot Richardson answered, "Blessed." Without her faith, a faith instilled in her at a young age by her parents, Richardson said she never could have forged ahead on the path that she chose. She said, "As a little girl, I knew that God had given me a talent in athletics because I loved sports so much and felt so alive participating in them."

Ignore Negativity

As a young girl, Dot Richardson was ostracized, made to feel strange and a "freak" by people who thought young girls and sports didn't mix. It would have been easy to give in to the criticism, to choose a more typical path. Richardson never did. "I am so glad that I never let the voices of others stop me from expressing the gifts God has given me," she said.

Always Consider Your Impact on Others

Dot Richardson has spent most of her life leading by example, but her agent, Tom McCarthy, taught her that sometimes there's more a person can do. He encouraged her to go on speaking tours, to tell her story and inspire others directly. "He believes that success is not measured by how much money one has, but instead by what difference one can make in the world," she said. "God brings people together for a reason, and I know he brought Tom and me together to make a difference."

Never Shy Away from a Challenge

Given the choice of softball or medicine, Dot Richardson chose both. The decision made her a better softball player and a better physician. She is wiser, stronger mentally, more patient, and more self-assured because she opted for the challenge. "I believe that pain and frustration lead us in the right direction to make us strong enough for our moments of truth in defining our self and our destiny," she explained. "It is not an easy road, but a road worth traveling."

Appreciate Your Parents

It is easy to give lip service to Mom and Dad, to say an insincere "Thanks" or wave a goofy "Hi, Mom" sign. Dot Richardson knows that without her parents, Ken and Joyce, she would never have pushed forward. She would never have believed in herself and her inner strength. "I always say that if I could be even half the person my mother is my life would be a success," she shared. "We didn't have much money, but with their love and support I felt so rich."

Never Stop Working

It would be easy for Dot Richardson to rest on her laurels. She has plenty, after all. Richardson hasn't retired to a life of anonymity. She is still on the front line for her sport, supporting the cause of softball and women's athletics. More important, as a doctor, she is still inspiring, growing, and learning. She explained, "The most important personality trait to be successful is humility, the ability to recognize that you can always do better."

∽24∾

Wilma Rudolph:
Faith

"Triumph can't be had without the struggle."

—WILMA RUDOLPH

She shouldn't have lived, really.

She certainly wasn't supposed to walk.

The should nots and will nots and cannots paved the path of Wilma Rudolph's young life, greeting her at every turn, trying to knock her down at every stage of her existence.

She blew past them as if they were competitors lined up on a dusty track.

Buoyed by the two things no medical textbook can ever account for—a mother's fierce love and a human being's own determination—Rudolph overcame the obstacles and became an inspiration.

She ran because they said she wouldn't walk; she succeeded because they said she would fail.

"*I can't* are words that have never been in my vocabulary," she once said. "I believe in me more than anything in the world."

When Rudolph won three Olympic gold medals in 1960, no American had ever come home with such a haul. But Rudolph did more than win, she recognized the responsibility that came with it and, with her dignified manner, paved the way for other African-American athletes.

Because of Wilma Rudolph there was Jackie Joyner-Kersee and Florence Griffith Joyner and Gail Devers.

Because of Wilma Rudolph there was a future for these women.

In an era when African-Americans were still discriminated against, when women athletes of any race weren't given the benefits of their male counterparts, Rudolph blazed through every barrier, shedding stereotypes and building hope along with her.

"She opened a crack in the door," her college coach, Ed Temple, told the *Minneapolis Star-Tribune* after Rudolph died in 1994, "and it was never closed again."

And when Rudolph returned from her triumphant Olympic experience, things were different. Not immediately, but the nuggets of change she had planted were waiting to be seized by the next generation.

"Wilma opened the doors for women, not just black women, but all women," Temple said in a 1994 interview. "When she won all those gold medals in Rome and we saw pictures in all of the magazines, we thought, 'Maybe this can be the beginning.'"

It's strange how the most innocuous of arrivals often are the forerunners of greatness. Wilma Rudolph was born on June 23, 1940, in the poor, segregated community of Clarksville, Tennessee. She was the twentieth of twenty-two children born to Ed Rudolph in two marriages. He was a railroad porter. His wife, Blanche, was a maid. Money was tight on the heels of the Great Depression, and so the arrival of tiny Wilma—born premature and just four pounds at birth—was hardly accompanied by horns and revelry.

Denied the best health care available at the time because of her race, she spent the better part of her infancy and childhood fighting off every disease imaginable: measles and mumps, scarlet fever and chicken pox, and double pneumonia.

Rudolph's mother helped her fend off each illness with staggering will and dedication. But at age four, Rudolph's left leg and foot grew weak and deformed, and the family was given the devastating news. She had polio.

In the 1940s, the polio outbreak terrified the country. Frightened parents refused to let their children outside as the spread of the disease seemed to spike during the hot summer months. The vaccine developed by Jonas Salk was still a decade away, leaving thousands of children dead and countless others paralyzed. The fortunate ones spent their days in an iron lung.

But race and poverty prevented Wilma Rudolph from even hoping for that most rudimentary care.

Undeterred, Blanche Rudolph contacted Meharry Hospital, the black medical college at Fisk University, and arranged treatment for her daughter. Twice a week for two years, Blanche made that fifty-mile trip. Doctors taught Blanche how to massage her daughter's leg, and she in turn taught her other children how to help their sister. Blanche Rudolph also insisted that her daughter not treat her leg as if it didn't work, to use it over and over again and to force it to function.

"The doctors told me I would never walk again," Rudolph once said. "My mother told me I would. I believed my mother."

It wasn't easy. Rudolph was a child and, like any child, longed to be like everyone else. As her brothers and sisters trotted off to school, Rudolph was left home as she battled frequent colds and bouts of the flu. Her face pressed against the window, longing to go to school as well, she would cry in sadness and loneliness.

"The only thing I ever wanted was to be normal," Rudolph told the *New York Times*. "To be average. To be able to run, jump, play, and do all the things the other kids did in my neighborhood."

Rather than wallow in her disappointment, though, Rudolph used her desires to be normal as motivation. That will and her mother's dedication formed a powerful union, and by age eight, Rudolph was walking with a leg brace. By age nine, she had graduated to an orthopedic shoe, and two years later, she didn't need the specially made shoe either.

"When I ran, I felt like a butterfly."

—WILMA RUDOLPH

Who knows how a body works? Had Wilma Rudolph grown up healthy, with the ease and freedom to run whenever she wanted, she may not have been pushed to compete so hard once the chance finally came her way.

But those leg braces were shackles in both the literal and figurative sense, and as soon as Rudolph shed them, she was off, never to be caught again.

She skipped school and scaled fences just to get on the track and enjoy the sensation of running as fast as she could. She challenged anyone who would take her up on it—boys and girls—and won almost every time. She played basketball with her brothers, more than holding her own.

At Burt High School, her basketball coach dubbed Rudolph "Skeeter" because of her lean and lanky body, which appeared to be all elbows and ankles. Never mind—Skeeter could play. She made it a point to learn what the school records were and then set about breaking every one. Twice she led her team to a state championship.

"The symbol of Wilma equaled that of Jesse Owens."

—OLLAN CASSELL, ONE-TIME HEAD OF USA TRACK & FIELD

Rudolph's raw talent and ability impressed one referee in particular by the name of Ed Temple.

A sociology professor at Tennessee State University in Nashville, Temple also coached the school's legendary track team, the Tigerbelles. He encouraged Rudolph to consider track.

Back then, the NCAA rulebook was still decades away, so when Temple invited Rudolph to train with his college team there was nothing to stop the fifteen-year-old Rudolph from signing on.

It was grueling training. Temple challenged his athletes and disciplined them equally hard. Rudolph struggled initially. She felt overwhelmed by the more talented and experienced college athletes, and she wondered if she could make it.

Her mother, never one to coddle Rudolph, spelled it out for her.

"Quit wondering," she said. "Work."

Rudolph did, and in 1956, at the age of sixteen, she qualified for the Olympic Games in Melbourne.

She won a bronze medal as part of the relay team, a great accomplishment for a young woman who wasn't even supposed to walk. But Rudolph's mother had taught her daughter to dream big.

After graduating from high school, Rudolph went to train with Temple full time as a student at Tennessee State University.

In the late 1950s, few colleges offered athletic scholarships for women, so Rudolph had to work to pay her way. She did clerical work or swept out the gym, whatever it took to stay in school and keep running.

Four years later, after four more years under Temple's tutelage as a full-time student, Rudolph blossomed into a superstar. She was a combination of fluid motion and raw power, yet she possessed an eerily calm demeanor. Her amazed coach often watched Rudolph sleep quietly off to the side between races.

"Any time I can catch a nap—even for a few minutes—I will," Rudolph explained once.

In 1959, Rudolph blazed to a world-record time in the 200 meters, paving her way to the 1960 Olympics and the moment that would change her life forever.

ುಲ .∞. ೂಲ

"I've heard Wilma described as a fighter, but I'd say she was a conqueror. She didn't fight. She won."

—Anita DeFrantz, former Olympian and one-time member of the International Olympic Committee

• ◆ •

The woman who wasn't supposed to live or walk instead became the fastest woman in the world, a symbol of grace, beauty, and athleticism. The three medals alone were impressive, but it is how Rudolph won them that separated her from other champions. She won the 100 meters by three meters, an absolute blowout; won the 200 meters in 24 seconds flat (the current record, set by Florence Griffith Joyner in 1988, an era of elite training, stands at 21.34); and in the anchor leg of the 4 × 100-meter relay overcome a second-place start behind Germany because of a bad baton pass to lead the United States to a gold medal and a world-record time.

"The feeling of accomplishment welled up inside of me," Rudolph said of her Olympic Games. "Three Olympic gold medals. I knew that was something nobody could take away from me, ever."

Deservedly, she won virtually every award that could be bestowed on her following that Olympic experience; the UPI Athlete of the Year and Associated Press Woman Athlete of the Year, the James E. Sullivan Award for good sportsmanship, and the European Sportswriters' Sportsman of the Year.

Because of her story of inspiration and dedication, Rudolph was the darling of the 1960 Games. Dubbed the "Black Pearl" and the "Black Gazelle" in the media, she was flocked by reporters and besieged by fans. During an international tour following the Olympics, *Sports Illustrated* reported that police in France had to keep fans at bay as they tried to get Rudolph to wave from her bus.

President John F. Kennedy even invited her to the White House.

It was an overwhelming, almost surreal experience for a woman raised with so little and who faced so many staggering setbacks in her early years.

"The 1960 Olympics was my greatest thrill," Rudolph once told the *New York Times*. "And when I think back on it, I still get frightened, to remember a capacity crowd in the stadium all standing and chanting my name."

As unprepared as she might have been for her moment of glory, the twenty-year-old Rudolph did not let the chance to use her popularity for the greater good pass her by.

Buford Ellington, the governor of Tennessee, said he wanted to welcome Rudolph back home with a victory parade. Rudolph agreed to the festivities, but offered a stipulation—there would be no segregation.

Consequently, the homecoming banquet and parade held in Rudolph's hometown of Clarksville was the town's first integrated event.

She retired from track two years later because, she said, she wanted people to remember her at her best. What else might she have accomplished had she stuck with her sport? Maybe competed in another Olympic Games?

Rudolph never had such thoughts. Not one for regrets or looking back, she simply forged ahead.

"What do you do after you are world famous at nineteen or twenty and have sat with prime ministers, kings and queens, the pope?" Rudolph wrote in her autobiography, *Wilma*. "You come back to the real world."

For Rudolph that meant earning her teaching degree from Tennessee State University, marrying her high school sweetheart, Robert Eldridge, and raising her four children.

Initially, she returned to Clarksville, where she taught at her elementary school and took over as track coach at her alma mater, Burt High School.

But she left her hometown not long after and moved to Maine and later to Indianapolis. She gave lectures and coached track for a time at DePauw University in Indiana. She even served as a U.S. Goodwill Ambassador to French West Africa.

"When I was going through my transition of being famous, I tried to ask God why was I here?" she once said. "What was my purpose? Surely it wasn't just to win three gold medals. There has to be more to this life than that."

Rudolph found her answer in 1967 when Senator Hubert Humphrey invited her to serve on Operation Champion, an athletic outreach program for underprivileged children across the country. Spurred by her work there, she began the Wilma Rudolph Foundation, a nonprofit organization dedicated to underprivileged children, a decision she later called her greatest achievement.

Because her own life had been such an inspiration, Rudolph had no problem getting her message across to youngsters who seemingly had little hope.

"I tell them that the most important aspect is to be yourself and have confidence in yourself," she said. "I remind them that triumph can't be had without the struggle."

Long after Rudolph's track career disappeared, the honors kept coming her way. She was inducted into the National Track & Field Hall of Fame in 1974, and in 1983 the U.S. Olympic Hall of Fame welcomed her into its shrine.

After ten years in Indianapolis, Rudolph returned to Tennessee in 1992, taking over as the vice president of Nashville's Baptist Hospital, but two years later she was diagnosed with brain and throat cancer.

She lived just four more months and died quietly at her home on November 12, 1994, at the age of fifty-four.

Rudolph left an indelible impression on her home state. In Tennessee, the same state that kept her and other people of her race separated for much of her childhood, a portion of Highway 79 is named in her honor, and a bronze statue stands in her hometown of Clarksville. On the Tennessee State University campus, some students live in the Wilma G. Rudolph Residence Center, and track and field athletes compete on the Wilma Rudolph indoor track.

Of course, Rudolph's reach extends far beyond Tennessee, and even beyond her sport. The woman who wasn't supposed to walk or even live instead lived and walked a life of example and inspiration to millions of people.

"Never underestimate the power of dreams and the influence of the human spirit," Rudolph said. "We are all the same in this notion, the potential for greatness lives in each of us."

Wilma Rudolph's Life Lessons

Nothing Replaces Self-Confidence

Wilma Rudolph had every reason to doubt herself. She was poor, she was sickly, and in a time when it was a huge disadvantage, she was black. But the one thing Rudolph had was an unflinching belief in herself. "I believe in me more than anything in this world," she said.

Never Underestimate the Power of Love

Polio was not just a diagnosis in the 1940s. It was a death sentence, or at best, a sentence to a handicapped life. Wilma Rudolph never believed that because her family never believed it. Together they defied odds and medical science, relying on each other and loving one another to overcome a horrific illness. "When you come from a large, wonderful family, there's always a way to achieve your goals," she once said.

There Is No Such Thing as Failure

The first time she trained with the Tigerbelles, the track team at Tennessee State University, Wilma Rudolph watched the older, more experienced runners fly by her. Dejected initially, she rebounded quickly to use their strength as her motivation. "Winning is great, sure," she once said. "But if you are really going to do anything in life, the secret is learning how to lose. Nobody goes undefeated all the time. If you can pick up after a crushing defeat and go on to win again, you are going to be a champion someday."

Develop Your Passion

Wilma Rudolph didn't run because she was good at it or because others told her to. She ran because she loved it, and as a result, she succeeded. "When I was running, I had the sense of freedom, of running in the wind," she once told the *New York Times.* "I never forgot all the years when I was a little girl and not able to be involved. When I ran, I felt like a butterfly. That feeling was always there."

Endure the Pain in Order to Enjoy the Success

Had Wilma Rudolph not grown up with polio, of course, she could still have appreciated her Olympic-winning moments. Yet because she endured the hardships and overcame the doubters, winning was much more than just feeling the weight of a medal around her neck. It was a redemptive and glorious moment. "The triumph can't be had," she said, "without the struggle."

❦ 25 ❧

Joan Benoit Samuelson:
Pacesetter

"Success in any field is about the level of your passion."

—JOAN BENOIT SAMUELSON

She blazed through the tunnel and onto the track at the Los Angeles Coliseum, eighty thousand crazed fans screaming as she carried an American flag around the final lap of the first women's marathon in Olympic history. Captured by television cameras and photographs worldwide, the image of Joan Benoit Samuelson heading to the finish line at the 1984 Olympic Games has defined her career.

Strangely, though, that is not the moment Benoit Samuelson recalled when asked about the most important event in her career.

"The 1984 Olympic trials were the most important ever in my sports career," she said. "It was not the most public period, but it laid the groundwork for my whole career."

That Benoit Samuelson chose a moment few followed or cared about, as opposed to the historical one shared by millions, says everything about the petite woman who has been the embodiment of women's long-distance running.

She is from Maine. That, however, is not merely where she is from. It is who she is. Like many Mainers, Benoit Samuelson is a quiet but witty

239

person, a warm woman who is nonetheless reticent with her words. A person of deep integrity, Benoit Samuelson has carried the mantle of her fame with dignity, even if she seems a bit confused as to how she got to be who she is. Far from a braggart, she is the woman who ran by a mural of herself while training for those 1984 Games and didn't even glance up.

Her life, however, offers deep meaning and inspiration. She became a champion in an era when Title IX was enacted but hardly enforced. With few opportunities for young women and even more stigmas about women athletes, Benoit Samuelson proved that women could succeed in the most grueling of disciplines, winning not just that Olympic gold medal but earlier two Boston Marathons.

Hers is not just a story of hard work and perseverance, but of balance. Benoit Samuelson is a wife and a mother who just so happens to be an Olympic legend.

"My life teaches the next generation about the constant need to keep all aspects of your life in the proper balance," she said.

The most important thing, though, that Benoit Samuelson teaches is to trust your own instincts. People scoffed at the notion of a woman running 26.2 miles, yet Benoit Samuelson ran. They argued that training in cool Maine would never prepare her for the heat of Los Angeles. Yet she trained in Maine . . . and won in Los Angeles. They argued that children and childbearing would destroy her career. And yet there she is today, still running, still competing.

> "It's a good thing to be nervous. If you're not nervous before a competition, something's not right."
>
> —JOAN BENOIT SAMUELSON

"Joan teaches all of us to be independent and seek your own path," Mark Bloom, author of *God on the Starting Line,* a book about Benoit Samuelson, and a senior contributor to *Runner's World* said. "Don't worry about doing what's popular."

Growing up, Benoit Samuelson watched her brothers try every athletic avenue granted them. But this was in the early 1970s, before the federal government enacted Title IX in 1979 and long before the impact of the law mandating equal opportunity in extracurricular activities (particularly sports) was felt.

It wasn't that young women weren't interested in sports. There simply weren't opportunities. Benoit Samuelson skied and played tennis, but those were only club sports and not considered terribly competitive.

"Joan once told me when she was a teenager in her little town of Maine, she'd go out to run and feel embarrassed that people were ridiculing her," Bloom said. "She'd make believe she was just out looking at flowers or something. That's how hard it was to break those barriers as a female athlete."

But after breaking her leg in a skiing accident, Benoit Samuelson needed to do something to get back in shape, and so she ran. She quickly realized she had an affinity for it and soon became the only girl on her high school's cross-country team.

She played field hockey as a freshman at Bowdoin College, but struggled with knee pain from the lateral cutting and so instead turned her attention to long-distance running. She transferred for three years to North Carolina State to improve her training regimen but returned to graduate from Bowdoin in 1979. Not long after receiving her diploma, Benoit Samuelson decided she was ready to run the Boston Marathon.

People who can run 26.2 miles in winning times rarely go unnoticed. They are a unique group of incredible athletes. Rarely does an unheralded, obscure individual emerge from the pack and cross the finish line first. It would be akin to a figure skater tossing her name into the mix and winning the U.S. nationals.

"When Joan started there were no women runners, but it didn't deter her. She felt something in her heart and stuck with it."

—Mark Bloom, senior contributor, *Runner's World*

Benoit Samuelson had run just one marathon before entering the 1979 Boston Marathon. She raced with friends in Bermuda, intending to run just half the distance, but when a race official told her she couldn't get a cab until the last racer crossed, she decided to complete the entire thing.

She entered Boston full of confidence but short on knowledge.

"The only thing I knew about the Boston Marathon was that there was supposedly this killer hill—Heartbreak Hill—somewhere along the way," Benoit Samuelson once said. "I kept waiting for it and waiting for it. I even passed a guy on the hill and asked how much longer it was until Heartbreak Hill. He looked at me like I was crazy."

There were a lot more confused people later when Benoit Samuelson, a Boston Red Sox cap atop her cropped hair, crossed the finish line in 2:35:15, blistering the American women's record by ten minutes.

"One word to describe me? Over-my-head."

—JOAN BENOIT SAMUELSON

"Whenever Joan would come to a curve in the road, she would go the long arc of the curve," running legend Amby Burfoot, who trained with Benoit Samuelson in 1984, said. "Most runners take the short arc and when they say they ran eighteen miles they actually went sixteen. When Joan runs eighteen miles, it's more like twenty. There are no shortcuts with Joan. You must put in the work."

Launched into the spotlight of the running world, Benoit Samuelson missed the 1980 Boston Marathon because of an appendectomy and, plagued by injuries, was forced to wear casts for much of 1981 and 1982 on both of her legs. In 1983 when she crossed the Boston finish line first again, this time beating a world record not long removed from an Achilles tendon injury, the shock and amazement was every bit as strong as in 1979.

As often happens, Benoit Samuelson was blessed with good timing as well as an athletic gift. In 1984, the Olympics finally allowed women to compete in its original event, the marathon. On the heels of her win in Boston, Benoit Samuelson should have been the favorite—an American racing legend running in America for the first Olympic marathon. But just months before the Olympics and only seventeen days before the Olympic trials, Benoit Samuelson had arthroscopic surgery on her knee.

She arrived at the Olympic trials a jumble of nerves, as unsure of her ability as her competitors.

"Joanie was petrified of the trials," her coach, Bob Sevene, recalled in a 1999 interview.

The thing about Benoit Samuelson, though, is she doesn't hide from a challenge. The same young girl who broke barriers by competing in boys cross-country shook off the notion that a knee simply couldn't go 26.2 miles only weeks removed from a surgical repair.

Benoit Samuelson is not a follower. She marches to her own beat, and it is a beat she trusts instinctively.

"I visited Joan six months before the Olympics," Burfoot said. "All the other top runners were training in Arizona or other warm weather locations to prepare for the summer heat in California. Not Joan. She was training in Maine while remodeling a broken down old farmhouse. That's typical of Joan. She remains true to her heart and proves that real strength is internal, not external."

Buoyed by that spirit and confidence, Benoit Samuelson won the Olympic trials, and though she still remained an underdog as the Olympic Games dawned, she emerged a legend.

"Joan had this deep-seated belief in herself and a vision of what she could become. That gave her the motivation to prove she was the very best."

—JOHN BABBINGTON,
BOSTON-AREA RUNNING COACH

On August 5, 1984, Benoit Samuelson started out with the pack of fifty runners, but after three miles, troubled by the slow pace, broke out on her own. Veteran race watchers questioned the move—Allan Steinfeld, then the chief referee for the Olympic marathons, told the *Portland Press Herald* he remembered thinking, "'Aw, what are you doing, Joanie?' I saw her run in the Olympic trials and knew she was an incredible woman, but this was the Olympics. There were some very strong women in that pack that could chop her up."

Except they didn't.

"For an athlete, she had a very quiet, laid-back personality, but she was a risk taker," said John Babbington, a Boston-area running coach who trained Benoit Samuelson when she was younger. "She often disregarded conventional wisdom because she wanted to go where others had never been."

Unable to challenge the diminutive American, the competition watched instead as Benoit Samuelson's lead only grew. By the time she reached the tunnel that would take her into the Coliseum, she was alone.

"I remember thinking on opening day what it might be like to run through that tunnel alone," Benoit Samuelson told the *Portland Press Herald.* "I told myself there's only one way to find out. You're going to have to do it."

The image of Benoit Samuelson emerging from the tunnel and into the sun-dappled stadium, carrying an American flag and a huge smile, is one that will forever live in Olympic lore. She seized the moment at exactly the right time—the first Olympic marathon ever run by women, won by an American woman in an American city.

"Joan Benoit Samuelson is a great athlete who achieved her success the old-fashioned way—focus and hard work."

—BILL RODGERS, U.S. MARATHON LEGEND

It was electrifying and exhilarating for everyone in the stadium.

Overcome and overwhelmed, Benoit Samuelson remembers funny things from that day. She told me she remembers a makeshift paper hat she wore through the race, one she took with her through drug testing and into the press conference.

"Then we went to lunch, and I put it down at the buffet line and never saw it again," Benoit Samuelson said. "People ask me all the time about that hat, and I have no idea where it is. Maybe it'll show up on eBay one day."

Benoit Samuelson vowed on the day she went from running legend to American legend that she wouldn't change.

To her credit she hasn't.

All you need to know about Benoit Samuelson is that her gold medal sits, she once told *Sports Illustrated,* in a drawer "with window cranks and batteries and Christmas ornaments. Occasionally the drawer swells because of the weather and I can't get into it at all."

Injuries hindered Benoit Samuelson's career after the Olympics. She won the Chicago Marathon in 1985 and ran the 1987 Boston Marathon, even though she was pregnant, but her body couldn't handle the rigors of the major races.

The injuries, though, didn't dampen Benoit Samuelson's spirit.

Humble doesn't begin to describe Benoit Samuelson. A woman who has achieved iconic status said she is most proud of her family, her husband and her two sons, and that when she defines her life it is in two eras: "B.C. (before children) and A.D. (after diapers)." Instead of orchestrating her family around her life, she does just the opposite, training and speaking and working whenever her children's schedule allows.

Aside from her family, her life revolves around helping others. She realized a dream when she began the Beacon to Beach 10K in 1997. The race, which begins at Crescent Beach and ends at Portland Head Light, the nation's first commissioned lighthouse, takes runners through some of Benoit Samuelson's favorite training grounds and through her beloved home state of Maine.

It also benefits Shine the Light for Kids, a nonprofit organization that donates proceeds from the race to a different Maine youth-based program each year.

"If Joan sees a need, she wants to reach out and make a difference," U.S. marathon legend Bill Rodgers said. "She's fun and smart and a delight to be around. Joan is a real role model for young girls. They should all try to be like Joan."

More, they should all try to learn about Benoit Samuelson. Today's generation of young girls and young women are the lucky ones. There are no barriers left to break, no hurdles left to leap. The women who came before them took care of that, paving the way not just for Title IX but for its enforcement. High school athletic facilities are as apt to be filled by young girls as young boys, and scholarship opportunities are plentiful for everyone.

No one has to stop and pretend to smell a flower, embarrassed to be training hard, as Benoit Samuelson did. She literally blazed the trail in every step of her training miles, her marathons, and mostly, in those Olympic gold medal 26.2 miles in Los Angeles.

"My mother used to say she had no idea where the fire in my belly came from," Benoit Samuelson said. "But I do know. Success in any field is about the level of your passion."

Joan Benoit Samuelson's Life Lessons

Perseverance

Done in by a knee injury right before the Olympic trials, no one would have blamed Joan Benoit Samuelson if she had thrown in the towel and pointed her star four years down the road. Aside from the physical pain, she had the emotional insecurity of wondering just what her body would allow her to do. Instead of letting fear grip her, though, Benoit Samuelson simply put her head down and ran. "You can't quit along the way," she said.

Persistence

It would be so easy to take a day off, to not train when the weather is rotten, to skip a run when your knees ache or your muscles are screaming. Joan Benoit Samuelson, like every other athlete, had those days. There were days when she wasn't sure if she could race, but as she once said, "I can always run." And so on the hard days, Benoit Samuelson plugged, or sometimes plodded, on, knowing that with every small step comes a greater reward. "Keep at it," she said, "a little bit every day."

Passion

There are few sports more solitary than distance running. Alone for hours with no teammates to motivate you and no coaches offering instruction, it takes discipline and single-mindedness. Foremost, though, it requires passion. It is too grueling a sport, demanding too much of a person's self to pursue without a true love. "I don't look at running as a career, successful or unsuccessful," Joan Benoit Samuelson told *USA Today* in 1993. "I look at it as a passion or challenge or opportunity to do something that makes me feel good, to do something I love."

Patience

No one laces up a pair of sneakers and runs 26.2 miles on the first day. Most folks don't make 2.2 miles on that first day. As much as distance running is about the long haul, it is also about baby steps. Joan Benoit Samuelson enjoyed surprising success, winning the Boston Marathon in 1979, but the out-of-nowhere aspect of her victory was only apparent to outsiders. To Benoit Samuelson, crossing that finish line was years in the making, years of lonely days in Maine during high school and challenging training runs in North Carolina during college. "It takes time," she said. "You can't rush success."

❦26❦

Annika Sorenstam:
Focus

"I don't try to be in the spotlight. I let my game speak for itself."

—ANNIKA SORENSTAM

Of all the athletes in all the sports who might pick a fight over gender equality, Annika Sorenstam would seem the least likely. A quiet, humble Swede who wants simply to play the best golf she can, Sorenstam is no latter-day Billie Jean King interested in waging a Battle of the Sexes II.

And yet on a May day in 2003, there stood Sorenstam, about to tee off at the famed Hogan's Alley and go head-to-head against the men in their own event, the Bank of America Colonial.

Critics and even supporters wanted to make it about a woman versus the men, Ladies Professional Golf Association (LPGA) versus Professional Golf Association (PGA), but to Sorenstam it was much simpler.

It wasn't about any broad meanings or defining moments.

It was about herself.

"A story that illustrates who I am would have to be playing against the men at Colonial," Sorenstam said. "This showed my drive, determination, and how I always strive to get better."

People try to complicate Sorenstam, to dig beneath that reserved veneer and find out what makes her tick. They want to understand a woman who has dominated a sport like none before her, a woman who makes a game as frustrating as golf look so easy.

Really, though, Sorenstam isn't that complicated. She is good because she works hard. She is successful because she is never satisfied, and she constantly improves because she's always looking for the next challenge.

Perhaps that seems a rather basic recipe to explain a woman who has redefined her sport, but as Confucius once said, "Life is really simple, but we insist on making it complicated."

For so many people, a passion becomes a burden. Living up to expectations and always trying to improve can sap the fun out of anything, and for athletes who compete in the bubble of public viewing, it can be even more difficult. Sorenstam rarely struggles with that. Of course, she has days when her game isn't at its best, but at the end of the day her disappointment never overwhelms her.

She won't allow it to.

When I asked her what her biggest fear is, Sorenstam said, "Not being able to do something that I enjoy." That's really what everyone wants to be able to do, but so often, we lose sight of that simple goal. Sorenstam never has, and it is a good measure of why she is her game's greatest player.

"I tell people if you're kicking yourself because you didn't see Michael Jordan or Wayne Gretzky or Nolan Ryan in their primes, you should see Annika play because athletes like this only come around once in a lifetime," former LPGA commissioner Ty Votaw has said of Sorenstam.

Since turning pro in 1994 and winning Rookie of the Year honors that year, Sorenstam has been compared to Tiger Woods, so strong has been her stranglehold on women's golf. The truth is, Woods ought to be compared to Sorenstam. Her dominance is more complete. A record eight-time Player of the Year, Sorenstam is the only LPGA player to five times win Player of the Year honors, the top spot on the official money list, and the Vare Trophy, given to the woman with the season's lowest scoring average. Twice she has won ten or more tournaments in a season and owns ten major championships trophies (to Woods' twelve). The first woman to break sixty, she is already a member of both the LPGA and World Golf Halls of Fame.

"I have to be honest, I do pinch myself sometimes when I look at my results," Sorenstam once said. "I mean, I feel like I'm just a little girl from Sweden that came over here to follow my dreams and hope to win a few golf tournaments. . . . I feel like, have I really done this? Is it really true?"

Her tournament title haul to date is sixty-nine. The record of eighty-eight belongs to Kathy Whitworth, and Sorenstam, who has said she'd like someday soon to have children, is by no means ready to retire.

"She psychs most players out before they tee it up," legendary coach David Leadbetter told *USA Today* in 2005. "It's a natural response, like the way players reacted to what Tiger did in 2000. When you win as much as she does, that aura rubs off on people."

Now ordinary people will have a chance to feel that aura. Not content to make her mark with just her clubs, Sorenstam recently opened her new golf academy near Orlando, Florida. Annika's Academy of Golf & Fitness is geared toward students of all ages and genders, with Henri Reis, her longtime coach, and Kai Fusser, her longtime trainer, providing the instruction.

Just as she takes charge of her golf career, Sorenstam has taken charge of this project. She has worked directly with building contractors to make sure the 5,400-square-foot center is designed just as she wants it. From the colors of the sofa in the lobby—blue and gold like the flag of her native Sweden—to the exercise equipment, Sorenstam's handprints are all over her facility.

"It's hard to compare this to golf, but it's like winning a major," Sorenstam told *USA Today*. "When I was a little girl growing up in Sweden, I had big dreams. One was to be an LPGA player. As I grew up, other dreams followed. My goal is to inspire. I hope I'm just at the beginning of my vision."

Students in the school might be a bit overwhelmed when Sorenstam joins their foursome, but the funny thing about Sorenstam is that off the links there is nothing intimidating at all about her. Quiet to the point of being shy, she is thrilled that she tends to blend into the background. When she was younger, Sorenstam said she would purposely play badly or three putt toward the end of a tournament just to avoid the victory speech left to the winner.

"My coach saw this was a problem for me," Sorenstam said. "So he encouraged the second and third place finishers to speak as well. I figured that I should start winning, as the others were made to give a speech, too!"

An unlikely superstar, yes, but Sorenstam is hardly a surprise success. Born into an athletic family—her parents, Tom and Gunilla, as well as younger sister, Charlotta, all skied and played tennis, volleyball, and badminton—Sorenstam was blessed not only with the ability to play sports, but the desire for excellence. A fan of tennis star Bjorn Borg she longed to be a tennis star and made that her first athletic focus.

The Sorenstam sisters—Charlotta also played—were a force in the junior tennis rankings, with Annika rising as high as twelfth among Swedish juniors and Charlotta to number ten.

"My parents are loving and supportive and always allowed me to explore different interests," Sorenstam said. "My sister is another strong influence in my life, always supportive and ready to challenge me. My family always made me believe that I could follow any dreams that I had, and my father taught me that there are no shortcuts to success."

Competitive as she was, though, Sorenstam soon grew frustrated with her inability to master tennis. Opponents realized she had a weak backhand and exploited it in matches. By sixteen, Sorenstam had enough. She quit the game on the spot, telling her father she was burned out, and she looked for another outlet for her athletic abilities.

"I love the challenge, and I love coming down the stretch and making the shots you need to."

—ANNIKA SORENSTAM

She found golf. Introduced to the game by her golf-playing parents when she was twelve and already working part-time with Henri Reis at fourteen, Sorenstam put all her efforts into the game once she set down her tennis racquet.

To a lot of people golf is, as Mark Twain once wrote, a good walk spoiled. A person can play the same course fifty times and never play it the same. But to Sorenstam, it was the perfect outlet. There is no opponent across the net to compete with, only yourself and the course. Mastery comes from repetition and hard work, two things that Sorenstam was very good at.

Reis, who still coaches Sorenstam, taught Sorenstam about tempo and rhythm and helped her develop a swing that by now is as effortless and natural to Sorenstam as a morning stretch.

"My biggest influence with golf has been my one and only coach, Henri Reis," Sorenstam said. "His teaching is simplistic, and he has made me the consistent player that I am."

Add Reis's instruction to Sorenstam's sheer will, and well, the simple recipe for greatness takes form. Sweden, of course, isn't the ideal setting for a golfer. Snow covers the ground for much of the year, but on the days snow blanketed her course, Sorenstam simply used orange balls.

"You can't believe her focus, her determination, her preparation over the winter months," none other than Tiger Woods said of Sorenstam to *USA Today* in 2005. "She didn't get to this level by just hoping she could play well. She went out and worked."

Like Borg, the tennis icon, Sorenstam was fortunate to have women in her own country to serve as golf role models. Pia Nilsson, who starred at Arizona State University and enjoyed moderate success on the LPGA, took the reins of the Swedish Golf Federation just as Sorenstam was coming into her own.

"Annika is a lot more
than a golfer."

—Pia Nilsson, former Swedish golfer

"She taught me to ask questions, to face my fears, and to think ahead," Sorenstam said of Nilsson.

Nilsson took Sorenstam under her wing, and in 1990, helped Sorenstam garner a golf scholarship from the University of Arizona. In two years in Tucson, Sorenstam was twice named an all-American, as well as College Player of the Year, and won one national title. As a sophomore she also qualified for the U.S. Open.

"Annika sets her vision so high," Nilsson said. "She's always striving for excellence and really believes she can shoot fifty-four or lower."

It is that inner confidence that convinced Sorenstam to join the professional ranks in 1993—despite finishing twenty-four strokes behind champion Patty Sheehan in that U.S. Open. When asked to describe herself in one word, she came up with the perfect answer.

"Committed," she said.

In 1993, Sorenstam joined the European Tour, figuring the competition wasn't as stiff as in the United States, so she could get her feet wet as a professional. In ten tournaments, she finished second four times and easily won the tour's Rookie of the Year honors.

A year later, she came to the LPGA. Up and down in the beginning of her season, Sorenstam proved her mettle to fans and media at the British Open where she weathered tough English conditions to finish in a tie for second place. Spearheaded by her strong season at the tough major, Sorenstam finished the year in strong form, earning Rookie of the Year in the LPGA.

"A lot of people can do what she does for one round. She does it four days in a row."

—JULI INKSTER, LPGA HALL OF FAME GOLFER

A year later, she was the tour's Player of the Year.

That's not normal, of course, certainly not in the intricate game of golf where the wiles of a veteran often overcome the sheer talent of up-and-comers. Only one other woman, in fact, followed a Rookie of the Year season with a Player of the Year season— the revered Nancy Lopez.

"Annika is a fabulous golfer," Lopez said. "I love the way she sets goals in her life and career and then goes after them with all she's got. I admire that a lot."

In 1995, Sorenstam finished in the top ten in four of her first five events and came to Colorado's Broadmoor Golf Club for the U.S. Open in fine form. For years, Sorenstam had set her sights on that one open, dating back to when her countrywoman Liselotte Neumann took the title in 1988. For Sorenstam, the U.S. Open represented the pinnacle of golf.

Heading into Sunday's final round, Sorenstam trailed leader Meg Mallon by five strokes, but with her calm approach belying the butterflies flitting through her stomach, Sorenstam put together a sixty-eight for the day and went to the clubhouse ahead of Mallon by one stroke. When the veteran missed a birdie putt on the final hole, Sorenstam won her first major and, at twenty-four, became the fifth youngest U.S. Open champion in history.

"Annika is like the little engine that could," LPGA announcer and former star Donna Caponi said. "She studied engineering in school and keeps chugging along the golf course. She just engineers her way around the course with a well-grooved swing. Her swing never changes and is locked in her muscle memory."

"With golf it's all about business. Annika wants to be the best woman golfer ever and sweep away all the records."

—Donna Caponi, golf analyst

Paired with a second consecutive runner-up finish at the British Open plus a ten-stroke win at the GHP Heartland Classic and a playoff win against legendary Laura Davies at the World Championships of World Golf, Sorenstam finished the year as the money leader on the U.S., European, and Australian tours, a feat never before accomplished.

Along with Player of the Year honors from the LPGA, Sorenstam was fêted as the World Player of the Year by *Golf World,* the first woman to win the magazine's award, and was named Sweden's Athlete of the Year.

It was only the beginning of a career that, though sidelined recently by a nagging back injury, still doesn't have a finish line in sight.

Most people would have been more than pleased with Sorenstam's early professional efforts. By 2000, she already had amassed enough points to qualify for the LPGA Hall of Fame (though she had to wait until 2003 for the ten-year Tour membership requirement to kick in).

But where others saw greatness, Sorenstam saw a hole. Winless in the major tournaments, she ended the 2000 season determined to become, believe it or not, better. She hired a personal trainer who put her through grueling sessions that included push-ups with weight plates on her back and pull-ups with leaded weights on her ankles. From kickboxing to cycling to running to swimming, the always athletic Sorenstam cross-trained herself into an even more gifted athlete.

"Annika is brutally honest with herself and doesn't play the blame game," Pia Nilsson explained. "She stubbornly sticks with trying to improve and is building her skills all the time."

With drives soaring as far as three hundred yards, Sorenstam tackled the

2001 season with a vengeance and, not surprisingly, quickly ended that major tournament drought when she won the LPGA Championship, the first major of the season. By year's end she became the first woman to cross the $2 million mark for earnings in a season and, at one point, won four consecutive tournaments.

"I focus on the basics and the positives in my life."

—ANNIKA SORENSTAM

A year later she became only the second woman to win eleven tournaments in one season and in 2003 won the British Open to complete the career Grand Slam.

Hardly resting on such laurels, Sorenstam won the 2005 Mizuno Classic in Japan, becoming the first player in LPGA Tour history to win the same tournament five consecutive times, and after an eight-tournament winless streak in 2006 caused some to wonder if she was slipping, Sorenstam roared back to win the U.S. Women's Open in an eighteen-hole playoff for her tenth major title, tying her for third on the all-time women's list.

"Of course I felt some pressure all week," Sorenstam said afterward. "That is what motivates me. That is why I play this game. To come here and do something like this, it's just very gratifying."

Despite such overwhelming supremacy, Sorenstam remains an everywoman of a sort. *Sports Illustrated* columnist Rick Reilly once spent a day with Sorenstam where a security officer at an autographing session asked Sorenstam if she had a visitor's badge. He had no idea she was the guest of honor. Other people in line to meet the famous golfer butchered the pronunciation of her name. "This is a golfer who has won fifteen more times than Tiger Woods since the beginning of 2002," Reilly wrote. "Can you imagine someone saying, 'So, Teeger, how do you pronounce your last name?'"

Sorenstam was just fine with the inattention. It appealed to her shyness and it also sat well with her simple desire to just be a golfer.

During a pro-am event at Donald Trump's Trump International Golf Club in 2003, the real estate mogul was asked if he thought Sorenstam was missing the boat on endorsements and appearance fees that could quadruple her already hefty income.

The Donald demurred. "Her whole thing is to be the best golfer she can be," he said of his pro-am partner. "That's what motivates her. She's not interested in anything that gets in the way."

This, of course, is what made Sorenstam's decision to play with the men so curious. Here was a woman who eschewed the spotlight walking right into the glare of it. Sorenstam, though, wasn't doing this for publicity or, frankly, for women's rights. As Trump explained, she wants to become the best golfer she can, and in her mind, the best way to challenge that is to play with the best.

And so, when officials from the Colonial Country Club in Fort Worth, Texas, home to a PGA Tour event since 1946, extended an invitation to Sorenstam, she accepted, becoming the first woman since 1945 to play in a PGA Tour event.

From professional golfers, both men and women, to weekend duffers, everyone had an opinion on her decision, and with more pressure than perhaps any golfer has ever endured, Sorenstam more than carried her weight. She finished five over par for two rounds, missing the cut by four shots but comporting herself with dignity and proving that she is among the game's best, man or woman.

"Success to me is reaching your personal goals and seeing the results of your achievements," Sorenstam said. "Success is not only the final destination but also the process and journey along the way. To me, success is not always about wins and losses, but rather knowing when to take one step back to be able to take two steps forward."

Annika Sorenstam's Life Lessons

Have Patience

"Have patience"—two simple words, yet two of the most difficult to live by. Greatness, not even for the great ones, rarely happens overnight, and for Annika Sorenstam success required hours and hours of solitary practice rounds and tedious drills. She did not blast onto the international golf scene so much as methodically plow her way to the top; Annika believed in taking her time and learning along the way because she has what so many people who lack patience miss out on—longevity. "For me, golf is a lifestyle," she said. "I have passion for the game, and I believe this is important."

Keep an Optimistic Outlook

If ever a game was invented to destroy an optimistic spirit, it is golf. Mere inches can decide victory or defeat, a great shot or a disaster. But in Annika Sorenstam you will never see the bad manners or angry reactions so often exhibited on a golf course. "I would like to be remembered as someone who loved the game of golf," Sorenstam said. "I want to be remembered as a woman with great sportsmanship."

When You Get an Opportunity, Take It

Turning down the chance to play in a PGA Tour event would have been the easy thing. Annika Sorenstam would have avoided the negative attention, the critics, and the inevitable questions. But saying no also would have denied Sorenstam the chance to measure herself against golf's greatest athletes, and that would have been far worse than any publicity she'd have to endure. "Pressure? I love it," Sorenstam once said. "That is what keeps me motivated and keeps me going."

Surround Yourself with Good People

Blessed with a loving family, Annika Sorenstam also has been fortunate to work with the same people for the better part of her career. The two coaches closest to her, Henri Reis and Pia Nilsson, have known Sorenstam since she was a teenager. They, like her parents and sister, care not just about Annika Sorenstam the golfer, but about Annika Sorenstam the person, and always have her best interest at heart. "I know I can count on them for anything," Sorenstam said.

27

Dawn Staley:
Inspirational

"No regrets. No sorrow."

—Dawn Staley

To outsiders, to people who don't know Dawn Staley, her life would appear charmed. She has segued from high school superstar to college superstar to international superstar to professional superstar to coaching superstar.

She is a point guard with a Midas touch, good at everything she tries, turning three Olympic medals into gold.

But a charmed life?

No, silver spoons aren't handed out in the Raymond Rosen projects where Staley grew up. Aristocracy and blue-bloodedness don't get you respect at the courts on the corner of 25th and Diamond in North Philadelphia, where Staley learned to play basketball.

"One word to describe me?" Staley said. "Odds-beater."

Staley is the first to admit her life now is charmed. She often finds herself caught between amazed and overwhelmed at the bounty that basketball has brought her. She has been lauded by her hometown, celebrated by USA Basketball, and honored by the Red Cross and the WNBA.

Ever humble, Staley isn't sure what she's done to deserve it, but a quick glance at her hoops resume might explain it. From the time she picked up a basketball, she has been a star: *USA Today* High School National Player of the Year, two-time NCAA Player of the Year, three-time Olympic gold medalist, United States' flag bearer at the 2004 Olympic Games, two-time USA Basketball Female Athlete of the Year, four-time WNBA All-Star, and two-time Atlantic 10 Coach of the Year. Those are just the highlights.

In Philadelphia, where a seven-story mural of her once hung from a downtown building, she is beloved, as respected and admired as the city's other native basketball child, Wilt Chamberlain. Tell a Philly kid that he plays like Dawn Staley, more than likely he'll say, "Thank you." Yes, even a boy. Staley isn't a good female basketball player. She's good. Period.

Staley, however, has never been satisfied being just a good basketball player. She's always strived to be more, to turn her own successes into opportunities for others. Her Dawn Staley Foundation, begun in 1996, is geared toward helping kids who grew up in neighborhoods just like hers, offering them after-school programs, basketball clinics, and most important, a shining example of a woman who has made it.

"There is no better teacher than the ups and downs of sports. You learn how to take tests every day and how to pass them."

—DAWN STALEY

And in 2000, though still a star player in her own right, Staley took over the moribund Temple University women's basketball program. She has resuscitated the program from doormat to dominant, leading the Owls to their first Atlantic 10 Tournament title—and their second and third—their first top twenty-five ranking, and into the NCAA Tournament three times in five seasons.

She did all that while continuing to play all-star caliber basketball for the Charlotte Sting of the WNBA, not retiring until the end of the 2006 season.

Charmed? Indeed.

Except Staley knows her own backstory. She knows what she's had to overcome and how difficult parts of the journey were. She knows that she remains the exception, the one who got away to a lifetime of success instead of the majority who succumbed to the hardscrabble world that surrounded them.

There is no charm in that, only hard work and sacrifice, perseverance and struggle.

"When I think about Dawn," Renee Brown, the WNBA vice president, said, "I think about hope."

In 1957, Estelle Staley moved to North Philadelphia. Life wasn't easy. A single mother with five children—three boys and two girls—she cleaned other people's homes to make ends meet.

Strong-willed and tough, Estelle didn't let her children get away with anything. Just because she might be at work, they were still expected to mind the rules.

"Dawn teaches players that you can be undersized and make it."
—LINDA HILL MCDONALD,
FORMER WNBA COACH

"My mother raised me and was my inspiration," Staley, the youngest in the family, said. "She instilled discipline in me and did it with her black belt. I was more scared of my mother than anything out there in the community. That was a good thing. I couldn't cut corners in my house, so I sure wasn't going to do it outside, either."

What Staley did do outside was play sports. She was, her mother once said, "a jock," plain and simple. As a kid, Staley tormented her older brothers to let her tag along for games of basketball, football, whatever they were into. Grudgingly, they'd bring her along, where invariably she'd be teased and ridiculed.

She never stopped tagging along.

The teasing, however, didn't last.

"Used to be the boys in the neighborhood knocked on the door looking for Dawn's brothers to play touch football," Estelle Staley told the *Philadelphia Inquirer* in 1996. "Then it was her brothers and Dawn they looked for. Then it was just Dawn."

With an okay from her mother, Staley would stay out until 2:00 AM playing basketball. She didn't look like much of a player, what with her five-foot, five-inch frame, but what Staley lacked in inches she made up for in spunk and attitude, hard earned in years of playing with the boys at the Hank Gathers Recreation Center.

"Too many times I get people who are so into the results they forget about the effort," Staley said in *It's How You Play the Game*. "It's effort that will get you where you have to be. I always look for the hustler over the natural talent. . . . Give me a player who hustles or a teammate who's trying and I guarantee I'll get results."

Blessed with an almost intuitive ability to see the court, she can razzle-dazzle with the best of them, but truer to her nature, Staley never set out to be a street performer with a basketball.

"I was eight years old when the 76ers drafted Maurice Cheeks in 1978," Staley said. "I loved to watch him play because he simplified the game. At one point I wanted to play the game like Magic Johnson, but then I decided to play the game in a simple and consistent way like Mo."

At Dobbins Tech, high school alma mater to Hank Gathers and Bo Kimble, Staley's simple and consistent game led her team to three Public League championships and earned her national Player of the Year honors, as well as a scholarship to the University of Virginia.

> *"Dawn takes total responsibility for the team and pushes them to their limits. The end result is she has the total respect of her teammates."*
>
> —WNBA Coach Nell Fortner

In Staley's four years at the University of Virginia, the Cavaliers went 110–21 and went to three Final Fours. In Staley's junior season, Virginia lost a 70–67 overtime heartbreaker in the national championship game. Staley, however, was named Most Outstanding Player of the Final Four, the first time the award had gone to a player from the losing team.

"Dawn has great character to go along with her drive to succeed," USC basketball coach Marianne Stanley said. "Dawn has laserlike focus, and in her mind, nothing is insurmountable."

A three-time all-American, Staley was named College Player of the Year in her junior and senior seasons. She is one of only three players to have her number retired at Virginia and the only Atlantic Coast Conference player (male or female) to amass more than 2,000 points, 700 rebounds, 700 assists, and 400 steals in her career.

"When Dawn was teeny tiny playing in the eighth grade, you could see she was something very special to the game from the minute you saw her play," Staley's college coach Debbie Ryan told *USA Today.* "She was always a very insightful player who understood the game. She exudes team play all the time, on the court and off the court."

With that summary, plus the liner notes from Virginia's record books where her name appeared frequently, Staley headed to Colorado Springs in 1992 for the U.S. Olympic trials. Not nearly arrogant enough to consider herself a lock, she was nonetheless devastated when she was the last player cut, and the team went to Barcelona without her.

It was the first time in Staley's basketball life that she really didn't know where to turn. There was no Women's National Basketball Associaton (WNBA), no professional league of any kind in this country for women.

"I asked the coaches why I got cut, and they said two reasons: too short and not enough international experience," Staley said. "I couldn't do anything about my height, but I got a job overseas and started getting the right kind of experience. That was a pivotal time for me. I could've packed it in, but I wasn't willing to do that."

Instead, Staley hopped around Europe and South America, playing in France, Italy, Brazil, and Spain.

One of Staley's favorite sayings, culled from, of all places, the movie *House Party 2,* is "Do what you don't want to do to get what you want." It's one of the life lessons she remembered and certainly fit this time of her life.

"I'd describe Dawn in one word—generous."

—Val Ackerman, former president of the WNBA

The nomadic overseas life wasn't easy—Staley once joked she smuggled contraband macaroni and cheese and Philadelphia-born Tastykakes into her luggage—but Staley had set out to prove her detractors wrong, and more important, she set out to represent her country.

She did what she didn't want to do to achieve her goal.

"Everywhere I've ever played, I've put forth my best effort and gave it all I had," she said. "I have no regrets about anything. I've never cried if I fail because I held nothing back. Here's how I like to put it—you can't force tears out of your eyes. No regrets. No sorrows."

In 1994, Staley returned to the States for the Goodwill Games and the World Championships. The United States won gold and bronze respectively, and Staley was named MVP of the Goodwill Games. USA Basketball, the same organization that had cut her two years earlier, named her its Female Athlete of the Year.

When it came time to announce the roster for the 1996 Olympic Games in Atlanta, Staley's inclusion was a given.

"I wouldn't want to mess up and let Dawn down," Staley's Olympic teammate and roommate Lisa Leslie said. "Dawn tried to bring out the perfection in me and kept my game at a high level. She has the heart of a lion. I learned how to fight and compete from her."

That Olympic team, of course, was the launching pad for women's basketball. The women's Dream Team went 60–0 en route to their Olympic gold medal and fed the frenzy that would become the American Basketball League (ABL) and, later, the WNBA.

As much as what Staley did on the court inspired others to play like her, what she did off the court inspired her friends and teammates to be like her. During an Olympic warm-up tournament in China, Staley coerced her teammates, enjoying the largesse that only comes with being an American Olympic athlete, to chip in their sneakers, shirts, and even their sports bras for the less fortunate Cuban team.

"She saw the girls were impoverished and didn't have anything," Brown remembered. "The Cuban girls had to sneak into the room, and we gave them all of the items we'd gathered. Dawn doesn't forget where she came from and has kept an open heart."

When Staley returned home from her Olympic experience, rather than taking center stage at a party in her honor, Staley went out and bought a bunch of barbecue grills and food, hired a DJ, and invited her neighborhood out for a Day in the Park.

It was the first event for the newly formed Dawn Staley Foundation.

But unlike many professional athletes who turn their multimillion-dollar paychecks into charitable foundations, Staley didn't really have a salary to draw from. There were no mega signing bonuses from the upstart ABL, no million-dollar endorsements to cash in.

Staley made the foundation happen because she wanted it to happen. She called on Nike, the company that had started working with her that year, for a donation and literally went from business to business, capitalizing on her name to cull sponsorships.

"Dawn has given so much back to Philadelphia," longtime basketball reporter Dick Weiss, who still lives in the Philadelphia area, said. "She's the best woman player ever to come out of this area and a real role model to the community."

Today, some twenty-five hundred people attend the annual Day in the Park, and Staley's foundation has helped countless at-risk kids. In 2005, the city of Philadelphia presented Staley with its prestigious John Wanamaker Athletic Award, given to a person or team that "reflects credit upon Philadelphia." Staley is the only individual woman to earn the award.

She's won it twice.

"My greatest success in life has been starting my foundation, working with kids in the North Philadelphia area," Staley said. "I love working with youngsters on a daily basis and making a difference in their lives. I want to give them hope in what might be considered hopeless situations."

There is no better inspiration, of course, than an example, and Staley continues to inspire. She joined the WNBA's Charlotte Sting in 1999 after the ABL folded and enjoyed four all-star seasons there.

In 2000, she took the job at Temple, leading the Owls to a 19–11 record that season and the Women's National Invitation Tournament.

That summer she hopped a plane for Sydney, bringing home a lovely trinket—her second Olympic gold medal.

For the next three years, Staley was a whirling dervish of basketball, splitting her time between Temple and the WNBA's Charlotte Sting. Though her schedule would exhaust most people, Staley thrived as well as survived. She took the Sting to the WNBA Finals in 2001 and the Owls to their first Atlantic 10 Tournament title in 2002.

In 2004, she added two-time Dream Team member to her resume, heading to Athens for her third Olympic Games.

The U.S. contingent at the 2004 Olympic Games was an uneasy contingent. The United States was just one year into the Iraq War, a decision condemned by many internationally, and anti-American sentiment was commonplace abroad. Athletes wondered how they would be received, if the Greek fans in attendance would actually boo when the American flag entered the stadium for the opening ceremonies.

Suddenly the honorary flag bearer, a position always of great distinction, was more than just a token job. It needed a person beyond reproach, as well as a person tough enough to handle whatever reception the fans might offer.

The girl from North Philly got the job.

"If America really wants to defend itself, if it wants to reshape perceptions, Staley is a great place to start," wrote *St. Petersburg (FL) Times* columnist Gary Shelton. "She is the best of us, an example that, in America, it is possible to mold a wonderful life from a humble beginning. She is smart, unselfish, talented, passionate, charitable. Which of these qualities should fans boo first?"

None, as it would turn out. The Americans were received, if not warmly then at least not rudely, and the Games went on.

"Dawn is as solid as a rock, and you can count on her in a pinch," WNBA coach Van Chancellor said. "Her word means everything. Dawn is a mature, warm human being."

It was to be Staley's swan song. Not surprisingly, she went out on top. Now a savvy veteran, she passed the torch to the next generation, a generation of players who watched her play, who fell in love with basketball because of her.

After switching teams to the Houston Comets, Staley retired from the WNBA in 2006, leaving in her wake a legacy of young stars who now strive to fill the sneakers of a five-foot, five-inch player who left a gigantic imprint.

"Dawn Staley is the best ambassador the WNBA ever had," WNBA player Nikki McCray said.

An international star, Staley returned to where it all began and quietly went back to work. As Temple enjoyed its best season in 2005, including a national record twenty-five-game winning streak at one point, media started to visit the coach who seemingly does it all and does it all well.

Staley, naturally, deflected the praise and attention from herself. She talked about her players—their hard work, their sacrifices.

"When I got this job in 2005, Dawn sent me a letter, and I still carry it around with me for inspiration," Donna Orender, president of the WNBA, said. "The gist of the letter is it's so important to make a difference. That's how she views the world."

If pressed, Staley could tell her players her own story. Her goal, as always, wasn't to impress.

She wanted to inspire.

"There was bleakness all around me and an attitude that you won't amount to much because of where you grew up," Staley said. "I always have wanted to prove the naysayers wrong and inspire the next generation that they can succeed, too. It doesn't matter where you come from if you find your passion and work hard at it."

Dawn Staley's Life Lessons

Do What You Don't Want to Do to Get What You Want

That is more than Dawn Staley's life lesson. It is her personal motto. To achieve her goals and realize her dreams, Dawn always has been willing to do things she didn't want to do. Homesick and lonely, she nonetheless endured the nomadic life of overseas basketball in order to do one thing: to make the Olympic team. "I could have packed it in," she said, "but I wasn't willing to do that."

A Disciplined Person Can Do Anything

Growing up, the odds weren't in Dawn Staley's favor. Born to a single mother, she lived in a rough neighborhood where expectations for children were low and dreams were rarely realized. Dawn ignored all of that and with single-mindedness and determination paved a path out of her bleak surroundings and into international success. "If you fail a test in life, you'll face it time and time again until you pass it," Dawn said. "The stakes keep getting higher if you don't learn how to pass."

Find Your Passion, Work Hard, and Stick with it

At five feet, five inches, Dawn Staley never measured up to the traditional basketball player, but inches can't measure heart and passion. Dawn's love for her sport sparked her work ethic, pushing and prodding her to greatness. "I've always put it all on the line," she said.

If You Can't Win Them All, Win Most of Them

Winning doesn't necessarily have to apply to games. Winning also is about overcoming odds and succeeding in life. Certainly on the basketball court, Dawn Staley won "most of them," putting together a high school, college, and international resume that could stand alongside anyone's. Staley, though, also wins in life. "My greatest success has been starting my foundation," she said. "I love working with youngsters on a daily basis and making a difference in their lives."

Be a Great Observer and a Nonstop Learner

Dawn Staley is arguably one of the most talented people, man or woman, to play the game of basketball. As a college basketball coach, she simply could call on her own experiences and her own talents to teach the game. She doesn't. She is constantly learning, trying to better herself. She is still a student of the game. "I've spent years perfecting my art," she said.

Trust Yourself

To pave her way to a better life, Dawn Staley had countless supporters, a loving mother, wonderful coaches, and friends. But in the end, the one person who really made her life a success was Dawn Staley. She believed in herself, not just in her talent, but in her instincts. "I want to be remembered as an odds-beater who persevered and remained steadfast," she said.

28

Pat Summitt:
Intensity

"No one has to start my engine in the morning."

—Pat Summitt

She was twenty-two, a graduate student taking four classes, trying to make ends meet on her paltry salary of $8,900. They told her she had a varsity basketball team, but really this was worse than high school. Players sold doughnuts to pay for uniforms, and as the head coach, she also washed those uniforms, drove the team van, and cleaned up the gym before and after games.

Today, the road she rides into her office is named after her, and Adidas makes sure her players are outfitted in the snazziest uniforms and as many pairs of sneakers as they might need. Her team not only is varsity, it is the standard by which all other women's basketball programs are measured.

To get from there to here, from sixteen wins to thirteen Final Fours, you have to understand the woman who has been the one constant at the University of Tennessee.

The word extraordinary is so often overused.

In describing Patricia Head Summitt, it is woefully inadequate.

"Pat's life teaches us that if you work hard, do it the right way, and never cut corners, you can go to the top," said Billie Moore, the longtime

University of California at Los Angeles (UCLA) coach and Summitt's mentor. "Pat has a passion for what she does. She loves the sport, and it shows."

That passion shows in the trophy cases in Knoxville, Tennessee, where seven national championship trophies are engraved with the University of Tennessee. Only one coach in basketball—men's or women's—can claim more. John Wooden, the wizard of Westwood, has ten at UCLA.

In recent history, Summitt and Tennessee have gone mano a mano with Geno Auriemma and the University of Connecticut, the two programs and two coaches creating a rivalry for the ages. The truth is—though Auriemma may beg to differ—there is no UConn powerhouse without Summitt.

Without Summitt, the women's NCAA Tournament doesn't get national television coverage as it does today on ESPN. Without Summitt, the women's Final Four doesn't break attendance records virtually every year.

"Pat teaches her players to play like today is your last day on Earth."

—BASKETBALL STAR LISA LESLIE, WHO PLAYED FOR SUMMITT AT THE OLYMPIC GAMES

Without Summitt, just maybe the WNBA doesn't come along.

"Women's basketball would not be where it is today without Pat Summitt," former WNBA president Val Ackerman said. "There is very little in the sport she has not been involved with."

She is a cornerstone in the game. Sure others came before her—the great teams at Immaculata College led by Cathy Rush—but Pat Summitt took women's basketball out of its niche and into the collective consciousness.

"She's the best women's coach of all time," longtime basketball writer for the *New York Daily News* Dick Weiss said. "Her consistent excellence set the standard for the entire sport and helped to popularize the sport. She started coaching in the 1970s, and four decades later, she's right in the middle of the mix. Truly amazing."

Her resume does nothing to discount that notion. The winningest basketball coach in NCAA history (men or women), Summitt eclipsed the nine-hundred-win plateau in January 2006.

Along with those NCAA titles and Final Four appearances, she coached the United States to its first Olympic gold medal in 1984. Named the Naismith Coach of the Century in 2000, Summitt is also a member of the Basketball Hall of Fame and the Women's Basketball Hall of Fame.

In thirty-one years, she has never had a losing season.

What's more impressive than the trophies and honors, though, is the lady herself. Tough as nails on the court, she is a presence that commands attention and a person who demands respect.

"Her vivacious manner touches all generations."

—BASKETBALL LEGEND TERESA EDWARDS

"What people will remember her for are the championships," former Tennessee star Michelle Marciniak told the *New York Times*. "But the people close to her will remember her for influencing lives. She has helped so many people and keeps in touch with a lot of her players. It means a lot to her."

Summitt's success is not borne out of some ingenious offensive scheme or defensive design. It is borne out of her values and her standards. She does not accept less than complete effort, and so her players give nothing less than complete effort. She demands respect and loyalty and teamwork, and so her players give her and each other respect and loyalty, combining the two to develop teamwork.

She wraps basketball around her life lessons, weaving the two into greatness.

Anyone can teach a player how to run a pick and roll. Summit teaches her players how to be champions.

"My mentor, Billie Moore, told me two things," Summitt related. "Never compromise your principles, and never lower your standards. Those two things have stuck with me through thirty-one years of coaching."

The irony is the woman who intimidates more than she could ever be intimidated came into this job a nervous, wide-eyed twenty-two-year-old. Hired in 1974 as an assistant coach at Tennessee, Summitt thought her job would be a great way to make ends meet while she took graduate courses and worked out in hope of landing a spot on the 1976 Olympic team.

Only weeks into her job, Summitt learned the head coach had left to pursue her doctorate. With no coaching experience and her own playing days only recently behind her, Summitt was a head coach.

It would scare the pants off most people, and to be quite honest, Summitt was a little flustered.

But then she's never been afraid of challenges. A true farm girl from Henrietta, Tennessee, Summitt was never coddled. Her father, Richard, believed in hard work. He worked the family farm while also running a feed store, grocery store, and tobacco warehouse and treated his two daughters the same as his three older boys. Each day Summitt and her siblings milked the eighty cows, once at 5:00 AM and again at 5:00 PM. She was expected to attend church on Sundays and school every day that the building was open. Summitt told me that in twelve years of school, she never missed a single day.

She also told me about her father's competitiveness, a trait obviously passed on to his children.

"We'd play checkers, Chinese checkers, Rook, and my dad never let us win," she said. "I was so thrilled when I could win at all. My dad beat my brother one day, and Derek began to cry. He said, 'You never let me win.' My dad said, 'You'll win when you learn how to beat me.'"

"I have an unbelievable focus, and I don't know why. That's just who I am."

—PAT SUMMITT

Richard Head, who died in 2005, was a huge presence in his daughter's life. He was the one who put the basketball hoop in the hayloft, so his kids could play after their long days of chores were done. But he was also the one who Summitt strove to please and impress.

"Principles my dad would also drill into our heads were: don't ever cry when you lose, and don't you dare show anyone you have any weakness in you, and never brag about what you have done," Summitt said in *It's How You Play the Game*. "If you are as good as you think you are, people will talk about you, and you'll get your due. Don't let it come from you."

In 1996, when Summitt's Lady Vols won their fourth NCAA title, beating Georgia in Charlotte, Summitt's first postgame remarks weren't about her team or even her growing legend. They were about her father.

"Tell you how big this game is," she said. "Today my dad hugged and kissed me for the first time in forty-three years."

Summitt never doubted her parents' love. She told me that she had "awesome parents," two people who wove a tightly strung fabric inside her.

She was buoyed by their toughness and demands, not afraid of it. Richard and Hazel Head gave their daughter the simplest, yet most vital life lesson, a principle that would guide her entire career.

"You can't wait around for others to do things you need to do yourself," Summitt said.

In college that meant defying not only doctor's orders but the medical prescription of the day. At the end of her senior season at Tennessee–Martin, Summitt tore her anterior cruciate ligament (ACL). Even today, ACL surgery requires upward of four months of rehab. In the 1970s, it often meant simply the end of a career. Summitt wouldn't accept that. In 1976, the United States would field its first Olympic women's basketball team, and she intended to be on it.

And so in between jumpstarting her program at Tennessee and taking graduate courses, Summitt put together her own rehab regime. Her schedule, as described in a 1998 *Sports Illustrated* article, was nothing shy of lunacy. "Three-mile run at 6:00 AM, weights at 6:30, shower, rush to the gym to teach, dash to the lecture hall to take the exercise physiology and

"Success is personal happiness, and that comes from being content with what you do."

—PAT SUMMITT

sports-administration classes, sprint back to the gym to coach a two-plus hour practice, hop in the car to go scout a local high school player, burn rubber back to the gym for two hours of basketball and sprints, shower again, and hightail it home by midnight to study for the biomechanics midterm."

Of course, Summitt not only coached the Lady Vols to a sixteen-win season, she made the 1976 U.S. Olympic team, at twenty-four the oldest woman on the roster, and helped the United States to a silver medal.

Seven months later, the University of Tennessee played in its first Final Four. The twenty-five-year-old Summitt had been on the job for three years.

"No one has to start my engine in the morning," Summitt said. "I think it keeps running at night while I'm sleeping. All I have to do is put it in gear when I get out of bed."

It is, of course, one thing to push yourself through pain and misery, to demand insanity of yourself.

It is another thing entirely to get others to push themselves through pain and misery, to not only demand greatness from them, but to get it.

"Pat's players idolize her," Ackerman said. "She's a true pro in her conduct."

Summitt's Lady Vols are a by-product of her personality. It is a roster of unparalleled basketball success, dotted with eighteen all-Americans on thirty different teams and twelve Olympians.

The players who come to Knoxville know what will be expected of them. They know that their coach sets her clocks at home twelve minutes ahead, so she's never late. They know that they will be ordered to sit in the front rows of their classes and never during their four-year college career have an unexcused absence from class.

And they know the stories, the tales that sound almost Bunyanesque about Summitt's maniacal expectations.

A smattering . . .

In 1989, Summitt kicked her team out of its own locker room and squeezed the players into the visitor's space because, she said, they hadn't played well enough to deserve their palatial room.

Once after a disheartening loss to South Carolina, Summitt marched the players off the buses, into the locker room, back into their still-dirty uniforms, and onto the court, admonishing them to "play the second half you didn't play now."

And most famous of all, a pregnant Summitt, married to her husband, R.B., for ten years, flew to Allentown, Pennsylvania, to recruit Marciniak. Already in the throes of labor, she barely finished her recruiting pitch when she dashed out of the house. Instead of going to the hospital, Summitt went to the airport, and when nervous pilots tried to convince her to land in

Virginia to deliver the baby, Summitt said, "No." The legend goes that Summitt didn't want to land in Virginia because the Cavaliers had beaten the Lady Vols in the NCAA Tournament that year.

The truth is a little less colorful. She wanted her husband to attend the birth. Naturally, son Tyler was born in Tennessee.

That says enough, doesn't it?

"I've got tunnel vision," Summitt once said, underscoring the understatement.

And yet despite all of this, the demands that outweigh the expectations, the basketball single-mindedness in the face of all reason, Summitt's players keep coming to Tennessee.

"She sets the bar high for her players and has high expectations of everyone in her program," WNBA senior vice president Renee Brown said. "Her players play with great confidence because Pat is confident. If the leader is confident you empower your players to perform with confidence."

How this basketball-centric woman empowers her team might surprise people. She doesn't talk hoops, not at first anyway. When Summitt sits down with her players at the start of each season, there is no talk of making the Final Four or winning a national championship. She talks about far less tangible methods to success, the "Definite Dozen" she calls them in her book *Reach for the Summit:* (1) respect yourself and others; (2) take full responsibility; (3) develop and demonstrate loyalty; (4) learn to be a great communicator; (5) discipline yourself so no one else has to; (6) make hard work your passion; (7) don't just work hard, work smart; (8) put the team before yourself; (9) make winning an attitude; (10) be a competitor; (11) change is a must; and (12) handle success like you handle failure.

Kids don't get it right out of the gate. They wouldn't be kids if they did.

But Summitt drives each point home day after day, practice after practice, and meeting after meeting.

"She has this great intensity," former WNBA coach Linda Hill McDonald said. "No one outworks her in preparation for practices or games. Pat takes her talented players and shows them how to play as a team."

And she lives the Definite Dozen herself, giving the best teaching tool of all: example.

"I believe leaders are made not born," she said. "Leadership opportunities arise from life experiences."

The untold secret to Summitt's success, though, is who she is when the suit is off and practice is over. She is the warmest Southern gentlewoman around.

"She doesn't have a selfish bone in her body," WNBA coach Nell Fortner said. "She is so real, honest, loyal, and gives it her all every day. As a friend, Pat is there for you and never stops giving. She even gives to her competitors, because she's all for the good of the game and the athletes."

Her schedule book looks like that of a CEO of a Fortune 500 company, but she does not shirk her responsibilities away from the court. She welcomes visitors and guests into her office with such affection that it is easy to think she has all the time in the world. The truth is, the next appointment is in five minutes, and there's another after that and film to watch, players to speak with, and heaven knows what else.

"Pat is the ultimate," former University of Mississippi coach and current Houston Comets coach Van Chancellor said. "She's at the top of her profession, but still the wonderful country girl I met in 1978. Pat's a good down-home person who has never forgotten her Tennessee roots. She's accomplished so much, but you'd never know that when you meet her. Fame hasn't changed her at all."

It is that genuine kindness and concern that tempers Summitt's basketball hard edges. Her players know the rest is tough love, that the same blue eyes that can bore into a player who makes a mistake can crinkle with laugh lines or crease with compassion and worry.

She is a coach who will make you cry in exhaustion, frustration or, yes, sometimes humiliation, but a coach who players realize sometime during their college careers or perhaps afterward has not only made them better players.

She's made them better people.

"I want to be remembered as a difference maker for others," Summitt said. "I want to be remembered as a great daughter, a great mother, and a great wife. I want to be remembered as making a difference in the lives of young women."

Pat Summitt's Life Lessons

Have a Passion Every Day

It is impossible to do all that Pat Summitt has done without passion because there are tough days and long days, days when nothing goes right, and nights where the team doesn't win. Yet every morning, Summitt told me, she wakes up ready to go, inspired and energized to go to work. "The one thing I know for sure?" Summitt said. "All I have is today, so make the most of it."

Make Relationships a Priority

Pat Summitt has a truckload of trophies and awards and has achieved more in women's basketball than any other person. Yet she said none of that hardware means nearly as much to her as the relationships she's built. "Success is not about trophies," she said. "Relationships with family, friends, and the athletes and their families mean more to me. It would be awfully lonely sitting in my house hanging out with a bunch of wooden trophies."

Discipline Yourself So No One Else Has To

There is a telling story about Pat Summitt in a *Sports Illustrated* article. The author tells of Summitt's father, Richard, driving his twelve-year-old daughter into the middle of a mound of hay, pointing to a tractor and a rake and saying simply, "Do it." He drove off, and Summitt went to work, toiling until the job was done. "You can't wait around for others to do things you need to do yourself," Summitt said.

Work Hard

Nothing in Pat Summitt's life came easily. She worked hard as a child on her family's farm, toiling in the fields and the barns alongside her siblings to make sure the chores were done. In college, she rehabbed a knee injury that would have ended most athletes' careers, defying the odds to make the U.S. Olympic team. As a coach, she jump-started a program from nothing, building it into the standard of excellence, despite being a woman in what was then a man's world. "My parents taught me about having a great work ethic and taking the initiative in life," Summitt said.

Compete to Be the Best You Can Be

Pat Summitt has never apologized for her never-ending quest for success. She knows that it may make people uncomfortable and that she may lose out on some popularity contests because of her desire to win. But Summitt also knows that competitiveness is something to bask in, not something to be ashamed of. "It's not the most sociable quality you can possess," Summitt wrote of competitiveness in her book *Reach for the Summit.* "People won't always like you for it; it won't win you a lot of friends and dates. If being well liked is your aim, I can't help you. But competitiveness is what separates achievers from the average."

Handle Success Like You Handle Failure (So Many People Have Such a Hard Time with This One)

Pat Summitt will be the first to admit she hates losing. "I know how it makes me feel," she wrote in her book *Reach for the Summit,* "which is basically sick." But she also knows there is value in failure and that the ability to handle losing with the same grace and dignity as winning is the true sign of a champion. "Losing makes you wiser," she wrote in her book. "There is nothing to be ashamed of in short-term failure, or in making a mistake, so long as you deal positively with it."

29

Jenny Thompson:
Excellence

"What keeps me going is finding out how far I can push myself."

—JENNY THOMPSON

No matter how hard she tried, Jenny Thompson couldn't stop the tears.

Every night she would stand in a hallway outside of her Indianapolis hotel room, sobbing to her mother who was across town in another hotel. Exhausted, overwhelmed, and extremely disappointed, the superstar of swimming felt like a failure.

Expected to qualify in as many as four individual events at the U.S. Olympic trials in 1996, Thompson missed on one and then another and eventually all four.

What makes a champion isn't just touching the wall or crossing the line first.

Champions also are defined by their spirit.

In what outsiders would consider her bleakest days, Jenny Thompson became a champion. She stopped listening to what people expected her to do, stopped fretting over her medal haul at the Olympic Games. She dug deep within herself and rediscovered what made her who she was.

"Jenny made a decision that changed the course of her life," her coach, Richard Quick, told *Sports Illustrated* in 2000. "She learned that swimming wasn't everything, that she could go on without it. When she discovered that, she became a better swimmer. And had a fantastic Olympics."

Most ordinary people aren't going to walk in Jenny Thompson's shoes. She is the most decorated American Olympian, a woman with twelve medals, including eight gold, two world records, and winner of a record eighty-five international medals as well.

Ordinary people can still draw inspiration from Thompson, in how she's fought to succeed, in how she's defied conventional wisdom, and in how she's defined her life by her passions, not results. A gifted athlete who has become a gifted doctor, Thompson learned long ago that excellence isn't about a time on a clock or even a degree on a wall, and that competition doesn't come from the swimmer in the next lane.

It's all from within.

> *"By the age of thirty, Jenny was an astounding champion with eight Olympic gold medals and as a doctor. Wow!"*
>
> —Longtime *Chicago Tribune* Olympic reporter Philip Hersh

"What keeps me going is finding out how far I can push myself," Thompson once said. "How fast can I be? How long can I stay on top? That striving for excellence, that feeling of knowing you have trained until you don't have one drop of energy left, that's what keeps me happy."

Unafraid to ruffle feathers—she once posed provocatively for *Sports Illustrated*—and speak her mind, Thompson has always been an individual. The toddler who wore a Wonder Woman swimsuit became a teenager sporting an American flag bandana and then became a woman secure in who she is.

She never won an individual Olympic gold; all of her first-place finishes came as part of a relay team. Critics will argue that is a hole in her pedigree, but Thompson makes no apologies for what others perceive as her shortcomings.

"When I show little kids at clinics my gold medals, no one asks if it was relay or individual," Thompson told longtime *Chicago Tribune* Olympic reporter Philip Hersh. "A gold medal is a gold medal, and I have eight. I think it's just an American value to want to do it on your own."

Thompson comes by her spunk naturally. It belonged first to her mother, Margrid.

Margrid Thompson was divorced when her youngest child, Jenny, was only two. Left to raise four children on her own, Margrid never wallowed in self-pity or gave time to self-doubt. Single parent or not, her children deserved everything, and so she made sure they had it. The kids played any sport they wanted, tested out musical instruments, and whatever fueled their passions, Margrid made happen.

"I have never judged my swimming by its proximity to perfection. I swim because of my passion for the sport, and that transcends performance."

—Jenny Thompson

Working as a medical technologist, Margrid spent her few spare hours taxiing her kids wherever else they needed to go.

Her youngest daughter tried flute, piano, and tap lessons but really took to swimming. It meant that, on top of her thirty-minute commute to work each day, Margrid would add an additional eighty-minute roundtrip run from Georgetown, Massachusetts, to Dover, New Hampshire. Margrid never complained.

Instead, encouraged by Thompson's quick improvement, Margrid made the agonizing decision to relocate the entire family to New Hampshire in 1986 so that thirteen-year-old Jenny could train more easily.

That it made life more difficult for Margrid, who now shuffled an hour each way to work every day, never mattered.

"She gave up a lot of her own life for us," Thompson once said of her mother.

Margrid Thompson died of esophageal cancer in 2004, but not before she saw her hard work and love realized in three Olympic trips (she died before the Athens Games) and four wildly successful children: Kris is a musician, Erik is a college professor, and Aaron is a high school math teacher.

"The love between them was something you could almost touch," Thompson's coach John Collins told Hersh in 2004. "As I got to know them better, I realized how big a part of the picture Margrid was. She took great delight in Jenny's swimming, but she was in no way the typical age-group parent, except in doing as much as she could do for her child. And Jenny gave her back a lot in return."

Thompson immediately rewarded her mother for the big decision to move the family. In 1987, when she was only fourteen, she won the 50-meter freestyle at the Pan American Games and took third in the 100-meter freestyle, narrowly missing a spot on the 1988 Olympic team.

By 1991, Thompson had her first world championship, helping the United States to the 4 × 100 relay title and, a year later, set the 100-meter freestyle record.

Thompson went to Barcelona for the 1992 Olympic Games a heavy favorite, but her time in the 100-meter freestyle—54.84—was good only for a silver as an unheralded Chinese swimmer blew by her.

Inviting controversy, she questioned the winning Chinese swimming delegation and criticized the Olympic doping policy.

"I want the play in my pool to be fair," Thompson said. In 1998, she was vindicated when vials of human growth hormone were found in the bags of the Chinese swimmers.

Thompson had to be happy with two golds in the relays.

"When the team element was in play, Jenny always swam her best," Mark Schubert, Thompson's swimming coach, said.

> *"Jenny never won an individual gold medal, but she was a champion in the way she worked and competed."*
>
> —Mark Schubert,
> Thompson's swimming coach

After Barcelona, Thompson took her swimming talents to Stanford, where the swim team went undefeated in her four-year career. She added twenty-six NCAA medals to her repertoire and pages to her legend when, in 1994, she broke her arm on a water slide and, two months later, won a world championship despite a titanium rod and seven screws in her arm.

By 1996, Thompson was arguably the best swimmer in the world.

All of which made those Olympic trials, where anxiety and pressure overcame her, more unbearable.

"I was a basket case," Thompson said at the time.

Faced with two choices in Atlanta, to dive in or drown in her sadness, Thompson not surprisingly chose the former.

Though she admitted it was hard to watch the individual events, Thompson summoned her spirit to anchor two relay teams to gold as well as swim in a preliminary heat in the medley relay. All this hard work earned her three gold medals in Atlanta.

"Some power comes over me when I swim relays," Thompson once said. "I get this sense I can't let the team down, that I have no choice but to win. Coming off the final turn, I felt an adrenaline rush that made me think there was no option but to get faster and faster and faster."

Already twenty-three when the '96 Games ended, most people figured that was Thompson's last chance.

Instead, Thompson just got better. In 1999, she broke Mary T. Meagher's eighteen-year-old world record in the 100-meter butterfly and returned to the Olympics in 2000, heading to Sydney in search of that elusive individual medal.

It never happened. Thompson took a bronze in the 100-meter freestyle and finished a disappointing fifth in the 100-meter butterfly.

Thompson hardly went home empty-handed. She won three golds as part of the powerful

"Every time she swims, Jenny gets better and better."

—Olympic gold medalist
Natalie Coughlin

American relay contingent, pushing her total to eight when she and her teammates set a world record in the medley relay, the final race of the Games.

That had to be it, right? By then Thompson was twenty-seven, ancient by swimming standards.

She enrolled at Columbia University's College of Physicians and Surgeons, pursuing an intimidating passion. "I went from being at the top in swimming to being at the bottom of the barrel and realizing I didn't know anything," she once said.

Most medical students can't find the time to do laundry. There was no way Thompson could continue as a competitive swimmer.

"If it's Jenny Thompson, anything can happen," German swimmer Sandra Volker once said. "She's a fighter, and she wants to win."

Inspired by another fighter—Margrid's cancer was diagnosed in 2001—Thompson jumped back into the pool a year after the 2000 Games ended. At first she just intended to use the lap pool in the basement of her New York apartment to get back into shape.

Old habits die hard.

"I really missed the way my body feels when I'm swimming," Thompson told Hersh in 2002, full into her comeback. "I think I have this kind of Zen relationship with the water. In a way, it's really sort of spiritual for me, training. Being in the water. Just being in the water. I'm a Pisces. Born to be a fish."

In 2003, Thompson took second at two U.S. national championship events and qualified for the world championships.

It defied logic and all sorts of swimming conventional wisdoms, where talented women are leading dry-land lives by their twenties.

"If she wants to do something badly enough," Margrid Thompson said of her daughter, "she has the ability to stick to it, no matter how hard it is."

Hard doesn't begin to describe the life Thompson chose. Swamped with schoolwork from one of the most demanding medical colleges in the country, Thompson added two-hour training regimens to her day, chug-a-lugging from Manhattan to the Bronx to practice.

"People ask me, 'Why are you still doing this?'" Thompson said to Hersh during the rat race. "No one asks Barry Bonds why he is still playing baseball. He is better than he has ever been. . . . There are a lot of misconceptions about how old a woman athlete should be."

Thompson turned most of them on their ear in 2003 when she stunned the world in Barcelona, winning two gold and three silver medals in her six events at the world championships.

A week later, she started her third year of medical school.

Inspired by herself and her mother, who lost her battle in February 2004, Thompson took a leave of absence from medical school to set her sights on the Athens Games.

"Talk about tenacity," swimming legend Janet Evans said. "Jenny was going to med school, training for the Olympics, and getting over the death of her mother, who was her inspiration."

Her perspective by then had changed. Wiser at thirty-one, she went to Greece simply proud to be competing. The results—two silvers for relay— were almost irrelevant.

"My swimming paradigm has shifted," Thompson once said. "The pressures don't weigh as heavily on me because I have realized there are things in life like war and illness that make anxiety about sport seem silly. When the pressures start to rumble in my mind, I take a deep breath, remembering that things could be worse."

By simply showing up in Greece, Thompson was an inspiration.

"At first I think everybody was shocked to see her come back," said sixteen-year-old Bridget O'Connor, who trained with Thompson in 2004. "Then we realized how great it is for someone to still swim and love it the way she does. She motivates us all."

That, however, was even enough for Thompson. She swam one last time at the world championships that year before retiring for good.

In 2006, Thompson received her medical degree from Columbia and began a one-year internship at the esteemed Memorial Sloan-Kettering Cancer Center in New York before beginning her first year of residency at Brigham and Women's Hospital in Boston as an anesthesiologist.

Though out of the limelight, Thompson continues to make a difference. Since 2003, Thompson has served as an athlete ambassador for Right to Play, a nonprofit organization that promotes health education and community development around the world and has been dubbed the athletes' Peace Corps.

In 2006, Thompson toured Zambia, visiting and working with countless children on everything from physical activity to AIDS prevention.

"This is the kind of thing where I feel I can make the most difference," she told the *Boston Globe*. "It really inspires me to hopefully take part in activities with medicine internationally and helping kids in other countries. It's remarkable how much you can do with very few resources. You can make a big difference without too much."

Or, as in Thompson's case, you can make a difference by simply believing in yourself.

Jenny Thompson's Life Lessons

Draw Inspiration from Everyday Events

That Jenny Thompson's mother, Margrid, sacrificed her own priorities for the benefit of her children is not surprising. Nothing teaches unselfishness quite like parenthood. What is surprising, though, is how Thompson took her mother's selflessness and molded it into her own life. A doctor today, Jenny has traveled to Africa to work to educate children about health care. "You can make a big difference without too much," she said. It is a motto her mother, a single parent of four, lived by.

Don't Let Others Define You

Rather than applaud what she has accomplished—a twelve-time Olympic medal winner—critics have always railed about what Jenny Thompson lacked: a medal in an individual event. For years, the criticism ate at Thompson until finally she realized that what she felt about herself, not what others thought of her, mattered most. "When I show little kids at clinics my medals, no one asks if it was relay or individual," Thompson told longtime *Chicago Tribune* reporter Philip Hersh. "A gold medal is a gold medal, and I have eight."

Embrace the Unexpected

At thirty-one and in the middle of the demanding world of medical school, Jenny Thompson decided she could swim in another Olympics. In a sport where swimmers peak in their twenties, it defied all logic and conventional wisdom. The reasons not to compete were many, but the single reason to compete—

because Thompson wanted to defy the odds and prove something to herself—was stronger. "At first I think everybody was shocked to see her come back," sixteen-year-old Bridget Connor said of Thompson's return to Athens. "Then we realized how great it was for someone to still swim and love it the way she does."

Forget About the Results

In a day and age where it is not nearly good enough to place or show, where winning is everything, Jenny Thompson instead measured her own worth by her own standards. Of course, she wanted to win every race she entered, but more, Thompson merely wanted to get out of the pool certain that she had given her best. "What keeps me going is finding out how far I can push myself," Thompson said. "That striving for excellence, that feeling of knowing you have trained until you don't have a drop of energy left, that's what keeps me happy."

‿❧ 30 ❧‿

Serena and Venus Williams:
Double the Drive

"I'm playing for those little girls who never watched tennis, who might say, 'I want to be like Serena,' or 'I want to be like Venus,' and I feel very proud to take on that responsibility."

—SERENA WILLIAMS

Not much more than a footnote in her sport, Virginia Ruzici won just fifteen tournament titles in her twelve-year career.

The little-known Romanian deserves the credit for forever changing the face of tennis.

In 1978, Ruzici won the French Open, earning $22,000 for her efforts. Sitting in his Compton, California, home, Richard Williams was flabbergasted. A former basketball, golf, and football dabbler himself, Richard Williams was simply staggered by the money and possibilities tennis offered.

He convinced his wife, Oracene, who already had three daughters from a previous marriage, that it was time for more children. Two years later Venus Ebone Starr was born, followed in fifteen months by Serena Jameka.

Nothing in tennis—not the power, not the training, and most important, not the color—has been the same since.

More than just champions, Venus and Serena Williams are modern-day pioneers, women who defied the odds as well as their circumstances to become the Jackie Robinsons of their sport. African-Americans had been winners in tennis before. Althea Gibson and Arthur Ashe blazed the trail long before Richard Williams even conceived the idea of breeding his own tennis stars. But until the Williams sisters arrived on the scene, African-American athletes never before had owned the sport.

Venus and Serena owned it on the courts, in the media, and in the public consciousness, bringing women's tennis into the homes of people who had never cared about it and opening the eyes of young girls who had never dreamed they could play.

The Williams sisters inspired, not so much by winning, but simply by being there, by outlasting the criticism and the quirkiness of their father, to showcase two well-rounded, well-adjusted, and respectable young women who also happened to know how to smack a tennis ball over 100 mph.

"If you listen to young people and you say, 'Who do you like?' no matter what culture they're from—girls and boys of all colors—they'll say, 'Oh, I love Venus,' or 'I love Serena,'" tennis legend Billie Jean King once said of the Williams sisters. "They cross every boundary, and they bring everybody together, and it's great. I think we should all have

"You can't sleep on anybody. They might not be here, or they might not be here for a couple of days, but they come back."

—SERENA WILLIAMS

heroes and heroines and 'she-roes' that are of all colors or religions or whatever; it shouldn't get down to just somebody that looks like you."

What's more, the Williams sisters achieved international stardom and success while still maintaining their own spirits. Far from one-dimensional, they have varied interests. Both love to design clothes, and Serena has dabbled in acting. Critics have argued that these side jobs have taken away from their tennis, but the Williams sisters counter, "Is that so bad? Is there anything wrong with having more than one passion and feeding them equally?"

Rather than define themselves by their tennis achievements, they have chosen to measure their success in their personal happiness.

"Success is doing what you love and standing up for what you believe in," Serena said.

Their stardom has not been without kinks. Criticized for having their heads in the stars instead of on the tennis court, the sisters were dismissed as cautionary tales caught up in the rush of celebrity, and as their tennis took a hit from both the naysayers and injuries, their eldest sister, Yetunde Price, was murdered.

"I love doubters. More than anything what I love, besides obviously winning, is proving people wrong."

—SERENA WILLIAMS

"You don't necessarily think of your heroes as human," Isha Price, another of the Williams sisters, told the *New York Times* in 2006. "You think they are capable of juggling a fantastic career, live fabulous lives. But to have surgery and lose your sister, we had in a short amount of time a lot of tragedy."

Writers and reporters have used many words to describe the Williams sisters since they burst onto the tennis scene. Traditional has never been one of them. They are as unique to their sport as they are to one another, women who detoured from the traditional path of tennis glory, yet found their way to the top anyway. Bold, confident, and unapologetic, they turned the gentrified sport on its ear, injecting much-needed verve and bringing tennis out of the country clubs and into the mainstream.

"They are the most unusual pair in the history of tennis," longtime tennis analyst and *Boston Globe* columnist Bud Collins said. "It's an almost impossible story of how they were raised to be champions. We've never seen anything like it and probably never will again. Serena and Venus are great athletes and competitors."

The simple explanation is that the Williams sisters' skin color set them apart, but it was much more than that. From brash outfits that included a catsuit for Serena and clickety-clacking beads for Venus, to predictions and promises of future success, tennis had never before seen anyone quite like the Williams sisters.

The rest of the world had. They were the offbeat kids in the neighborhood who expressed themselves through funky clothing or the best athlete in town who never backed down from a challenge. Sometimes giggly, sometimes serious, they were what every other kid in America had always been, and now those kids suddenly had someone just like them holding rackets in their hands.

"People who didn't traditionally look at tennis began to watch it," former touring pro Leslie Allen told the *Washington Post* in 2005. "And they weren't necessarily people of color. Their reach was so broad, so universal, because they were the atypical tennis player. They weren't from that country-club model and had more universal appeal. They were interesting people; they wore interesting outfits, and they had dynamic games."

A polarizing figure who has not always made life easy for his daughters, Richard Williams nonetheless deserves heaps of credit for the Williams sisters' success, as well as for who they are. Much like Tiger Woods's father, Earl, pushed him to become a great golf champion, Richard Williams did the same for Venus and Serena. That he did it when others laughed at him makes his single-mindedness all the more remarkable. He knew nothing about tennis but bought instructional videos and taught himself how to play.

On tennis courts used more for drug transactions than matches, Richard toted four-year-old Venus to practice, lugging tennis balls in milk crates and asking the nearby gang members to guard the courts, so his child could practice in peace.

Richard Williams's dedication certainly helped the Williams sisters, but providence also played a hand, blessing Richard Williams with two unusually coordinated children who were as eager to play tennis for hours as other kids were to skip on the playgrounds. Lithe and tall, Venus would grow to six feet, one inch, and Serena, though shorter, would become a compact pile of muscle.

"It's easy to feel that you have to win, but then playing isn't fun. It's better to not let yourself feel the pressure."

—Venus Williams

"It is unbelievable that two black sisters who started playing tennis at age six would have a father telling the world, 'My daughters will be the number one and number two players in the world,' and then fifteen years later, it happened," tennis analyst Betsy Nagelsen McCormack said.

As good as her father promised, Venus breezed through the competition as a kid, winning sixty-three consecutive matches to quickly become Southern California's reigning number-one player in the twelve-and-under division. By age ten, she was on the front page of the *New York Times*. In a story headlined "Status: Undefeated. Future: Rosy. Age: 10," Venus was hailed as the next big thing. "In a sport where first names like Billie Jean, Martina, Chrissie, and Steffi have become synonymous with success, Venus sounds like a winner," penned the *Times*.

Not to be outdone by her big sister, Serena came along and blazed the same trail, winning her ten-and-under Southern California division as well as forty-six of the first forty-nine tournaments she entered.

Just as the tennis world was starting to hear about the Williams sisters, their father yanked them out of junior competition. It was an unconventional move that was loudly booed by people who adhered to tennis' traditional paths, but applauded by others who had seen one too many tennis prodigies burn out before their teen years.

"The important thing is that they go slowly and do the right thing," Billie Jean King said of the sisters after an exhibition doubles match with them in 1992. "That's what makes champions."

"I think the best part about having a sister is that it's very inspiring."

—VENUS WILLIAMS

Richard Williams's problem wasn't with the junior circuits but the single purpose of it. Tennis is rife with overbearing parents who prepare their children for little outside of the lines on the court. Richard Williams refused to let that happen. He wanted his girls to go to school, to see things outside of tennis, arguing, "When they've finished their tennis careers, I don't want a couple of gum-chewing illiterates on my hands."

Now enrolled in the Art Institute of Florida and leading their own lives, the sisters often have thanked their father for his brave choice. Serena said she is an avid reader, and in her spare time, Venus used to teach herself foreign languages.

Moreover, the sisters never looked at their passion as a profession but have been able to enjoy tennis as professionals just as they did as children.

When asked what she thought the next generation could learn from her, Serena said, "Have fun in whatever it is you do."

Richard Williams relocated the family from the mean streets of Compton to the tennis haven of Florida, signing the girls up with Rick Macci, a tennis coach in Delray Beach. In between school lessons, the girls had tennis lessons, hitting as many as two hundred serves a day.

In 1994, the WTA Tour, backhandedly agreeing with Williams, instituted new eligibility rules that would allow young players to play only restricted schedules. That was Richard Williams's intention all along. From 1994 to 1996, Venus, who had turned pro in 1994 at the age of fourteen, played limitedly but nonetheless attracted crowds. At her first professional match in October 1994, the world's media descended on Oakland, California, to watch the newest tennis prodigy. Venus didn't disappoint, dispatching Shaun Stafford in straight sets and then taking a 6–3, 3–1 lead over Arantxa Sanchez Vicario, then the number one player in the world, before dropping eleven consecutive games to lose the match.

Asked how the loss compared to others in her career, the precocious Venus answered, "I don't know. I've never lost before."

The tennis world didn't quite know what to make of the Williams family, unsure if Venus was arrogant or honest, cocky or confident, and when Reebok inked the as-yet-untapped talent of Venus to a $12 million contract in 1995, it did little to earn the family fans among the conservative tennis community.

Many considered Venus (Serena, at the time, competed in virtual anonymity) nothing more than a brilliant marketing ploy by a calculating father, complaining that her tennis strokes were far from solid and that as she aged and the competition grew fiercer, she would be exposed.

In 1997, the critics were permanently quieted. In the same year that Althea Gibson would turn seventy, the seventeen-year-old Venus streaked to the U.S. Open final, the only unseeded player to ever play for the championship.

That same year, Serena made her professional debut. She lost her first professional match in straight sets, but a month later, the world learned of the littlest Williams sister when Serena upset Mary Pierce and Monica Seles in only her second WTA main draw competition. By year's end she had risen from number 304 in the rankings to number 99.

Already the tennis world was buzzing with the idea that a tandem of sisters might soon own its sport when, in 1998, Venus and Serena met on the court for the first time. A psychological battle as much as a physical one, their matches against one another always were fraught with unforced errors and sloppy tennis. The complexity of their relationship, and their deep love and respect for one another, made it extremely difficult for one to try to beat the other. The first time they met, big sister Venus won in straight sets.

"Family comes first, no matter how many times we play each other," Serena told *Sports Illustrated*. "Nothing will come between me and my sister."

That notion, however, soon would be tested. In 1998, Serena inked a lucrative endorsement deal with Puma, one that would deliver even more riches if she were to crack the top ten. By June of 1998, just eight months into her professional career, she joined the top twenty, and by year's end, Puma was signing that check. Serena Williams was ranked in the top ten.

"I think of how hard I worked," Serena said in the book *Sports Leaders and Success.* "People say, 'Oh, you're so lucky to have this.' But luck has nothing to do with it, because I spent many, many hours, countless hours, on the court working for my one moment in time, not knowing when it would come."

"I'm alive, so that means I can do anything."

—Venus Williams

The moment came in September 1999. When she beat Martina Hingis in the U.S. Open final, Serena Williams became the first African-American to win a Grand Slam since Althea Gibson in 1958.

The win catapulted Serena to number four in the rankings and jump-started what had previously just been whispers, the notion that perhaps the younger Williams might be better than her big sister. As happy as she was for Serena, Venus struggled watching her kid sister hoist the family's first Grand Slam trophy.

"It was almost like a death for Venus," the girls' mother, Oracene, said of Serena's triumph. "She thinks since she's the oldest, she should have been the first."

But Venus is nothing if not the typical older sibling. More reserved and quiet than Serena, she is a born nurturer, one who graciously allowed her little sister to enjoy the spotlight while she stepped aside.

Serena, too, learned something in her victory. The quintessential youngest of the family who grew up idolizing her older sisters, she finally realized with that victory that she was her own person, with her own style and her own passions.

"When we would go out to eat, my parents made me order first because if I didn't order first, I would order everything Venus ordered," Serena once said of her desire to copycat her big sister.

Not surprisingly, Serena after that win started to break out of here sister's shadow, favoring far more outlandish tennis attire and embracing her out-going personality.

"I wanted to do everything that they did," Serena said of her sisters. "They were all older, and I wanted to do everything they did. They were and are amazing women, and they all had goals. I learned how to set goals from them."

The sisters' emergence captured tennis almost like a craze. Famed toy store FAO Schwartz marketed Venus and Serena Williams dolls, while newspapers and magazines chronicled their every move.

Bold and confident, they blew the doors off the staid world of tennis by speaking their minds and blistering those little yellow tennis balls like no other woman before them. With speeds clocked upwards of 100 mph and the athleticism to cover the court like quick cats, the Williams sisters simply overwhelmed finesse players such as Martina Hingis, who previously had dominated the sport.

Venus, for a time, would reclaim her position at the top. In 2000, she enjoyed a year unlike any since Steffi Graf's Golden Slam in 1988. Venus won her first Grand Slam title, taking the Wimbledon crown and then quickly added her second, claiming the U.S. Open championship when she topped Serena in the first "Sister Slam."

Asked if she had anything left to accomplish in tennis, Venus replied, "I've never been ranked number one."

She checked that off the following year. After defending both Grand Slam titles, Venus Williams became the first African-American tennis player to hold the world's top spot.

Her time in the sun, however, would be short lived, eclipsed by the one woman on tour who was simply stronger and better than she was—her kid sister.

Unlike Venus, who struggled with Serena's Grand Slam title, Serena saw nothing but motivation in Venus's accomplishment.

"After her win, I've been supermotivated," she said. "I've got this great new battery pack that's never going to end."

In 2002, Serena realized the potential that tennis aficionados knew was coming. She went 56–5 that year, winning the French Open, Wimbledon, and the U.S. Open, and then started 2003 by winning the Australian Open, becoming only the ninth woman to win all four Grand Slam titles.

To add to the Williams sisters' luster, Serena beat her big sister all four times and wrested the number ranking from Venus as well. Venus remained at number two.

Just as their tennis started to take over the world, the sisters branched out. Venus enrolled in the Art Institute of Florida to study design and began her own design company, V Starr Interiors. Not to be outdone, Serena took interest in designing her own tennis outfits, putting together bold ensembles the reserved sport had never seen before. Her catsuit at the 2002 U.S. Open caused as much a stir as her play. In 2003, she signed an endorsement contract with Nike, one that allowed her to design a line of tennis clothing.

Serena also tried her hand at celebrity, walking the red carpet at various functions and enjoying a handful of cameo roles on television programs as she pursued her love of acting.

Tennis pundits argued that people who didn't put all of their focus in tennis could never master it, but the Williams sisters never apologized. Richard Williams may have dreamed of girls collecting big paychecks and earning tennis glory, but he also was the man who pulled them out of juniors competition, desperate to preserve some sense of normalcy for them.

"My desire to go out and do something I love wakes me up," Serena said. "I love tennis, acting, and designing."

More than their outside interests, it is the loss of their sister, who also served as a personal assistant, that has slowed the sisters. Yetonde Price was murdered in Compton, California, in a gang-related shooting, leaving three children without their mother.

"No one knows that pain," Serena Williams told the *New York Times* in

2006. Serena and Venus took time off to grieve, but both were hampered by injuries when they tried to return. Venus was slowed by wrist problems, while Serena battled knee injuries as well as an extensive surgery to repair torn tendons. Withdrawing from event after event, the pair tumbled down the rankings.

In their absence, others caught up. Following the lead of the Williams sisters, who brought a new level of physical fitness and strength to tennis, players like Maria Sharapova have developed power games and now are ruling the roost.

Of course, just as people started to count the Williams sisters out, Serena proved that was never a good idea. In 2007, the unseeded Serena, ranked number eighty-one after injuries limited her to just four tournaments in the 2006 season, stormed into the Australian Open final. Still not in the best of shape, she combined God-given talent with steel will to upend the game's top player, Sharapova, to win her first Grand Slam title in two years, a lifetime in Williams sisters' standards. Serena dedicated the victory to her late sister, Yetunde.

"I've got a lot more left in my tank," Williams told the *New York Times* during her run to the championship. "Nobody thought I'd be able to get this far but me and my mom. I like being the underdog, but you can't be an underdog forever. I won't be number eighty-one anymore. I like being number one, expected to win. I like that pressure."

Whether they ascend to the world's number one ranking again or simply go off to pursue their other interests, the Williams sisters will have made their mark on not just tennis, but the world. The comparison may seem trite, but they are the Tiger Woods of their game, two young women who showed that like the American dream promises, anyone can become anything if they work hard enough at it.

"When I first came along, I said, 'I'm not playing for anybody. I'm just playing for myself,'" Serena said. "But in reality, I know I'm playing for a lot of people. I'm playing for those little girls who never watched tennis, who might say, 'I want to be like Serena,' or 'I want to be like Venus,' and I feel very proud to take on that responsibility."

Before his untimely death, Arthur Ashe fought hard to bring the sport he loved to the masses. Through his inspiration and hard work, he jump-started inner-city tennis programs across the country.

The Williams sisters didn't follow his model. Where Ashe was humble and quiet, the Williams sisters were proud and loud, but no one doubts Ashe somewhere is smiling as two girls from Compton, California, help realize his dream.

"I have seen so many effects by the Williams sisters," tennis star James Blake said to ESPN. "The Williams sisters have become so prominent to all young girls that want to be involved in sports. They have made such a great, positive difference. I think that's something Arthur would be proud of."

The Williams Sisters' Life Lessons

Embrace Challenges

Their practice courts were manned by drug dealers. Their sport was dominated by white people with money. Their father knew nothing about tennis. What's amazing about the Williams sisters isn't that they came so far, it's that they ever got started. But along with their tennis talent, the young women were blessed with courage. They welcomed obstacles, knowing that overcoming them would only make them stronger. "To overcome any hurdle you have to be and think positive," Serena said. "God will never give you more than you can handle, keep this in mind. It will help anyone get through plenty."

Remember Your Values

Bad behavior runs through society like a rampant disease. Athletes who could make a difference in the world by showing young people how to behave instead corner the market on boorish behavior. For all of the complaints people have misguidedly lodged at the Williams sisters, no one can ever argue that the young women have failed to live up to their charge. They are role models, young women who have avoided scandal and embarrassment, all while toting the burden of opening their sport to an entire race. "Winning, losing, money, riches, or fame don't make you happy," Venus said. "For my tennis career, it's great, but as far as me being Venus, it doesn't really make a huge difference."

Never Underestimate Your Will

It is easy to get bogged down in the negative. If enough people say you can't do something, it's hard to remember why you think you can. The little voice deep inside, though, is the one to trust. Fed well it can overcome even the harshest critics. Before she stunned the tennis world by winning the 2007 Australian Open, Serena Williams could have filled a phone book with the people saying she was out of shape, lacking the discipline and the dedication to win. But she believed in herself and ended up with her eighth Grand Slam trophy. "More than anything, what I love, besides obviously winning, is proving people wrong," she said afterward.

It's Okay to Enjoy Your Success

Humility certainly is an admirable trait, but hard work rewarded ought to be celebrated. The only way to reach for the next goal is to enjoy the first one. When Venus and Serena Williams won their first Grand Slam tournaments, they were rightfully elated, relishing their places in history and their moments in time. Once they tasted that feeling, it only made them hungrier for more. Asked how she felt after an early exit from her initial Wimbledon appearance, Venus replied, "It's my first Wimbledon. There will be many more."

Have an Intense Desire to Win

Winning certainly isn't everything, but champions crave winning like children crave sweets. As Serena Williams once described it, winning creates an "insatiable" appetite. Chastised for always dreaming so big, the Williams sisters knew they could achieve their goal because they knew the hunger inside of them wouldn't allow them to settle for anything else. "There's nothing like being hungry for the sport of tennis," Serena Williams said after her surprising 2007 Australian Open title. "I love winning. I don't care if it's Uno or running a race. I love winning."

∾ 31 ∾

Babe Didrikson Zaharias:
Originality

"You can't win them all, but you can try."

—BABE DIDRIKSON ZAHARIAS

Her sports resume included tennis and track, basketball and golf, boxing and swimming, volleyball, handball, bowling, billiards, skating, and cycling.

Asked if there was something she didn't play, Babe Didrikson Zaharias gave an answer that only she could provide.

"Yeah," she said. "Dolls."

Atypical doesn't begin to describe her. Didrikson was the antithesis of every other woman of her generation, a tomboy with a sassy tongue and brash confidence.

In an era when women, like children, were meant to be seen and not heard, folks frankly didn't know what to make of her, let alone do with her. "It would be much better if she and her ilk stayed at home, got themselves prettied up, and waited for the phone to ring," reporter Joe Williams wrote in the *New York World-Telegram*.

She is remembered now as a woman who blew open the notion of traditional roles for women, who proved that athletics weren't simply for the folks with XY chromosomes, and she is held in high esteem as a pioneer for the women's movement.

The truth is, Didrikson didn't set out to tote the banner of the feminist cause. She performed for herself, her own joys and her own self-satisfaction.

"I was determined to show everybody," she said after her high school basketball team said she was too short to play.

It would be the motto of her life.

Babe Didrikson showed everybody, showed them her talent and her skill, showed them that women could do more than make a good casserole, and most important, showed them what hard work, dedication, and determination could accomplish. Naturally gifted as she was, Didrikson would have been great without even trying.

"Concentration is the ability to think clearly of several things in proper sequence."

—Babe Didrikson Zaharias

Because she tried so hard, she became a legend.

"Oh, how that girl would work for the things she wanted," Babe's sister, Lillie said.

She wanted to be considered in a class by herself, and as her sports summary proves, she did it. Voted the greatest female athlete of the first half of the twentieth century, it could be argued that Didrikson is simply the greatest female athlete ever. There was then and is now no one like her, a multisport sensation who is almost impossible to categorize.

Is she a basketball phenom? A track superstar? A great golfer? Yes, yes, and yes.

"She is beyond all belief until you see her perform," legendary sportswriter Grantland Rice wrote of her. "Then you finally understand that you are looking at the most flawless section of muscle harmony, of complete mental and physical coordination the world of sport has ever seen."

Born to Norwegian parents in 1914, Mildred Ella Didrikson quickly differentiated herself from the other girls of her era. Running around the streets of Beaumont, Texas, she wore her hair short and her face plain, turning her nose up at pretty clothes and lipstick in favor of scrappy fights and athletic endeavors.

Life wasn't easy, with a father who often headed out to sea as a sea captain and a mother who never really assimilated into the American culture.

Her mother, Hannah, was steadfast in her housekeeping and put her daughter in charge of mopping the floors. Ever the athlete, Didrikson often would fasten scrub brushes to her feet and skate around the floor when her mother wasn't watching.

"Practice should be approached as just about the most pleasant recreation ever devised, besides being a necessary part of golf."

—BABE DIDRIKSON ZAHARIAS

But the family made time for fun, playing baseball in the backyard or swimming in the nearby river. Didrikson's father, Ole, built a wooden gym for his seven children, complete with chin-up bar and makeshift weightlifting equipment that consisted of flatirons tied to the ends of broomsticks. Didrikson recalled, "He put it there for the boys, but Lillie and I would work out, too."

The two would scale neighborhood hedges as if they were hurdles, and Didrikson impressed everyone with her dead-eye aim with a rifle and throwing arm.

"Before I was even into my teens, I knew exactly what I wanted to be when I grew up," Didrikson wrote in her autobiography. "My goal was to be the greatest athlete that ever lived."

Ironically, her first endeavor at organized sports went awry. The Beaumont High School basketball team told Didrikson that at five feet, six inches, she was too small for the rigors of basketball.

Much like Michael Jordan, who was cut by his high school basketball coach in his sophomore season, that criticism only fueled Didrikson to achieve more.

She went to the boys' coach and told him to make her better.

He was some teacher. Once Didrikson joined the girls' team, they never lost a game.

Didrikson's talents didn't go unnoticed.

Colonel Melvin J. McCombs of Dallas's Employers Casualty Insurance Company offered her $75 to drop out of school and become a secretary. He wasn't interested in her typing skills. He wanted her to play for his AAU basketball team, the Golden Cyclones, but knew that for Didrikson to keep her amateur status, the company would have to pretend she was just an ordinary secretary.

Didrikson agreed, and for three consecutive years—1930, 1931, and 1932—took the Golden Cyclones to the AAU Championship.

That, however, wasn't enough for this woman who always aspired to do more, be more, and win more.

She convinced McCombs that the Golden Cyclones needed to get involved in track and field. He gladly acquiesced for his new star.

Most women who competed in track and field opted for one of the ten events. Didrikson wanted to try them all.

"I really worked hard at that track and field," Didrikson said. "I trained and trained and trained. I've been that way in every sport I've taken up."

"I was determined to play the game well or not at all."

—Babe Didrikson Zaharias

On July 16, 1932, in Evanston, Illinois, that hard work paid off at the AAU Championships, which also served as the track and field Olympic qualifying event.

McCombs sent his entire team: the eighteen-year-old Didrikson.

"I think if you enter enough different events and give your regular performance, you can do something that's never been done before," McCombs told Didrikson, a story she recounts in her autobiography, *This Life I've Led.*

Up late the night before with stomach pain brought on by unbelievable anxiety, Didrikson overslept and frantically hailed a cab from her Chicago hotel to get her to the competition on time. She emerged with minutes to spare, already in her yellow warm-up suit.

Three hours later, she had competed in eight of the ten events, winning five outright, tying for first in the high jump, and setting world records in the javelin, eighty-meter hurdles, high jump, and baseball throw. She recalls in her autobiography racing from one event to the next, never pausing long enough to enjoy one performance before beginning another.

On her own, Didrikson amassed thirty points. The runner-up team, with twenty-two athletes to choose from, mustered twenty-two points.

No longer just a regional hero, Didrikson found herself on the front page of newspapers nationwide, all lauding her incredible afternoon, which is still considered the best in history for any man or woman.

Jaded sports reporters, not easily impressed by women, called her a "super athlete" and "wonder girl," while UPI wire service reporter George Kirksey summed up her performance as "the most amazing series of performances ever accomplished by any individual, male or female, in track and field history."

And Didrikson was just getting started.

A few weeks later, Didrikson went to Los Angeles for the Olympic Games. Women at the time were only allowed to compete in three events, so Didrikson, who had qualified in five, opted for the javelin, 80-meter hurdles, and high jump. She came home with two gold medals, robbed of a third by a questionable disqualification that ruled Didrikson's head had cleared the bar before the rest of her body in the high jump, a rule that no one brought to light in earlier competition and no longer exists.

"She was not against sexual liberation. She was an athlete, and her body was her most valuable possession."

—WILLIAM JOHNSON AND NANCY WILLIAMSON, AUTHORS OF *WHATTA GAL! THE BABE DIDRIKSON STORY*

By now she was a media darling. Her brash confidence may not have endeared her to her fellow competitors, but sportswriters, recognizing a good quote when they heard one, lapped up her every word.

Didrikson never apologized for her comments and never felt she should. She wasn't trying to be insensitive or arrogant. She was just being herself, talking openly and wearing her pride like a flag. "Her honesty is uninhibited either by vainglory or false modesty," Harry Paxton, the man who would help her write her autobiography, wrote. "Babe lays it right on the line, without striving for any calculated effect. The Babe doesn't pretend to be anything more than she is. Nor does she pretend to be anything less."

Today, Didrikson would have been on the cover of every Wheaties box, endorsing Gatorade and her own signature sneakers. But in the 1930s, the world wasn't quite sure what to do with her, and she was left to forge her own path of celebrity.

She tried vaudeville, and her fans loved it. They called for encores, and she was booked for cities weeks in advance.

If Didrikson was consistent in anything in her life, it was being true to herself, and a dog and pony show wasn't what she was about.

"I don't want the money if I have to make it this way," she told her sister Nancy after one week of her popular show.

Having accomplished all there was to accomplish in track and field, Didrikson turned her attention toward golf.

Think again of Michael Jordan. When he gave up basketball for the first time, he decided to give baseball a try, but the world's greatest basketball player could barely get by in the minor leagues.

Now consider Didrikson. She tucked her gold medals away, picked up a golf club . . . and went on to win every available golf title by the end of 1950. Fiercely determined, she worked on her game like a woman obsessed, driving as many as one thousand golf balls a day and playing to the point where her calloused hands had to be taped. On weekends it wasn't unusual for Didrikson to spend twelve to sixteen hours a day working on her golf game.

In 1935, the exhaustive work resulted in a Texas State Women's Golf Championship.

Not long after that, though, the United States Golf Association (USGA) ruled that Didrikson was ineligible for amateur status because she had received payment for exhibition performances in between the Olympics and her first golf championship. It was a bogus allegation, but Didrikson shrugged it off and worked even harder. She played in golf tournaments open to anyone, winning the Western Women's Open in 1940.

Three years later, the USGA reinstated her, and Didrikson quickly became the most popular female golfer in the country. Fans loved her attacking game, her strength, and by now even her brashness. Asked how a woman with such a sleight frame could hit the ball such a long way,

Didrikson replied in pure Didrikson fashion. "You've got to loosen your girdle and let it rip."

Between 1946 and 1947, Didrikson won seventeen consecutive tournaments and, when the year ended, decided to turn pro. She, along with her manager Fred Corcoran, helped start the Ladies Professional Golf Association (LPGA) two years later.

In the spring of 1953, Didrikson finally met a worthy opponent. She was diagnosed with colon cancer. The diagnosis, along with the colostomy, would mean retirement for most athletes.

When was Didrikson ever like most athletes?

"All my life I've been competing—and competing to win," Didrikson said. "I came to realize that in its way, this cancer was the toughest competition I'd faced yet. I made up my mind that I was going to lick it all the way. I not only wasn't going to let it kill me, I wasn't even going to let it put me on the shelf."

True to form, fourteen days after surgery Didrikson was playing in a golf tournament, and three months later, she entered the All-American Golf Tournament in Chicago.

Her game wasn't where it used to be. That was understandable to fans and golf aficionados, who wondered if Didrikson would come back at all, but it was incomprehensible to the ever-competitive Didrikson. Midway through a poor third round—after two bad early rounds—Didrikson simply sat down and bawled. Demoralized and defeated, she was wondering if the naysayers were right, if she truly was done.

Her husband of fifteen years, George Zaharias, and fellow golfer Betty Dodd, went to her and told her it would be okay to simply pick up her ball and quit.

"I don't pick up the ball," she screamed at them.

Instead, Didrikson kept playing, kept working, and the following year won five titles, including the U.S. Women's Open.

By now Didrikson considered herself much more than a golfer.

She considered herself a survivor and an inspiration. Of course, Didrikson had been an inspiration since the day she picked up a basketball, but the cancer made her recognize the importance of that role. Active with the American Cancer Society, she said she never considered quitting after "that cancer business," as she flippantly referred to her diagnosis.

"Every time I get out and play well in a golf tournament, it seems to buck people up with the same cancer trouble I had," she said.

Cancer, though, is a lot like Didrikson. It doesn't quit.

In 1955, during an operation for a ruptured disk, doctors found that the cancer had returned.

This time there would be no comeback. The illness continually worsened, sending Didrikson in and out of the hospital.

On September 27, 1956, Didrikson died at the young age of forty-five.

Her legacy, however, lives on. It lives on in elementary schools and middle schools and high schools, where young girls proudly sport team uniforms with nary a second glance. It lives on in colleges, where the battle over Title IX is still waged, but where women are considered equals. It lives on in the LPGA, where Annika Sorenstam is every bit as popular, as amazing, and as well regarded as Tiger Woods.

"My autobiography," Didrikson said in the final line of her book, "isn't finished yet."

Indeed not.

Babe Didrikson Zaharias's Life Lessons

Define Your Passions

Babe Didrikson Zaharias knew even as a little girl that she wanted to be great. More important, she knew the road she was meant to travel was in sports. Didrikson listened to her heart, she listened to her gut, and she realized what it was she loved, what it was she was meant to do. "Before I was even into my teens . . . my goal was to be the greatest athlete that ever lived," she said.

Steamroll over Obstacles

Cancer could have, probably should have, cut Babe Didrikson's career down long before it did. No one would have called her a quitter. But Didrikson approached the disease like she approached a sand trap on a par four. "You have to face your problem and figure out what to do next," she said.

Work Hard; Then Work Harder

When Babe Didrikson decided to try golf, she worked on her game until her hands literally bled from the blisters. She knew what all great athletes, all great people, know. Natural gifts and inherent abilities aren't enough. "The formula for success is simple," Didrikson said. "Practice and concentration, then more practice and more concentration."

Stay True to Yourself

After her amazing run through the Olympic Games, Babe Didrikson could have settled into easy money, attracting fans and the curious to her vaudeville act. But Didrikson knew she wasn't meant to be a sideshow. She turned her back on Easy Street to pursue her next passion. "I don't want the money if I have to make it this way," she told her sister Nancy.

Accept Help

To be great isn't to be above a little instruction, and Babe Didrikson knew that. When her high school team told her she was too small to make the basketball team, she turned to the boys' coach to make her better. When the USGA revoked her amateur status, she turned to Gene Sarazen, the best male golfer at the time, to improve her game. "I kept asking him questions and questions," she said of her partnership with Sarazen. "If I was going to be the best, I wanted to learn from the best."

Have Fun

As competitive as she was, Babe Didrikson never let it get in the way of her true spirit. She ignored political correctness and said what was on her mind and unabashedly reveled in her notoriety. "Okay, Didrikson's here! Now who's going to finish second?" was Didrikson's favorite way to greet her competitors.

32

Donna Lopiano:
The Difference Between
Being Good and Being Great

ew people are better suited to speak about women athletes of influence than Donna Lopiano. Denied the opportunity to play Little League baseball as a child, Lopiano has dedicated her adult life to furthering women's athletics. The former all-American softball player is the CEO of the Women's Sports Foundation, an organization dedicated to ensuring equal rights for all girls and women in sports. Lopiano, who was recently named one of the ten most influential women in sports, frequently speaks about "The Difference Between Being Good and Great," and has graciously shared her ten talking points, as well as some favorite champion athlete quotes on the subject.

1. BELIEF IN PERFECTION

No player can perform perfectly all of the time, and we certainly aren't perfect as people. But perfection in the performance of a sport skill is possible. Most players have experienced "the perfect shot," "the perfect swing," or "the perfect fake" at some moment in their careers. If you try to give your best effort every time you do something and don't quite achieve it, the result will be twice that of those people who didn't give their best. Perfection will happen as long as you give your very best effort.

- "What's the measure we set for ourselves? It's all relative. It's just a matter of giving your personal best." Bonnie Blair, gold medal speed skater
- "I am not looking for perfection. I look for the best in me." Martina Navratilova, tennis champion

2. ACCEPTING BLAME FOR ERRORS/SUPPORTING YOUR TEAMMATES

Great players always look inward to see what they could have done differently to have prevented a loss or an error. They never blame a teammate or look for excuses. Great players support each other and encourage their teammates.

- "No matter what accomplishments you achieve, somebody helps you." Althea Gibson, Hall of Fame tennis player

3. REPETITION IS KEY TO THE PURSUIT OF EXCELLENT PERFORMANCE

If you want to be a great writer, write a thousand pages. If you want to have a great tennis forehand, hit ten thousand forehands. If you want a great curveball, throw ten thousand curveballs. People who are great at what they do always count repetitions, never the amount of time they spend at practice.

- "You don't win because you do one thing right or two things right. You win because you do one thousand little things right throughout the year." Susan Butcher, champion dogsledder

4. PLAY AGAINST THE VERY BEST

An athlete doesn't get good by playing against someone she can easily beat. If you win against someone who is not very good, you know you are a little better than "not very good." When you win, or measure yourself against the best and achieve your goal, you know you are the best. Always seek competition against someone better than you are. Always seek the most demanding challenge. When great players practice, they envision themselves in the most difficult and challenging situations, so there's no surprise or nervousness when they actually find themselves in that situation.

- "There's no one I hate to play against. I consider everyone a challenge." Steffi Graf, tennis champion

5. NEVER SAY, "I CAN'T," "IT'S IMPOSSIBLE," OR "BUT"

If you think it is "impossible," or think you cannot do it, it will be impossible. Don't ever let yourself think or say the words "impossible" or "I can't." Try not to use the word "but" either. "But" always prefaces an excuse why you can't. Great athletes always say, "Why not?" or "I can do this."

- "When anyone tells me I can't do anything, why, I'm just not listening any more." Florence Griffith Joyner, gold medal sprinter

6. CONCENTRATION

Concentration is "sequential attention to detail." Great athletes create and use checklists in their minds. When the time comes to do a skill, they think sequentially according to that list—one step at a time in the order each step occurs, leaving no detail forgotten. When you are concentrating on a list of important things there is no time to be nervous, worried, or distracted. If you are working on your checklist, all of your attention is focused on the essentials of performance.

- "You're playing chess; my body's the board, and my arms and legs, my fingers, my eyes, and ears are all the pieces." Juanita Harvey, champion wrestler

7. NEVER MAKE THE SAME MISTAKE TWICE

People who are great always make mistakes because they are always looking for a better way to do something. The reason they are great is because they don't make the same mistake twice. If a person never makes a mistake, it's probably because they aren't challenging themselves to become better. They certainly are not trying new things.

- "Be bold. If you're going to make an error, make a doozy, and don't be afraid to hit the ball." Billie Jean King, Hall of Fame tennis player

8. BE A STUDENT, A SCIENTIST

Great players are perpetual students, reading everything they can about their sport, constantly talking to people about how to better perform a skill, and always asking, "Why?" When you stop learning and questioning, you stop being great.

- "Natural talent only determines the limits of your athletic potential. It's dedication, a willingness to learn, and discipline in your life that makes you great." Billie Jean King, Hall of Fame tennis player

9. DEMONSTRATE HOW GOOD YOU ARE BY EXAMPLE, NOT TALK

Great players know that it is easier to talk rather than to do. They don't waste time talking. They demonstrate their greatness by performing. They also recognize that whenever they play, young people will be watching and will try to imitate them. They recognize that they are always admired and emulated, whether they want to be or not, on and off the court.

- "In an age of Charles Barkley, I can't dunk, but still think I should be held accountable as a public figure." Martina Navratilova, tennis champion
- "As simple as it sounds, we all must try to be the best person we can by making the best choices, by making the most of the talents we've been given, by treating others as we would like to be treated." Mary Lou Retton, gold medal gymnast

10. ILLUSION OR REALITY OF CONFIDENCE

Great athletes either have confidence or they make believe they are confident. It doesn't really matter which. All great athletes are worried about performing well and are nervous before or during a contest. The great athletes simply hide it. They learn to act confidently and not show their fear. The illusion of confidence is as good as confidence itself.

- "Everybody tells me I don't belong out here. Sometimes it gets to me, but no one's going to run me off." Ila Borders, the first woman to pitch on a men's college baseball team

More than just talk about these ideals, Donna Lopiano lives them. As an outspoken voice for women, and sometimes outspoken critic against those who are impinging on women's rights, she is an inspiration who has never backed down from a fight or challenge. Lopiano selflessly and tirelessly has dedicated her entire career to making life better for others and each day reminds us of the difference between being good and being great.

Closing: Lessons Learned

$\mathcal{Y}$ou think you know a person.

After more than fifteen years in the sportswriting business, the last eight at the *Philadelphia Daily News,* I have had the good fortune to come across more than a few of the impressive women in these pages. Those I haven't covered or written about, certainly I'd heard of and read about along the way.

I thought I knew them all pretty well. I knew about their championships and gold medals, their record-breaking performances, and even some of their heart-breaking losses. I knew the who, the what, the where.

What I failed to understand was the why. Why were they so great? I presumed it was simply God-given talent. I was wrong. It is something far deeper than that, a feeling and even a personality that burns within each one that separates them from everyone else.

Most of us will never compete in an Olympic Games or blaze down the track in a Triple Crown event. Our lives will follow the more ordinary trajectory of friends, family, and work. But as I learned about each of these inspiring women, I realized that what burned inside of them burns inside me, and while it may not fuel me to become a world-class athlete, it can fuel me to become a world-class person.

The life lessons these women have offered—to take risks, to embrace challenges, to not worry about what other people think—are lessons I hope to live my life by and, more important, lessons I hope to teach my two children. All parents want what's best for their children. What we need to remember is what's best isn't about buying the greatest toy or even getting into the top school. What's best for our children is helping them to believe in themselves, teaching them that, whatever their dream, they should reach for it, and that failure is a necessary evil on the path to success.

If Dawn Staley can rise above her neighborhood, if Wilma Rudolph can overcome polio, if Martina Navratilova can leave behind her family, if Billie Jean King can outlast the critics, surely I can do my part.

This book has been a part of my life for two years now, so I'd be remiss if I didn't thank some people for bearing with me. First and foremost, I need to say thank you to Pat Williams for introducing me to these wonderful women and for offering me his constant enthusiasm and friendship. His energetic voice rang in my ear even when the clock on the wall told me to go to sleep.

I also need to say a special thank you to Phil Jasner, Dick Weiss, Dick Jerardi, and Mike Sielski. The fact that four people that I admire and respect so much would have the faith to recommend me for this project is overwhelming and humbling.

I'd also like to thank my coworkers at the *Daily News,* particularly my sports editor, Pat McLoone, who in his always encouraging way told me to go for it when I asked him about tackling this book.

Finally I need to thank my family—my husband, George, my daughter, Madigan, and my son, Kieran—for understanding when Mommy disappeared into the office for hours on end. They are all the inspiration I'll ever need to become a better person.

—Dana Pennett O'Neil
Philadelphia, Pennsylvania

Acknowledgments

With deep appreciation I acknowledge the support and guidance of the following people who helped make this book possible:

Special thanks to Alex Martins, Bob Vander Weide, and Rich DeVos of the Orlando Magic.

Thanks also to my writing partner Dana O'Neil for her superb contributions in shaping this manuscript.

Hats off to four dependable associates: my assistant Latria Graham, my trusted and valuable colleague Andrew Herdliska, my longtime adviser Ken Hussar, and my ace typist Fran Thomas.

Hearty thanks also go to my friend Peter Vegso and his capable staff at Health Communications, Inc. Thank you all for believing that we had something important to share and for providing the support and the forum to say it.

And finally, special thanks and appreciation go to my wife, Ruth, and to my wonderful and supportive family. They are truly the backbone of my life.

—Pat Williams

For More Information

You can contact Pat Williams at:
Pat Williams
c/o Orlando Magic
8701 Maitland Summit Boulevard
Orlando, FL 32810
Phone: 407-916-2404
E-mail: pwilliams@orlandomagic.com

**Visit Pat Williams' website at
www.PatWilliamsMotivate.com**

If you would like to set up a speaking engagement for Pat Williams, please write Andrew Herdliska at the above address or call him at 407-916-2401. Requests can also be faxed to 407-916-2986 or e-mailed to aherdliska@orlandomagic.com.

We would love to hear from you. Please send your comments about this book to Pat Williams at the above address.

Thank you.

More in the series

Code #0545 • $12.95

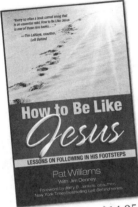

Code #0693 • $14.95

Code #1584 • $14.95

Code #2319 • $13.95

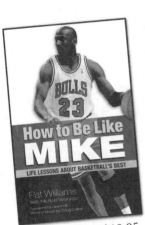

Code #9551 • $12.95

Code #1738 • $14.95

To order direct: Telephone (800) 441-5569 • www.hcibooks.com
Prices do not include shipping and handling. Your response code is BKS.